YOUR PERSONAL STYLE

Your Personal Style

Nancy Plummer

International Academy
of Design and Technology, Chicago

FAIRCHILD BOOKS

NEW YORK

DIRECTOR OF SALES AND ACQUISITIONS: Dana Meltzer-Berkowitz
EXECUTIVE EDITOR: Olga T. Kontzias
SENIOR ASSOCIATE ACQUISITIONS EDITOR: Jaclyn Bergeron
SENIOR DEVELOPMENT EDITOR: Jennifer Crane
DEVELOPMENT EDITOR: Rob Phelps
ART DIRECTOR: Adam B. Bohannon
ASSOCIATE ART DIRECTOR: Erin Fitzsimmons
PRODUCTION DIRECTOR: Ginger Hillman
ASSOCIATE PRODUCTION EDITOR: Jessica Rozler
COPYEDITOR: Aimee Chevrette Bear
COVER DESIGN: Erin Fitzsimmons
COVER ART: Stephen Sullivan
COVER MODEL: Heide Lindgren
COVER HAIR AND MAKEUP: Bryan Lynde
COVER STYLING: Collette LoVullo
TEXT DESIGN: Sara E. Stemen
PAGE COMPOSITION: Sara E. Stemen and Tom Helleberg

Copyright © 2009 Fairchild Books, A Division of Condé Nast Publications.

All rights reserved. No part of this book covered by the copyright hereon may be reproduced or used in any form or by any means—graphic, electronic, or mechanical, including photocopying, recording, taping, or information storage and retrieval systems—without written permission of the publisher.

LIBRARY OF CONGRESS CATALOG CARD NUMBER: 2008924426
ISBN: 978-1-56367-590-4
GST R 133004424

PRINTED IN CHINA

TP15

Dedication

This book is dedicated to all the wardrobe planning educators, image consultants, and family and friends who have contributed to my own personal style—especially to my parents, Phyllis and the late Leroy Plummer, who were my examples of ultimate style.

Contents

xv	Acknowledgments
xvii	Introduction
1	**PART I. GETTING STARTED: WHO ARE YOU?**
3	Chapter 1: Fashion Personality Types
41	Chapter 2: Personal Style Evaluation
59	Chapter 3: Closet Evaluation
81	**PART II. WARDROBE EVALUATION: WHAT SHOULD YOU WEAR?**
83	Chapter 4: Body Type Evaluation
105	Chapter 5: Wardrobe Selection Factors
153	Chapter 6: Cluster Concept
179	**PART III. TAKING ACTION: WHAT SHOULD YOU ADD AND WHY?**
181	Chapter 7: Foundation Basics
209	Chapter 8: Accessories! Accessories! Accessories!

235	**PART IV. FOCUS ON THE FUTURE: WHERE DO YOU GO?**
237	Chapter 9: Shopping Basics
249	Chapter 10: A Global Perspective: International Shopping
277	Chapter 11: Going Green with Your Personal Style
301	**PART V. DISCOVERY: UNIQUELY YOUR STYLE**
303	Chapter 12: Tying It All Together…Your Personal Style
323	Glossary
337	Credits
339	Index

Extended Contents

vii	Contents
xv	Acknowledgments
xvii	Introduction
xvii	Active Learning
xviii	Structure and Use
xxix	Threads
xxix	The Value of Personal Style
xxix	Resources
1	**PART I. GETTING STARTED: WHO ARE YOU?**
3	Chapter 1: Fashion Personality Types
3	Chapter Objectives
4	Where Are You Now?
5	First Impressions
8	Effective Communication
9	Fashion Personality
15	Fashion Personalities
25	The Clothing Message
26	Fashion Personalities
35	Who Should You Wear?

37	Clothing Cues
37	Discovery
37	Taking Stock
39	Key Words
39	Resources
41	**Chapter 2: Personal Style Evaluation**
41	Chapter Objectives
43	What is Your Personal Style?
44	Demographics
47	Psychographics
51	Values and Beliefs
52	Generation
54	Goals
56	Getting on Track
57	Key Words
59	**Chapter 3: Closet Evaluation**
59	Chapter Objectives
60	Taking a Look Inside
61	Beginning
64	Wear
70	Discard
73	Alter
77	Other Uses for Old Clothing
77	Practical Beauty
78	Key Words
79	Resources

81	**PART II. WARDROBE EVALUATION: WHAT SHOULD YOU WEAR?**	
83	Chapter 4: Body Type Evaluation	
83		Chapter Objectives
84		Let's Get Physical
84		Body Normal in the Fashion Industry
88		The Four Major Body Types
95		Proportion
96		Interesting Body Shapes
97		Clothing Choices As They Relate to Proportion
99		Body Type Recognition
102		Body Normal
102		Key Words
102		Resources
105	Chapter 5: Wardrobe Selection Factors	
105		Chapter Objectives
106		What Is Style?
108		Wardrobe Selection Factors
117		The Twelve-Hue Color Wheel
149		Be an Expert
150		Key Words
151		Resources
153	Chapter 6: Cluster Concept	
153		Chapter Objectives
154		The Emerging Style Icon
154		Getting Started
168		Building from the Basics
177		Key Words
177		Resources

179	**PART III. TAKING ACTION: WHAT SHOULD YOU ADD AND WHY?**
181	Chapter 7: Foundation Basics
181	Chapter Objectives
182	Shape Your Body
182	The Complete Bra Wardrobe
192	The Complete Panty Wardrobe
197	Body Shapers—Do You Need Them?
198	The Complete Slip Wardrobe
201	Prioritize to Perfection
202	Hosiery
206	What Every Great Wardrobe Relies Upon
207	Key Words
207	Resources
209	Chapter 8: Accessories! Accessories! Accessories!
209	Chapter Objectives
210	Characterizing Your Personality
210	Handbags
225	Footwear
229	Jewelry
232	Punctuate Your Style
233	Key Words
233	Resources
235	**PART IV. FOCUS ON THE FUTURE: WHERE DO YOU GO?**
237	Chapter 9: Shopping Basics
237	Chapter Objectives
238	Your Shopping Strategy

238		What's My Clothing Allowance?
239		Plan to Shop
242		Retail Formats
245		Big Shopping Days and Sales
246		Plan, Plan, Plan!
247		Key Words
247		Resources
249	**Chapter 10: A Global Perspective: International Shopping**	
249		Chapter Objectives
250		A Global Perspective
255		Fashion Market Characteristics
264		Transumerism and the Leasing Option
268		Internet Retailers
271		Travel—Pack Like a Pro
272		What Makes You Unique?
274		Key Words
275		Resources
277	**Chapter 11: Going Green with Your Personal Style**	
277		Chapter Objectives
278		Balancing the Earth and the Individual
279		What Do We Mean by Green?
292		Green—The Designers and Retail Stores
297		Green Cluster
298		Achieving Green
299		Key Words
299		Resources

301	**PART V. DISCOVERY: UNIQUELY YOUR STYLE**
303	Chapter 12: Tying It All Together...Your Personal Style
303	Chapter Objectives
304	Your Personal Image
310	The Total Look
315	Fashion Personality Total Look
320	Your Personal Style Journal
321	The Total Package
322	Key Words
322	Resources
323	Glossary
337	Credits
339	Index

Acknowledgments

Special thanks to all my colleagues and students at the International Academy of Design & Technology (IADT), Chicago, who have participated in the formation of this book. A big thank you to my interns Vanessa Pabon and Sheena Schwindt, who have helped me in ways too numerous to list. Thank you to all of the image instructors who tirelessly taught the material I passed on to them with enthusiasm: Gloria Petersen, Kimberly Turner, Kristi Kelley, Helga Marcial-Bravo, Kristen Engelman, Michele Lukovich, and Robin Baab. Thank you also to the members of the Association of Image Consultants International (AICI), whom I have learned so much from on the topic of image. Thank you to my clients and associates who have helped me perfect my techniques on wardrobe planning, especially Pamela Duvall, Asuncion Madrigal, and Jessie Besic of Salonblonde. I would also like to thank the reviewers, Camille Aponte, Katherine Gibbs School; Jan Haynes, Delta State University; and Mary Nelson, Monterey Peninsula College. Your valuable insights provided the finishing touch to the completion of this book. To everyone at Fairchild who helped to make this happen: Olga Kontzias, Executive Editor; Dana Meltzer-Berkowitz, Director, Editorial Acquisitions and Sales; Jaclyn Bergeron, Acquisitions Editor; Jennifer Crane, Senior Development Editor; Rob Phelps (profusely!), Development Editor; Michelle Levy, Development Editor; Blake Royer, Assistant Development Editor; Jessica Rozler, Associate Production Editor; Erin Fitzsimmons, Associate Art Director; and Adam Bohannon, Art Director. I am extremely grateful for all of your hard work, patience, and professionalism to make this a top quality book.

To my sisters and brother, Brenda, Christina, Debbie, Eloisa, Felicia, and Paul, who are never at a loss for words when it comes to style. You were all inspirations on many of the descriptions of the fashion personalities featured in the book. And lastly, my mother Phyllis, the definitive style maven, whose advice and support is always appreciated.

Introduction

What is personal style? How do you get it? How can you make it work positively for you in your current lifestyle?

This textbook is for fashion design and merchandising management students as well as for entrepreneurs and image professionals, all of whom seek to answer and expand their knowledge of these essential questions for their studies and careers.

If you are a student in a wardrobe planning class at any college or university, then you will be able to obtain a basic understanding of your own fashion sense by following the guidelines outlined in this book. If you are a fashion entrepreneur, beginner or advanced, you can immediately apply this book's exercises to your own business. If you are an image professional, constantly seeking to expand your knowledge in wardrobe planning, you can utilize your talents in conjunction with any or all of the material found within these pages. *Your Personal Style* is packed with fashion tips and will serve as a handy reference guide for the student and professional alike.

ACTIVE LEARNING

Your Personal Style will give you the opportunity to perform the necessary steps to achieve personal style in an easy-to-follow, logical manner. As you read each chapter your knowledge will increase on ways to achieve your own personal style. Studies have shown that in lecture-based college classrooms, students are not attentive 40 percent of the time (Pollio, 1984). *Your Personal Style* takes an active learning approach that allows you to participate in your journey of reaching magnificent style. You will be able to do the following to reach an understanding of personal style:

* Complete exercises that will help you retain what you have read.

* Review style tips to help form an association with what you have just learned.

* Observe photographs and drawings to see examples of what is being discussed.

* Study terminology to put in use as you expand your knowledge in personal style.

* Experiment with others by teaming up with a learning partner.

Although *Your Personal Style* is geared towards the female reader, males can take an active role in participating in the journey by partnering up with a female. The male reader will be able to apply the specific skills learned with their female partner or with a client depending on his lifestyle. Regardless of your gender, you will be able to discuss, critique, question, and test each other to help you reach your goals.

As you participate in active learning, you will begin to focus on the activities and exercises you have completed. Your goal will be to apply and reflect back on these teachings in order to identify and explore your own personal style.

STRUCTURE AND USE

This textbook has plenty of style of its own. Not only can the student learn from it and the professional keep it as a handy resource for years to come, but also its size and design, replete with colorful visuals, is intended for the coffee table. Instructors will benefit from the logical easy-to-follow format consisting of sequenced parts and chapters that include objectives, activities, bolded glossary terms, and chapter summaries. "Threads," or style tips, interspersed throughout the book are intended to inspire you with fresh ideas, which you'll want to immediately try out yourself. Photographs, drawings, worksheets, and charts will enable you to immediately identify with what it takes to achieve your personal style. Photographs of readily identifiable celebrities provide reference points to which you might aspire. Celebrities are constantly in the public eye and often have stylists helping them look their very best; therefore, celebrities provide a template, an assortment of sizes, shapes, and styles, to which we can relate.

Finally, in addition to this book, an instructor's guide offers further exercises; active learning suggestions; guest speaker and field trip tips; Internet site suggestions; and assignments for each chapter.

Part I. Getting Started: *Who* Are You?
What do you want to do? Where do you want to go? You can't get to where you want to be without knowing who and where you are now. The best way to begin is to look within yourself, at others, and also in your closet.

This section has three chapters: Fashion Personality Types, Personal Style Evaluation, and Closet Evaluation. Upon completion of the three chapters, you will be able to assess your personality, begin to evaluate your style, and then see what is in your closet that will help you to begin to form your own personal style.

Chapter 1: Fashion Personality Types

Everyone possesses a *personality*—an individual's unique way of expression. And everyone has *style*—a way of dressing, speaking, and acting. Personality and style are interdependent. The more you understand your personality and enhance your best qualities, the better your chances for creating and developing a personal style that exudes your energy.

CHAPTER 1: FASHION PERSONALITY OBJECTIVES After reading this chapter, you will be able to:

* Develop a fashion mission statement that shows how you want others to perceive you and the basic clothing pieces that will help you to do this.

* Prepare a budget worksheet for a clothing resource evaluation.

* Describe the five fashion personality types: sporty, romantic, classic, dramatic, and natural.

* Identify celebrities that fit into each fashion personality.

* Categorize dress classifications suitable for each personality type.

* Give examples of colors and fabrics that relate to each fashion personality type.

* Evaluate lifestyles that correspond to each fashion personality.

* Select hairstyles and accessory items for each fashion personality.

FEATURES OF CHAPTER 1: FASHION PERSONALITY TYPES This chapter features:

* Celebrity photos matching each fashion personality type.

* A summary chart detailing each fashion personality along with lifestyle choices, clothing styles, fabric choices, and color selections.

* A vendor chart outlining the clothing manufacturers that match each fashion personality.

Chapter 2: Personal Style Evaluation

Now that you know where your personality lights up on the fashion radar screen, you can begin to assess yourself on a realistic level. Who do you think you are and with whom do you identify? Examine your personality and beliefs from a realistic point of view. What first impression is formed when someone meets you for the first time?

In this chapter, you will assess demographics such as age, race, marital status, income level, and education. You will evaluate psychographics which are values, beliefs, attitudes, and opinions.

CHAPTER 2: PERSONAL STYLE EVALUATION OBJECTIVES After reading this chapter, you will be able to:

- List personality traits that are consistent with your behavior.
- Define demographically who you are.
- Discuss values and beliefs that are important to you.
- Categorize findings about yourself into a specific target market.
- Identify clothing stores that match your target market.
- Compare generation clothing characteristics to your own findings.
- Complete a lifestyle evaluation chart.

FEATURES OF CHAPTER 2: PERSONAL STYLE EVALUATION This chapter features:

- A personality assessment exercise.
- A chart listing identifiable demographic characteristics such as gender, age, race, and income.
- A chart listing common values and beliefs.
- A generational clothing identity chart.

Chapter 3: Closet Evaluation

An individual's closet reveals valuable information on one's clothing choices. In the conclusion of this first part, evaluating who you are, you will examine your closet(s) from a "wearable" point of view. In order to do this task, you will analyze the closet by breaking it into three parts: what you should *wear*, what you should *discard*, and what you should *alter*. Upon completion of each part of the closet evaluation, you will analyze your current clothing choices. In addition, as a final exercise, you will complete a design-your-own ideal closet.

Analyzing your closet at this stage is an important step in finding out *who* you are now. Your clothing choices speak volumes about your personality. As you complete the closet exercises in the chapter you will begin to notice a pattern and similarities in your clothing choices. As you gain additional knowledge the closet will be used as a tool that will help you throughout your style journey to add and/or delete clothing.

CHAPTER 3: CLOSET EVALUATION OBJECTIVES After reading this chapter, you will be able to:

- Examine your closet from your fashion-personality point of view.
- Sort clothing in your closet from the three-part closet evaluation perspective.

- Identify favorite clothing charities or institutions to give away the discarded clothing items.
- Prepare clothing items in need of alterations to take to a tailor.
- Select and analyze items you will wear and place them back in the closet in an orderly fashion (e.g., light to dark, left to right item classification).
- List ideal closet hardware and extras needed to complete ideal closet exercise.

FEATURES OF CHAPTER 3: CLOSET EVALUATION This chapter features:

- Photographs of before and after closet makeovers.
- Lists and photographs of common hardware and equipment items necessary for an ideal closet.
- List of charities and nonprofit organizations available for discarded items.

Part II. Wardrobe Evaluation: *What* Should You Wear?

Now that you know the basics of who you are, it is time to begin to build the foundation of *style* and establish your wardrobe. In the second part of the book, you will match one of the fashion personalities to wardrobe selections. An understanding of personal style begins with a wardrobe that truly exemplifies who you are, inside and out.

Chapter 4, Body Type Evaluation, begins the evaluation process. You will examine your body, noting the pros and cons of your body type. Those body parts that enthusiastically make you shine are the ones you want to accentuate. A positive body part for you may not be one for someone else. As you begin to look inside yourself you will start to realize you have curves you need to accentuate and call attention to. Positive features of your body are easy-to-dress and make you stand out amongst others. Those body parts that you have less than enthusiastic feelings about are the ones you will not want to call attention to. These body parts are harder to dress, making it difficult to find ready-to-wear that doesn't call for a little nip and tuck. Most of us can find clothes that fit our shape and size but also require some alterations. Examining your body includes an understanding of proportion and body types. As you read how to evaluate your body type, you will begin to understand that there is indeed plenty to celebrate about who you are at this very moment.

Chapter 5, Wardrobe Selection Factors, explores a variety of factors such as fit, color, fabric, quality, style, and care. Describing your look involves examining each of these factors individually; this will give you a better understanding of your personal style.

Experts believe people who have personal style also have the ability to *cluster* their wardrobes. In Chapter 6, Cluster Concept, the terms "cluster" and "cluster concept" will be defined. The cluster concept will begin the style progression process. The clusters that each student will evaluate are the work cluster, the sporty cluster, the casual cluster, the dressy occasion cluster, and the seasonal cluster. In this chapter, you will learn how to take 10 pieces of clothing and make 20 to 30 outfits.

Completing chapters 4, 5, and 6 allows you to establish a stylish wardrobe that is unique to your individual self.

Chapter 4: Body Type Evaluation

The human form has unique body shapes, yet we can categorize our individual shapes into four major types: hourglass, triangle, inverted triangle, or rectangle. Our choices of clothing and achieving a unique style depend on how well we can match our clothing choices to our body types. We will use the principle of proportion via the Golden Mean Ratio of 3:5:8 to identify how our individual bodies are segmented. An overview of clothing choices as it relates to body types concludes the chapter.

CHAPTER 4: BODY TYPE EVALUATION OBJECTIVES After reading this chapter, you will be able to:

* Identify and define the four major body types.
* Carry out the body type tracing exercise to identify body type.
* Define *proportion* and its relationship to body types.
* Carry out the body length proportion exercise.
* List the characteristics of an ideal proportion body type using the Golden Mean Ratio of 3:5:8.
* Identify pear, apple, and other body types outside of the norm.
* Identify clothing choices suitable for each body type.

FEATURES OF CHAPTER 4: BODY TYPE EVALUATION This chapter features:

* Celebrity photographs and pencil drawings identifying the four major body types.
* A body length proportion example drawing.
* Celebrity photographs that exemplify the proper way to highlight style as it relates to your body.

Chapter 5: Wardrobe Selection Factors

What is style? Each of us has style, but some people seem to have more than others. Words that exemplify what style means are elegance, good taste, smartness, grace, and panache. Those that have it, definitely combine the following six factors with ease: fit, color, fabric, quality, style, and care. Upon completion of this chapter, you will be able to unite these six factors in the proper combination to achieve your own personal style.

CHAPTER 5: WARDROBE SELECTION FACTORS OBJECTIVES After reading this chapter, you will be able to:

- Define the word *style*.
- Define the word *fit*.
- List the tips to accurate clothing fit.
- Discuss the three additional figure descriptions that can alter clothing fit.
- Identify the bust, waist, and hip measurements for women's, women's petite, and women's plus sizes.
- List the color seasons and their relationship to clothing choices.
- Recognize the colors on the color wheel and the terminology associated with the colors on the wheel.
- Demonstrate the color draping technique.
- Compare and contrast the differences between natural and manmade fabrics.
- List the basic fabric characteristics and their relationship to individual clothing choices.
- Comprehend the difference between excellent, good, and poor quality clothing.
- Compute the cost-per-wearing formula.
- Be aware of the variety of clothing styles available and how it relates to each individual.
- Define the word *emphasis* and understand its relationship to style.
- Recognize care labels and the requirements for proper clothing care.

FEATURES OF CHAPTER 5: WARDROBE SELECTION FEATURES This chapter features:

- Before and after photographs showing proper and improper fit.
- A color wheel with each color identified.
- Photographs of famous people identifying the four-color seasons.
- A fabric chart listing examples of fabrics of the woven and non-woven fabric types and their characteristics.
- A quality chart identifying excellent, good, and poor quality clothing identifiers.
- Pencil drawings showcasing different styles of jackets on individual models.
- Fabric care symbols and language chart.

Chapter 6: Cluster Concept

How often do you see someone who is dressed impeccably, but insists he or she doesn't have a lot of clothes? How come a man can own only two or three suits and still never give the impression that he's repeating himself? Clustering your clothes is one way to expand your wardrobe without spending a fortune. In this chapter, you will work on the *cluster concept* by taking 7 to 10 pieces of clothing to result in 20 to 30 outfits. You will begin with classics and continue to expand on a continual basis to widen your wardrobe when the need arises. This chapter will take you through the necessary steps to begin a work cluster, a sporty cluster, a casual cluster, a special occasion cluster, and a seasonal cluster.

Now that you have completed your body evaluation, the next step is to form your own personal style with pieces of clothing especially suited to you. Part II concludes with this concept of clustering, which is most important in establishing and keeping your own personal style.

CHAPTER 6: CLUSTER CONCEPT OBJECTIVES After reading this chapter, you will be able to:

* Define cluster concept.
* Complete your lifestyle analysis to begin your cluster process.
* Identify one main piece in your wardrobe to begin their first cluster.
* Examine your closet to review additional items that will round out your cluster.
* Complete the cluster worksheet based on clothing items chosen for your first cluster.
* Review additional clothing items for possible additional clusters.

FEATURES OF CHAPTER 6: CLUSTER CONCEPT This chapter features:

* A lifestyle analysis weekly grid worksheet.
* Cluster planning worksheets.
* Clustering for your fashion personality.

Part III. Taking Action: What Should You Add and Why?

Concluding an individual's journey to personal style does not stop with one's clothing items. A woman's complete image involves proper lingerie, a stylish hairdo, and simple foundations. Chapter 7, Foundation Basics, will examine the necessary items needed to make any wardrobe a standout. Essential bras, panties, body shapers, and hosiery will be discussed. Chapter 8, Accessories! Accessories! Accessories!, explores details that are crucial to completing your style portfolio. Accessory items include handbags, belts, jewelry, scarves, and footwear.

Chapter 7: Foundation Basics

There's nothing worse than not wearing your clothing well. You don't want to end up on anyone's "fashion don't" list! Accentuating your positive body assets begins with proper lingerie. Chapter 7, Foundation Basics, will examine the necessary foundation items that any woman should invest in as part of her basic wardrobe.

CHAPTER 7: FOUNDATION BASICS OBJECTIVES After reading this chapter, you will be able to:

* Identify the bras that are part of an essential bra wardrobe.
* Compare the variety of underwear available for perfect clothing presence.
* Recognize optional body shapers available to women of all shapes and sizes.
* Evaluate the variety of hosiery options available.
* Identify slips and liner options available to all women.

FEATURES OF CHAPTER 7: FOUNDATION BASICS This chapter features:

* Photographs of different body types wearing proper underwear, bra, panties, and body shapers.
* Pictures of the variety of hosiery available.
* Pictures of slips, liners, and camisoles available in major department and specialty stores.

Chapter 8: Accessories! Accessories! Accessories!

What woman doesn't like to add her personal touch to a basic wardrobe? Accessories are the essential ingredients to complete your style portfolio. In this chapter, we will review current footwear, handbags/briefcases/wallets, belts, jewelry, scarves/ties, eyewear, and hats. You will add your own personal touch to this discussion as well.

CHAPTER 8: ACCESSORIES! ACCESSORIES! ACCESSORIES! OBJECTIVES After reading this chapter, you will be able to:

* Define the word *accessory* and its usage with style and wardrobe planning.
* List the current trends in all categories of accessories.

* Categorize your accessory style items.

FEATURES OF CHAPTER 8: ACCESSORIES! ACCESSORIES! ACCESSORIES! This chapter features:

* An accessory planning worksheet.
* Cut-and-paste magazine cutouts journal exercise.
* Photographs of the major categories of handbags/briefcases/wallets.
* Photographs of the major categories of footwear.
* Photographs of models wearing belts, scarves/ties, jewelry, and footwear in accordance with their body types.

Part IV. Focus on the Future: *Where* Do You Go?

Your Personal Style has taken you through an evaluation of your inner self, an examination of your current wardrobe, and a review of your own personal accessory extras to complete your personal style. Chapters 9 and 10 review the basics of shopping in your own neighborhood and abroad. In addition, the future is explored reviewing globalization and green issues as they relate to the fashion industry and style. How much do you know about the future of these hot topics? Where do you go from here?

Chapter 9: Shopping Basics

Continuing forward on your style journey, Chapter 9, Shopping Basics, helps you finalize your wardrobe. A review of all the major store categories—department, specialty, and resale—will provide you with the necessary tools to go shopping and complete your style wardrobe.

CHAPTER 9 SHOPPING BASICS OBJECTIVES
After reading this chapter, you will be able to:

* Discuss various types of retail store formats.
* List clothing items needed to complete wardrobe clusters.
* Complete a wardrobe journal identifying each of your personal style selection factors.
* Recite the best places to shop online for unique categories of clothing.

FEATURES OF CHAPTER 9 SHOPPING BASICS This chapter features:

* A retail chart identifying and defining types of retail stores.
* Blank journal sheets for chapter highlights and notes.
* International websites summary chart.

Chapter 10: A Global Perspective, International Shopping

The term *globalization* is common with the millennial generation. As fast as time flies in this world we live in today, we are already beginning to see more and more diversity amongst us. Foreign travel is becoming more accessible to most people because of the variety of travel options and the simple fact that the Internet lets us roam the globe without even leaving home!

Achieving personal style is all about achieving uniqueness, or that which makes one stand out. Looking across the globe for clothing styles that meet your clothing objectives is one way to satisfy your style needs and desires.

CHAPTER 10: A GLOBAL PERSPECTIVE, INTERNATIONAL SHOPPING OBJECTIVES
After reading this chapter, you will be able to:

* Identify what makes each of the top fashion markets around the world distinct.
* Define *transumerism* and its effect on the shopping industry.
* Explain leasing options for luxury items.
* Prepare and pack a simple and complete travel wardrobe.
* Shop globally like a celebrity.
* Research fashion from a global perspective.

FEATURES OF CHAPTER 10: A GLOBAL PERSPECTIVE, INTERNATIONAL SHOPPING
This chapter features:

* A comparison of American and British fashion terminology.
* A table listing fashion weeks by country.
* A review of the top five fashion capitals.
* Travel packing tips by clothing category.

Chapter 11: Going Green with Your Personal Style

The terms *green, eco-friendly, sustainable, recyclable,* and *repurposed* would not be a part of anyone's discussion 10 years ago. Now, within the fashion industry, terminology and fashion that focus on helping to save the planet are the new buzzwords amongst designers and the fashionable elite. Chapter 12 explores the world of "green," what it is, who are the players in this new industry, and what you can do if you want your fashion to speak green.

CHAPTER 11: GOING GREEN WITH YOUR PERSONAL STYLE OBJECTIVES After reading this chapter, you will be able to:

* Define the term *green* and its relationship to the fashion industry.
* Categorize types of green fashions.

- Identify key brands and designers in the green fashion movement.
- Prepare, select, and analyze an action plan for current or future green clusters.
- Identify sources of all natural, green fabrics.
- Explain the difference between recycled, sustainable, and organic clothing.
- Describe the relationship of eco-fashions and the millennial generation.

FEATURES OF CHAPTER 11: GOING GREEN WITH YOUR PERSONAL STYLE This chapter features:
- An overview of retailers that are considered to be in the forefront of the green movement.
- Photographs of organic, repurposed, and recycled clothing.
- A Green Cluster Journal to supplement and use as you begin to finalize pieces for your cluster.

Part V. Discovery: Uniquely Your Style

And finally, Chapter 12, Tying It All Together...Your Personal Style, pulls together everything that you have learned with this book. In this final chapter you will review the previous steps taken in all of the chapters to reach your goal of personal style.

Chapter 12: Tying It All Together... Your Personal Style

The final touches to your wardrobe are not complete without you adding your own special touch, uniqueness, or flair. In this chapter you will review all the necessary steps to achieve personal style.

CHAPTER 12: TYING IT ALL TOGETHER...YOUR PERSONAL STYLE OBJECTIVES After reading this chapter, you will be able to:

- Compare and contrast total looks for each of the body types—hourglass, rectangle, triangle, inverted triangle, pear, and apple.
- Compare and contrast total looks for each of the fashion personalities.
- Establish personal style techniques and criteria for each of the fashion personalities.
- Complete your own personal style journal.

FEATURES OF CHAPTER 12: TYING IT ALL TOGETHER...YOUR PERSONAL STYLE This chapter features:

- Photographs of the appropriate clothing styles for each body type.
- Checklist detailing the steps you need to take before you walk out the door.

THREADS

Scattered throughout the book are Threads, or bits of style information worth remembering, that relate to the chapter. Threads are analogies to help you reinforce the principles learned throughout each chapter. There are various types of threads that will help you reach your goal. A thread can be:

* An exercise to help you evaluate lessons learned.

* A topic from fashion history that relates to what you've just read.

* A look at a celebrity that illustrates the topics.

* An extra bit of fashion information related to the chapter discussion.

Threads are meant to offer additional advice and suggestions that are fun and useful. As you read *Your Personal Style,* utilize the thread tips to consider other possibilities you may explore.

THE VALUE OF PERSONAL STYLE

"If style is the culture then fashion is the history."

Style comes from your background, your traditions, and your way of life. Fashion is the approach, or method, you take to present your style. As you begin to establish who you are and to develop your personal style, you will realize that you are a unique individual unlike anyone else. Your personality, environment, and lifestyle all form the framework that guides you to your clothing choices.

As you read *Your Personal Style* and continue to explore the possibilities that are available to you, your own style will begin to emerge and you will see yourself authentically and see others as they would like to be seen. Achieving individuality in your clothing choices will assist you in bringing out the beauty within you and allow you to see differences in yourself and others as unique qualities to value and respect.

Your style journey is just beginning. As you turn the page to begin Part I, you should ask yourself, *Who am I?* Continuing to Part II, ask yourself, *What should I wear?* In Parts III and IV, you will take action and focus on the future. And concluding with Part V, you will see the progression of a new you, a real you, a you that has style.

RESOURCES

Silberman, M. (1996). *Active Learning 101 Strategies to Teach Any Subject.* Needham Heights, MA: Allyn & Bacon.

PART I

Getting Started:
Who Are You?

CHAPTER ONE

Fashion Personality Types

"Personality is to a man what perfume is to a flower."
—CHARLES M. SCHWAB, EARLY U.S. STEEL INDUSTRY ENTREPRENEUR. HE WAS THE SON OF A TEXTILES WORKER.

CHAPTER OBJECTIVES
After reading this chapter, you will be able to:

* Develop a fashion mission statement that shows how you want others to perceive you, and that includes the basic clothing pieces to help you achieve this.
* Prepare a budget worksheet for a clothing resource evaluation.
* Describe the five fashion personality types: sporty, romantic, classic, dramatic, and natural.
* Identify celebrities who fit each fashion personality.
* Categorize dress classifications suitable for each personality type.
* Give examples of colors and fabrics that relate to each fashion personality type.
* Evaluate lifestyles that correspond to each fashion personality type.
* Select hairstyles and accessory items for each fashion personality type.
* Complete a lifestyle evaluation chart.

WHERE ARE YOU NOW?

Everyone possesses a **personality**—an individual's unique way of expression. Everyone also has **style**—a way of dressing, speaking, and acting. Personality and style are interdependent. The more you understand your personality and enhance your best qualities, the better your chances for creating and developing your personal style, or the style that exudes your own personal energy.

What do your clothes say about you? Your fashion personality shows up to the minute you start to get dressed in the morning. Your body is like a blank slate waiting for you to add your **taste** to its form. Your taste is your individual preference. Terms such as *natural, classic, dramatic, sporty,* and *romantic* are used to describe a range of fashion personalities that are most likely to be associated with particular preferences. (These fashion personalities will be discussed later in this chapter.) For example, a fulltime college student's clothing choices may consist of comfortable, relaxed, and simple pieces. A college student's *natural* personality will reveal a lifestyle that is not elaborate, fabrics that are easy to care for, and neutral colors. In contrast, a working professional may choose *classic* pieces that never go out of style, colors that work well with her overall complexion, and textures that range from smooth to rigid. Celebrities, constantly in the public eye, will exude a range of tastes and preferences based on where they are in their current life. *Dramatic* articles of clothing will not be so unusual on a celebrity because people look for these unique, bold, and daring looks to complement the lifestyle we think the celebrity is living. Bright colors, unusual designs, shapes, and patterns, and a variety of fabrics are all complementary to this dramatic personality. The clothing tastes of sports figures and other individuals who lead an active lifestyle lend themselves to the clothing of their particular sport or to clothing that has stretch or spandex and moves well with the body. *Sporty* personalities are constantly on the go and appreciate clothing that exhibits their active lifestyles yet still looks good for everyday wear. When you think of a *romantic* personality, you may envision femininity, lace, and ruffles. The clothing preferences for this individual may include skirts, sheer blouses, and delicate fabrics. All of these fashion personalities directly relate to the individual personality and illustrate a union of mind and body. You are the artist, dressing your body to express to others who you are.

FIRST IMPRESSIONS

Image consultant Jill Bremer believes that a first impression may be formed within the first 30 seconds of meeting. Within this time subconscious decisions may be made about your economic and education level. Jill also believes that "after about four minutes, they've also made decisions about your trustworthiness, compassion, reliability, intelligence, capability, humility, friendliness and confidence. At this point you've probably had the opportunity to speak, so they're now taking into account the way your voice sounds, the content of what you say and how you say it." (Bremer, 2004)

Seeing how quickly a judgment can be made is reason enough to always try to look your personal best. Crime television shows provide a perfect example of how quickly first impressions are made by analyzing their dead victims for clues. Looking at the victim's clothing, jewelry, and other accessories provide a multitude of clues to the victim's status in life. Designer clothing, shoes, jewelry, and other expensive accessories can narrow the focus of the crime investigator's search. In addition, the visual clues obtained during the body search may reveal how well the victim has taken care of his or her overall appearance, which in turn can lead to a judgment on economic status. In a small amount of time, so many clues may be found. Remember, you never get a second chance to make a first impression. Do you know what type of first impression you make on others? Take the following quick and simple quiz developed by the Royal Borough of Kensington and Chelsea to see what type of first impression you project.

First Impressions Quiz

1. There are three toilets. Which one do you choose?
   a) The one in the corner
   b) The one in the middle
   c) The one next to the tap

* If you chose "the one in the corner," you are a very vigilant person. You are very obstinate and find it difficult to get on well with people. This will put you in a very vulnerable position. A suitable career for you would involve art or using other skills.

* If you chose "the one in the middle," you are a leader with a laudably tolerant spirit, with high motivation. If there is someone to promote you it is very possible that you will be successful.

* If you chose "the one next to the tap," you don't care what other people think about you, and have sensible ideas. This kind of person is very clever, good at dealing with people, and has good relationships with people. You will be a good advisor although you don't have many leadership skills.

2. If you had to choose an animal to represent yourself, which would you choose?
   a) Dog
   b) Cat
   c) Horse
   d) Cow

* If you chose the "dog," then you don't make a deep impression on people. People are likely to forget you if you go to a crowded place.

* If you chose the "cat" and you are a man, then people don't have a good impression of you. If you chose the "cat" and are a woman, then

you are very motivated and always want to get attention from other people. You can make a very big impression on people.

* If you chose the horse, then you have high ideals for the future. People will always have a good impression of you.

* If you chose the "cow," then you can make a very deep impression on people, but often it's a bad impression.

3. Which makes you feel more confident?
    a) Your voice
    b) Your hands
    c) Your eyes
    d) Your body

* If you chose your voice, then you can easily influence people and they will normally follow you. Your confidence in your voice means that the first impression other people have of you is that they can rely on you and trust you.

* If you chose your hands, then the first impression people have of you is not very clear. People who stay with you a long time will discover that you are not very confident. You should think about how to improve your confidence.

* If you chose your eyes, then you are confident of your beauty. You often look at people's eyes while you are talking to them. This will help you to make a very good impression on other people.

* If you chose your body, then you don't have much motivation. You will cover your talents in front of people as you believe that you give a good impression but things may not be going as well as you think.

EFFECTIVE COMMUNICATION

Individuals see what you are wearing and they may form an impression of your personality, your occupation, and even your age. Dr. Albert Mehrabian is an author of more than 150 research publications including topics on non-verbal communication. Professor Mehrabian is known for his research on body language and is well known for establishing the classic statistic of effective communications. According to Mehrabian's communication model:

- ✳ 7 percent of meaning is expressed through the words that we speak.
- ✳ 38 percent of meaning is paralinguistic, or expressed through the way our words are said.
- ✳ 55 percent of meaning is expressed through facial expression.

Communication specialists have used Mehrabian's model to emphasize the "importance of meaning, as distinct from words" (Chapman, 2006).

Analyzing the highest percentage of Mehrabian's communication model, 55 percent, effective communication is based on the way we look, and it involves our total appearance, including our gender, age, hair and skin color, body type, grooming, and any extras such as piercings and tattoos. A person doesn't have to say anything; one's clothes communicate the message. From just one look, a person can be perceived as being:

- ✳ Poor—wearing tattered, dirty, smelly clothing.
- ✳ Rich—wearing very expensive-looking, quality clothing.
- ✳ Eclectic—wearing original-in-design, colorful, artful, and unique clothing.
- ✳ Athletic—wearing spandex, formfitting, body awareness type clothing.

We all make **assumptions** based on what we see. And as the saying goes "you never get a second chance to make a first impression."

The second highest percentage of Mehrabian's communication model is the way we sound, which amounts to about 38 percent of a first impression. Your communication style becomes part of your total appearance. Mehrabian describes this part of effective communication as the "way that the words are said." In spoken communication we have the **speaker**, or the person conveying the meaning, and the **listener**, or the person interpreting the meaning. This 38 percent applies to the spoken, as opposed to the written and read, such as the popular email communication. The way that we sound can be described as: loud, confident, creative, quiet, unassuming, or dependable.

What's left after how we look and sound? The balance of effective communication is in the words that are spoken, and this amounts to only seven percent. As the percentages convey, communication relies on the meanings we interpret largely from sensations (e.g., sight and sound) and much less from information we must process, even when that processing takes only that extra millisecond. John Ruskin, the nineteenth-century English art critic and social commentator, conveyed this observation when he said "The essence of lying is in deception, not in words."

Our appearances are powerful! Invest in your appearance, make it portray the real you. Begin now to make it a priority.

FASHION PERSONALITY

What is a **fashion personality**? It's an individual's unique way of expressing oneself through clothing. You can tell where someone is going, what they plan on doing, and even the mood of the wearer through their clothing choices. As stated previously, you begin each morning as a blank slate and then start the process of deciding what to wear today. Just as an artist begins to draw on a blank canvas, you begin to ask yourself, How do I feel? Where am I going? and How do I want to look?

Consider your feelings and how clothing can outwardly express your feelings. Would you wear bright colors when feeling sad and blue? Probably not, because the brighter the color the more attention you will attract. Consider the time of day of your activity. Are you going to a day or evening, formal or informal event? A cocktail dress for an informal event will definitely make you feel out of place. Consider how you want to look. What image, values, and perceptions do you want others to see? Your clothing choices will help you achieve the goals you want. How does this work? Consider your perceptions as you perform Exercise 1.1 below.

Exercise 1.1: Clothing Lines, Shapes, and Colors
How much can you tell about this woman from Figure 1.1?

1. What do you think she is doing?
2. What clothing cues help you to identify this woman's life?
3. How easy is it for you to identify personality traits?

FIGURE 1.1
The side view of this woman as she grocery shops can reveal a variety of interesting scenarios. What is your first impression?

A **cue** is an identifier, a sign, or indication. Clothing cues help us identify each other and interpret who and what we are. According to image consultant and educator Judith Rasband, "Change one symbol, element, cue, or clue and you change the entire message. The more of the same cues, the faster the message gets across to you and to others." Rasband also identifies clothing cues based on the **values** we have (Rasband, 2005). A value is the goal or standard held by an individual. It is something you would hold in high esteem; family life, respect, money, and time are examples of values that individuals may posses. Preview the following chart to see where your clothing cues are in relation to your values.

Table 1.1

CLOTHING CUES AND PERSONAL VALUE STATEMENTS

Personal Value	Value Meaning	Behavior	Clothing Cue
Accomplishment	Achievement Success Triumph	Always does the right thing Hard worker	Classic styles Designer brands Quality fabrics Neutral, timeless colors
Adventure	Escape Venture Quest	On-the-go Active Seeks new opportunities	Sporty comfortable styles Easy-care fabrics Bright colors
Accuracy	Correct Exactness Precision	Precise with all tasks Checks and re-check for exactness	Very detailed, classic styles High-quality, firm fabrics Pure, rich colors
Beauty	Lovely Attractive Pretty	Nice No flaws Pleasant to be around	Modern Up-to-date styles Quality fabrics Colors pleasing to the eye No patterns
Calm	Peaceful Tranquil Quiet	Still Quiet Relaxed	Simple styles Natural fabrics Peaceful Neutral colors such as white, beige, and sky blue No patterns

Personal Value	Value Meaning	Behavior	Clothing Cue
Creative	Original Artistic Inspired	Seeking out new and different opportunities to showcase original ideas May have tattoos and exhibit other personal artifacts	One-of-a-kind clothing Unusual shapes and styles Variety of colors Patterns and prints
Cleanliness	Spotlessness Purity Dirt-free	Very neat, not a hair out of place Pulled-together look	Tailored, classic styles Few details Smooth fabrics. Pure colors
Community	Group of people Neighborhood Village	Teamwork Enjoys working with other people Connection with everyone	Popular styles Simple, washable, fabrics Seasonal colors
Discovery	Breakthrough Sighting Detection	Inquisitive Alert Attentive	New, modern looks and styles Latest fabrications New, undiscovered colors
Excellence	Distinction Superiority Quality	Perfectionist Seeks what's right Inquisitive	Classic, tailored looks and styles High-quality, firm, and stable fabrics Modern, new colors

Personal Value	Value Meaning	Behavior	Clothing Cue
Family	Relations Relatives Lineage	Exhibits similar actions and behaviors of family members	Styles that resemble family background and heritage Colors and fabric of the country
Faith	Trust Confidence Belief	Willingness to trust authority Positive attitude Optimism	Simple, clean styles Natural fabrics Neutral, dark colors No loud prints or patterns
Fun	Enjoyable Amusing Pleasurable	Laughter Smiling Happiness	Unique styles Bright colors Patterns Variety of shapes
Global View	Worldwide Universal International	Seeking adventure and knowledge of foreign countries Love of unique personalities	Unique clothing styles from other countries Ethnic fashions Unusual prints, patterns, and colors
Harmony	Agreement Accord Synchronization	No fuss Easy-going Willing to conform	Matched suits Classic styles Basic suiting fabrics such as gabardine and wool Straight lines and matched patterns

Personal Value	Value Meaning	Behavior	Clothing Cue
Innovation	Novelty Originality Modernization	Not afraid to be the first in anything Inquisitive Risk-taking	Original new and trendy styles from new designers Mix of colors Unique patterns and prints
Money	Cash Wealth Riches	Stress-free Giving Relaxed	Couture and designer brand clothing High-quality fabrics Modern, new colors Latest untapped look
Power	Control Dominance Authority	Exerting influence Outspoken Dominating presence	Classic yet modern styles Neutral, bold colors High-quality fabrics, solids No prints or patterns
Simplicity	Effortless Minimalism, plainness	Quiet No fuss Helpful	Non-confrontational Simple styles with few lines, neutral colors Natural fabrics No prints or patterns
Variety	Assortment Diversity Multiplicity	Choosing excitement Seeking adventure Bored easily	Explore all styles Variety of fabrics and textures Prints and patterns

Source: Adapted from Judith Rasband's "Clothing Cues and Values Communications," © Conselle LLC.

A uniform defines where and who you are currently in life. How much can you tell about this woman from Figure 1.2?

1. What do you think she is doing?
2. What clothing cues help you to identify this woman's life?
3. How easy was it for you to identify personality traits?

FASHION PERSONALITIES

There are **five basic fashion personalities** that everyone can relate to:

1. Sporty—wears casual, comfortable, athletic clothing.
2. Romantic—wears feminine, delicate, lovely clothing.
3. Classic—wears tailored, conservative, basic clothing.
4. Dramatic—wears bold, unique, colorful clothing.
5. Natural—wears simple, untreated, neutral color clothing

How do you know which fashion personality you are, and can you be more than one fashion personality? In order to succeed in achieving the look for which you want others to perceive you, consider the following steps to reaching your true fashion personality.

Consider Your Lifestyle

The first step is to consider your lifestyle at this point in time. What activities, at this point in your life, represent your current lifestyle? Looking at each of these activities, does your clothing match your lifestyle? Follow the directions and fill out the grid in Thread 1.1.

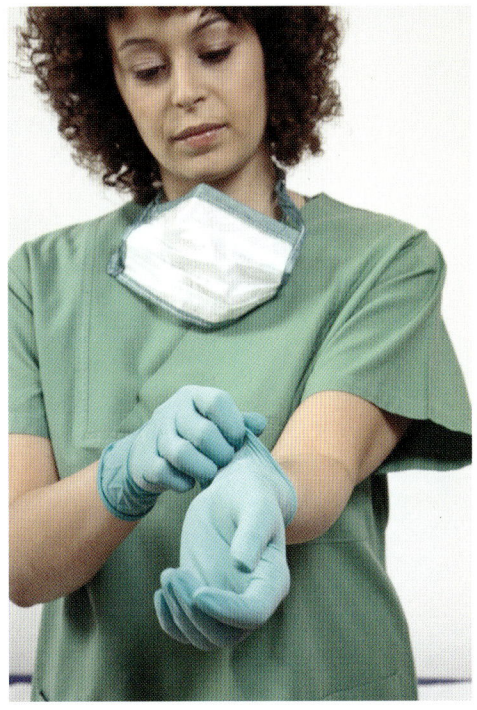

FIGURE 1.2
A person in uniform is readily identifiable. This woman's lifestyle can be determined in a few words just by looking at her uniform.

Consider Your Personality
The second step is to consider what type of personality you are. Do you consider yourself shy and introverted, or gregarious and outgoing? Your clothing speaks volumes on who you are and who you want to be. Complete the personality assessment in Thread 1.2 to see what adjectives express your personality, or your inner self.

Upon completion of the assessment you will know what others need to know about you. You will then be able to express yourself with your clothing choices. Your goal is to match your fashion personality with your inner personality.

Evaluate Your Resources
The third step asks how much you can comfortably spend on clothing. What do you currently own? Resources include how much money you have to spend on clothing and what is currently in your closet. Because your existing wardrobe is an essential part of planning the clothes suitable for your personal style, analyzing your closet will be covered in its own chapter (Chapter 3, Closet Evaluation).

A WEEK IN YOUR LIFE LIFESTYLE GRID
Your current lifestyle dictates your clothing choices. Upon completion of the grid you will see the percentage breakdown of your current life. If you work 60 percent of the time, then 60 percent of your clothing choices should match your work image.

You will refer to this grid throughout the book.

This grid represents who you are now and what your life entails. It will be used to see more than your clothing choices. Keep it!

Directions: Color code the various activities listed below. Complete the grid using the appropriate color in the right time slot. Once complete, you will be able to see the color blocks formed from each activity.

Table 1.2

A WEEK IN YOUR LIFE LIFESTYLE GRID

DAY

TIME	Sun	Mon	Tues	Wed	Thurs	Fri	Sat
7 a.m.							
8 a.m.							
9 a.m.							
10 a.m.							
11 a.m.							
12 p.m.							
1 p.m.							
2 p.m.							
3 p.m.							
4 p.m.							
5 p.m.							
6 p.m.							
7 p.m.							
8 p.m.							
9 p.m.							
10 p.m.							
11 p.m.							
12 a.m.							
1 a.m.							
2 a.m.							
3 a.m.							
4 a.m.							
5 a.m.							
6 a.m.							

■ **Sleep** ■ **Work** ■ **School** ■ **Exercise** ■ **Travel** ■ **Dressy** ■ **Casual Home** ■ **Casual Away**

THREAD 1.1

Experts recommend spending no more than eight percent of your monthly income on clothing. Looking at total yearly income, money experts feel clothing is only one part of the equation. Total living expenses equal 25–35 percent of your yearly income. In addition to clothing, there are groceries, supplies, postage, and other sundry items in this category. Complete the **budget worksheet** in Thread 1.3 to see how much money you spend on clothing.

High Net Worth

The United States is beginning to see a rise in the middle class. While there is a rise in the middle class there is also a rise in the number of high net worth individuals (**HNWIs**). The 2007 World Wealth Report by Merrill Lynch and Capgemini have predicted that the number of HNWIs (individuals with net assets of at least $1 million, excluding primary residences and consumables) in the world increased 8.3 percent to 9.5 million. With this population continuing to expand and disposable income becoming larger, consumers are ultimately spending more money on clothing.

Create a Fashion Mission Statement

The fourth step, creating your own **fashion mission statement,** will give you something to look back at when you are questioning your lifestyle, personality, or budget. It is your guide—your clothing mission. The completion of the last of these four steps will put you on the right track to your style goal of matching your personality to your clothing choices.

Exercise: 1.1: Fashion Mission Statement

Complete your Fashion Mission Statement—your philosophy on your personal style. There are two parts in completing a focused fashion statement that will exemplify your true fashion sense.

PART I: WHY? Complete the following statement: I want others to view me as . . . (Use adjectives that describe your personality and express values that you believe in.) *(continued on page 23)*

YOUR PERSONALITY CLUSTER

Directions: Your responses to the following statements will give you a sense of what general traits define your personality. There are no "right" or "wrong" responses. Simply place a check by those statements that apply or that are mostly true for you.

1. _____ I prefer being active most of the day.
2. _____ I often let my heart rule rather than my head.
3. _____ I tend to set goals and work hard to obtain them.
4. _____ I take more risks in life than the average person.
5. _____ What you see is what you get when it comes to my personality.
6. _____ I act rather than wait for something to happen.
7. _____ In a group I prefer to have an intimate conversation with one or two individuals rather than have a group conversation.
8. _____ I prefer to take calculated risks rather than act spontaneously in a situation.
9. _____ I can generally come up with many different solutions to a problem.
10. _____ Being authentic and true to myself is more important than being accepted by most people.
11. _____ I enjoy juggling a number of activities.
12. _____ After a special event, I enjoy spending time reflecting on my favorite moments.
13. _____ Most people would consider me to be a practical person with a lot of common sense.
14. _____ I often act before I think.
15. _____ I act according to my values rather than contemporary trends.

16. _____ I see opportunities rather than challenges.

17. _____ I enjoy books that focus on interpersonal relationships rather than ideas and facts.

18. _____ I am more conservative than liberal in my thinking.

19. _____ I generally stand out in a group for my uniqueness.

20. _____ I would confront a friend or a co-worker who was acting unethically.

21. _____ I manage change in my life well.

22. _____ As a gift, I prefer that someone give me a present that was personal rather than practical.

23. _____ On vacation I prefer a planned itinerary rather than go with the flow.

24. _____ I could be described as strong-willed.

25. _____ I believe the future will be better than the past.

26. _____ When I get together with friends we prefer to enjoy activity more so than conversation.

27. _____ It is more important for me to consider people's feelings more so than the facts when making a decision.

28. _____ I am known for being reliable and following through on my commitments.

29. _____ I enjoy tackling problems.

30. _____ On a vacation, the journey is more important than the destination.

31. _____ I would prefer to play a sport rather than watch a sports game on television.

32. _____ On vacation, luxury hotel accommodations and scenic views are important to me.

33. _____ I remain steadfast to my ideas and perceptions rather than be influenced by others.
34. _____ I have strong likes and dislikes.
35. _____ I could live anywhere and pretty much enjoy life.
36. _____ I do not shy away from conflict.
37. _____ I am uncomfortable when people I care about do not get along.
38. _____ I prefer to stick to the tried and true rather than new and untested.
39. _____ I take criticism well and am open to feedback about myself.
40. _____ I make friends from all walks of life.
41. _____ I consider myself more of a spontaneous than organized person.
42. _____ I pay attention to details in my work and personal life.
43. _____ I practice the adage "less is more."
44. _____ I prefer frequent change over things staying the same all the time.
45. _____ I would prefer to go with the flow rather than follow an itinerary.
46. _____ I prefer to do things on the spur of the moment rather than a planned itinerary.
47. _____ If I had to choose I would prefer to have a close friend rather than a new car.
48. _____ I am careful about what I do and say.
49. _____ I practice the adage "variety is the spice of life."
50. _____ I am more practical than innovative.

YOUR PERSONALITY CLUSTER SCORING

Directions: On Table 1.3, place a mark in the box for the numbers you have checked. After you have completed marking those boxes for the checked items add the columns for your score. The number represents your endorsement of the personality traits representative of that cluster described below.

Table 1.3
YOUR PERSONALITY CLUSTER SCORING GRID

	Sporty	Romantic	Classic	Dramatic	Natural
	1	2	3	4	5
	6	7	8	9	10
	11	12	13	14	15
	16	17	18	19	20
	21	22	23	24	25
	26	27	28	29	30
	31	32	33	34	35
	36	37	38	39	40
	41	42	43	44	45
	46	47	48	49	50
TOTALS					

YOUR PERSONALITY CLUSTER INTERPRETATION

Your highest score represents your dominant personality cluster. You may not have a dominant cluster but possess a certain degree of each of these personality aspects in your total personality represented by your score for each cluster. Your personality cluster may or may not match your fashion personality style. If your personality cluster matches your fashion style you are most likely dressing to represent your personality. If your personality cluster does not match your fashion style, reflect on what you are trying to express with your clothing. Fashion personalities will be further described in Chapter 1 and later chapters, but can be generalized for the purpose of this exercise as follows:

Sporty Personality: Outgoing, exuberant, enjoys activity, and making things happen, spontaneous, flexible.
Romantic Personality: Warmhearted, sensitive, melancholic, idealistic, loyal, detail-oriented, and people-oriented.
Classic Personality: Traditional, efficient, organized, thoughtful, matter-of-fact, responsible, reliable, and dependable.
Dramatic Personality: Bold, ingenious, stimulating, resourceful, and seeks change.
Natural Personality: Authentic, open, trustworthy, stable, forthright, and conscientious.

Source: Dr. Deborah Plummer, Ph.D., DL Plummer & Associates, Cleveland, Ohio, 2008.

PART II: HOW? Describe the clothing items that are important to your overall look and image.

CREATE YOUR FASHION MISSION STATEMENT Combine Parts I and II to achieve a fashion mission statement upon which you can base your clothing selections. Your mission statement should be brief—no longer than a maximum of one or two sentences. When you read it you will know exactly what items will get you to your personal style wardrobe, and when others read it, they will be able to identify your personal style. Completing this statement is the first step in achieving your own personal style.

BUDGET WORKSHEET

Complete the monthly budget worksheet to see where your money is going. How much are you actually spending on clothing? Are you above or below the average? Upon completion of the budget worksheet you will be able to see what categories of spending exceed the average. Use the revisions column to make adjustments up or down in categories where needed. At this time you are able to see the importance of clothing to your overall image and why it's important to spend your money wisely. Does your wardrobe need improvement?

Table 1.4
BUDGET WORKSHEET

Percentage Range	Category	Percent Chosen	Dollar Amount	Revisions
Fixed Expenses				
18–25%	Housing			
18%	Taxes			
1–5%	Insurance			
0–10%	Debt Repayment			
0–10%	Savings			
0–10%	Emergencies			
Living Expenses				
5–12%	Utilities & Phone			
8–15%	Food			
5–15%	Transportation			
2–5%	Medical			
2–8%	Clothing			
2–9%	Durable Goods			
1–5%	Personal Grooming			
1–10%	Recreation			
0–9%	All Other			

Here are two sample fashion mission statements:

* I, (insert name), want others to view me as a business professional intent on attaining recognition and financial security. I will invest in classic, neutral color, basic clothing items from vendors like Ellen Tracy, Armani, and Calvin Klein.

* (Insert name here) is a gregarious, free-spirited individual whose focus is helping others be happy. A denim jacket, khaki pants, and a white cotton button-down shirt from GAP will illustrate who she is.

THE CLOTHING MESSAGE

There are goals we all should strive to achieve when we wear clothes. Your goal is to have the **receiver**, the person receiving your clothing message, know exactly what it is that you, the **sender** of the clothing message, are trying to say. Let's examine the following clothing choices and form an assumption on what each individual is trying to convey. We will assume, or form an opinion, on the individual's personality based on that person's clothing choice. The following table illustrates typical assumptions based on individual clothing choices.

Ask yourself, is this the message you're trying to portray? Clothing is your art form so use it wisely.

Completion of the lifestyle grid, personality assessment, budget worksheet, and fashion mission statement, will guide you to achieve your fashion personality assessment. In addition, browsing fashion magazines and looking at what the celebrities are wearing and the physical features they possess, will help you to narrow down choices and assess your true fashion personality. Personalities not only shine through our clothing but also in other categories of our life. Individuals often choose their automobiles based on their personalities. Consider why you drive the car you drive and what prompted you to buy it?

Table 1.5
CLOTHING ASSUMPTIONS

The clothing assumptions listed below are based on you being seen in a *public* setting: at school, the work place, religious community, health club, or any other activity where people are engaged. Make a note that your job might require you to wear clothing that others not engaged in that activity might cause people to form negative assumptions. For example, a ballet dancer wears leotards and tights to perform. In practice and performing this is fine, but out in public, grocery shopping for example, it is best to cover up so others do not make the wrong assumption about you or your body.

Clothing Choice	Assumption
Turtleneck sweater	Shy, demure, conservative
Miniskirt	Youthful, showy, daring
Low cut blouse	Sexy, open, and risqué
Tight fitting dress	Body-revealing, conspicuous, lack of self-esteem
Baggy sweats	Comfort, uncaring, indifferent
Jacket	Power, authority, confident
T-shirt with slogans	Casual, fun, active

FASHION PERSONALITIES

The following personality celebrity table will assist you in your identification process. Celebrities are in the spotlight at all times. Oftentimes, stylists are dressing these stars to project a certain image. A celebrity or star is someone who is a public figure, a famous person and a personality. Included in this celebrity category are individuals who are not only in the music or movie industries, but also politicians, business leaders, athletes, and other notable public figures. Noticing and observing what these individuals wear provides you with

a benchmark to gage yourself against. Choose a celebrity whose style you admire and notice the styles, shapes, colors, and patterns they wear. Do they receive positive or negative press and why? Do you agree or disagree with the assessment of the press?

Previewing the following chart you can easily see the fashion personality that each star exhibits to the public. What we the public sees from these stars is not always who they really are, but who they want to be. Remember, clothing is a powerful tool that forms our first impression.

Not everyone will fit exactly in any single fashion personality category. Depending on your current lifestyle, you may exhibit more than one fashion personality. It's best to analyze *who you are* and *who you want to be* so you won't confuse yourself and others.

FIGURE 1.3

Celebrities strive to look their best when presenting themselves to the public. Thought goes into each and every outfit as they walk the photo-packed carpet. Note the fashionable image each star is portraying, from left to right: Venus Williams, Paris Hilton, Lucy Liu, and Ivanka Trump.

FASHION PERSONALITY TYPES 27

Table 1.6
PERSONALITY CELEBRITY TABLE

Fashion Personality	Physical Features	Celebrities	Car Most Likely to Drive
Sporty	Strong Athletic Casual Relaxed	Venus Williams Candace Bergen Jamie Lee Curtis	Jeep
Romantic	Large eyes Beautiful features Great figure and hair	Michelle Pfeiffer Jennifer Lopez Marilyn Monroe	Cadillac
Classic	Average features Poised and gracious Serene and well mannered	Grace Kelly Diane Sawyer Gwyneth Paltrow Catherine Deneuve	Mercedes
Dramatic	Tall Striking features High fashion	Diana Ross Tina Turner Cher Barbra Streisand	Ferrari
Natural	Little or no makeup Youthful appearance Friendly Casual manner Joyful outlook	Sarah Jessica Parker Katie Couric Goldie Hawn Lauren Hutton	Small BMW Sedan

Minor Fashion Personality Categories

One may also consider other minor fashion personality categories. I consider these fashion personalities minor because they are defined more by physical appearance and looks and not by just the three factors we have analyzed previously—lifestyle, personality, and resources. The first personality is based more on physical appearance than anything else. This is the **ingénue fashion personality**. "A young woman or naïve girl" is the description of this person. Similar to the natural fashion personality, the ingénue is youthful in appearance, yet one with a child-like innocence. Small in frame yet exhibiting a "little-boy" look is one way to describe this fashion personality. Celebrities in this category include Britney Spears, Sally Struthers, and Nicole Richie. A Volkswagen would be the type of cars these individuals would most likely drive.

FIGURE 1.4

Three celebrities who make eclectic fashion statements are (from left to right): Sarah Jessica Parker, Gwen Stefani, and Amy Winehouse.

The **sexy siren or alluring personality** is another category that can be singled out. To visually convey this look the individual would wear plunging v-neck tops, stilettos, and red lipstick. Ava Gardner, Raquel Welch, and Salma Hayek are celebrities that exhibit this fashion personality.

The **eclectic** fashion personality is one of constant change and originality. This person is care-free and full of life. Always expect the unexpected in dress with the eclectic fashion personality. Clothing in this category is often self-made by the individual expressing the "theme of the day" or making use of a variety of looks and styles from various manufacturers and designers. High-end designers that exemplify this eclectic style are Betsey Johnson, Vivienne Westwood, and Alexander McQueen. The celebrity personalities that exhibit the eclectic look are Amy Winehouse, Cindy Lauper, Sarah Jessica Parker's *Sex and the City* character Carrie Bradshaw, and Gwen Stefani. There is not just one standout look with the eclectic personality but an assortment of prints, patterns, colors, lengths and styles. The goal is to be unique and different. It is important to note the true eclectic personality does have style and does look put-together.

It's important to note that these minor personality types will also fall into one of the major personalities. An ingénue may be a sporty and a sexy may be a natural. The eclectic personality may also exhibit one of the major fashion personality types at times. The five personality types encompass a wide range of people. To describe the five fashion personalities more fully let's look at each one individually.

The Sporty Fashion Personality

The **sporty fashion personality** is described as someone who is casual and relaxed, strong and athletic. If your lifestyle grid shows more than 50 percent of your average week involved in casual activities, then this is where you will begin to evaluate your wardrobe. Basic clothing items that will be included in a sporty fashion personality closet are included on Table 1.7.

Table 1.7

SPORTY FASHION PERSONALITY CLOTHING CHOICES

Comfortable denim jeans	Denim jacket
White, traditional button-down shirts	Casual trench coat
T-shirts, long- and short-sleeved	Cable knit cardigan
Khaki pants	V-neck or zip hoodie
Knit drawstring skirt	Ribbed turtleneck sweater
Denim skirt	Polo dress in a neutral color

Table 1.8

ROMANTIC FASHION PERSONALITY CLOTHING CHOICES

Ruffled blouses	Cropped cardigan
Lace and silk chiffon blouses	Print bell-shape jacket
Bow cardigans	Corset dress
Dupioni silk dress	Tulip skirts
Denim jeans with embroidery, lace, or jewels	Bell sleeves on shirts, jackets, or outerwear

The Romantic Fashion Personality

For the next fashion personality, **romantic**, one thinks of femininity. Most vintage pieces fall in this category because they emphasize a woman's femininity. The basic clothing items for the romantic fashion personality are included on Table 1.8.

Table 1.9

CLASSIC FASHION PERSONALITY CLOTHING CHOICES

Black turtleneck	Suede and/or leather jacket
White stretch cotton blouse	Cashmere cardigan
Black pencil skirt	Little black dress
Classic neutral color trench coat	Shirtdress
Black pinstripe jacket and pant	100-percent cotton t-shirts
Dark denim five-pocket jeans	Black gabardine pants and jacket
Jersey skirt	

Table 1.10

DRAMATIC FASHION PERSONALITY TYPE

Bright color-patterned tops	Cropped jackets
Slim fit denim jeans	Mini skirts
Bold print jackets	Giant rings and jewelry
Dresses with plenty of detail	Belted trench coat
Fitted sweaters	Bubble, halter, or any trendy dress for the season
Animal print clothing items	
Color, color, color in all items!	

The Classic Fashion Personality

Basic clothing items for the most versatile of all fashion personalities, the **classic fashion personality**, include items everyone should have in their wardrobe. This fashion personality invests in quality, timeless pieces that are included on Table 1.9.

Table 1.11
NATURAL FASHION PERSONALITY TYPE CLOTHING CHOICES

Stretch flare leg pants	Shirtdress in a neutral color
Organic cotton tees	Relaxed fit denim jeans
Cotton and spandex white shirt	Khaki pants
Notch collar neutral color jacket	Cotton turtlenecks
Relaxed fit denim flare skirt	Basic cotton denim jacket

The Dramatic Fashion Personality

The **dramatic fashion personality** is an individual that likes to stand out in the crowd. One way to stand out in a crowd is through the clothing choices you choose to wear. The items you wear may seem like trendy clothing items to most other people but your clothing expresses who you are, so to the dramatic personality its drama! The clothing items in the dramatic closet are found on Table 1.10.

The Natural Fashion Personality

The **natural fashion personality** is interested in the overall simplicity and quality of her fashion. This individual is no fuss; keep it quick and easy when it comes to dressing. This personality would be interested in organic fashions. Chapter 12, Going Green & Your Personal Style, will discuss the fashion designers a natural personality may consider. Natural, simple, basic, clean, ordinary, and normal, this fashion personality is unpretentious in her outlook on fashion. The basic clothing items in the natural's closet are similar to the sporty yet not as casual. A cross between the sporty and the classic, the natural has the pieces found in Table 1.11 in their wardrobe.

Table 1.12

FASHION PERSONALITY VENDOR TABLE

Sporty	Romantic	Classic	Dramatic	Natural	Ingénue
GAP	Jessica McClintock	Chanel	Dolce & Gabanna	J. Jill	Marc Jacobs
Tommy Hilfiger	Valentino	Calvin Klein	Yves Saint Laurent	Eileen Fisher	Theory
DKNY	Vera Wang	Dana Buchman	Alexander McQueen	Tahari	BeBe
Ralph Lauren Polo	Tracy Reese	Anne Klein	Versace	Banana Republic	L.A.M.B.
Burberry	Anna Sui	Armani	Jean Paul Gaultier	Chico's	
J. Crew	Nanette Lepore	St. John	Issey Miyake		
Armani A/X	Betsey Johnson	Ellen Tracy	Escada		

WHO SHOULD YOU WEAR?

Now that you've classified yourself into one of the fashion personality types, it's time to identify the best clothing designers and manufacturers that match your personality. Designers have their own fashion styles that translate into their clothing. Once you identify who you are, you can begin to narrow your choices and fashion likes to a designer similar in personality. If unsure of your clothing choice and without a stylist to help you, knowing the designers' fashion style will narrow your clothing choices. **Personality Vendor Table 1.12** will be a valuable resource in leading you in the right direction. Included on this table is the minor fashion personality ingénue.

HAIRSTYLES AND WARDROBE INFLUENCE

Hairstyles and how-to's of a good cut is a huge topic and best left to the professionals to cover. Of course your hairstyle is a part of your total look. The hair frames the face and completes the personality area. For this reason, there are certain rules we all should adhere to:

* Your hairstyle should flatter your facial shape. Proportion applies also to the face, and the hair should be in proportion to the face.

* Your hairstyle should suit your age and lifestyle. For example, if you are athletic and sporty, a simple cut is necessary. If you are a senior with very long hair, the look may date you as oppose to making you look younger. Hair length depends not only on your age but also lifestyle and facial shape.

* Your hairstyle should be simple and easy to manage.

* Don't forget to check the back of your head! Your hairstyle encompasses the entire head, front and back.

* Work with a stylist to determine the best look for you. Hair trends come and go as does apparel, so be careful when choosing a look.

THREAD 1.4

Table 1.13

IMAGE CUE TABLE

Image Cue	Sporty	Romantic	Classic	Dramatic	Natural
Colors	Bright, primary, sport colors	Pale, pastels, white, soft colors	Neutrals –black, navy, brown, camel, white	Deep, rich, bold, bright colors	Neutrals—especially camel and khaki
Fabric	Cotton, spandex, denim, French terry cloth, mesh, ripstop, tencel	Lace, eyelet, brocade, peau de soie, chiffon	Gabardine, houndstooth, crepe, wool, worsted flannel, glen plaid, tweed, cashmere	Satin, chintz, jersey, velveteen, charmeuse, faux fur, stretch nylon, crepe	Linen, cotton, gauze, chambray, denim
Hairstyles	Short, easy-to-care-for, wash-n-wear	Soft curls, flowing long locks	Bob, clean lines, neutral tones	Broken lines, futuristic colors	Unaltered, simple styles, no color
Accessories	Sport watch, small stud earrings, or no jewelry at all	Small chains, delicate jewelry, posts	Pearls, small to medium hoops, family heirlooms	Bangles, bracelets, stones, diamonds, gold, glitzy	Simple drop necklace, rustic earthy jewelry, wood bangles

CLOTHING CUES

By this time you can successfully place yourself in a fashion personality category. There are additional **clothing cues** that will assist you in your fashion personality journey. These cues include *color, fabric, hairstyles,* and *accessories* that help to identify the unique qualities of each fashion personality. Because of their importance to personal style, cues such as these will be discussed fully in their own chapter, with the exception of hairstyles, which will be touched on but left to the hair professionals to expand upon. The preceeding image cue table will provide an overview of the effect each cue has on every individual fashion personality.

DISCOVERY

Discovering your fashion personality is the beginning step to achieving amazing personal style. Make it a **habit** to fulfill the steps necessary to achieve individuality. Clinical hypnotist Patrick Glancy says that "90 percent of our day is controlled by subconscious activity." Our normal everyday activities such as walking, breathing, cooking, exercise, and driving a car are based on habits: "a pattern of action that is acquired and has become so automatic that it is difficult to break." (Glancy, 2008). Bad habits are easy to develop and difficult to break, whereas good habits are difficult to develop but easy to drop. Modifying your behavior is a technique hypnotists like Glancy use to change bad habits. This behavior modification is useful when you begin to examine who you are. Knowing how you want others to perceive you are good habits to develop. Follow your instincts to attaining *your own personal style*.

TAKING STOCK

You can now identify the differences between the five fashion personalities: *sporty*—casual, comfortable, and athletic*; romantic*—feminine, delicate, and

FIGURE 1.5
Throughout history, women have made a fashion statement with their clothing. In 1924 these women expressed themselves in the color, style, and shape of their clothing choices. Times have definitely not changed.

lovely; *classic*—tailored, conservative, and basic; *dramatic*—bold, unique, and colorful; and *natural*—simple, untreated, and neutral in color. Color, fabric, hairstyles, and accessories are *image cues* that will help pinpoint your own fashion personality. Browsing through fashion magazines and identifying celebrities you can relate to can help you identify your true fashion personality. The exercise given will lead you to a path of achieving a genuine fashion personality identity.

Knowing the "inside" of who we are is the beginning of achieving a total look that clearly represents who we are on the outside. Fifty-five percent of what individuals notice about you is expressed through your clothing choices. Continue to strive to match the inside with the outside to obtain your own personal style.

KEY WORDS

assumptions	five basic personality types	romantic fashion personality
budget worksheet	habit	sender
classic fashion personality	HNWIS	sexy siren alluring personality
clothing cues	ingénue fashion personality	speaker
cue	listener	sporty fashion personality
dramatic fashion personality	natural fashion personality	style
eclectic	personality	taste
fashion mission statement	personality vendor table	values
fashion personality	receiver	

RESOURCES

Bremer, J. (2004). First impressions. Retrieved on March 15, 2008 from www.bremercommunications.com/First_Impressions.htm.

Chapman, A. (2006). Mehrabian's communication research: Professor Albert Mehrabian's communications model, *Business Balls,* Retrieved on April 21, 2008 from www.businessballs.com.

Glancy, P. (2008). *Understanding Habits.* Retrieved March 16, 2008 from www.glancyhypnosis.com/habit.html.

Posner R. (2008). *The Power of Personal Values.* Retrieved on March 16, 2008 from www.gurusoftware.com/GuruNet/Personal/Topics/Values.htm.

Rasband J. (2005). *Values Communication Through Personal Style.* Conselle L.C. Retrieved on March 16, 2008 from http://ce.byu.edu/ed/edweek/handouts/2007/29.pdf.

Royal Borough of Kensington and Chelsea. (2008). *First Impressions Quiz.* Retrieved on March 16, 2008 from www.rbkc.gov.uk/kccmagazine/regulars/impressions_quiz.asp#top.

Zennadi, B. (2008). *Can I Afford This?* Retrieved on March 16, 2008 from www.amaisd.org/nheights/budget_worksheet.htm.

CHAPTER TWO

Personal Style Evaluation

"Fashion can be bought. Style one must possess."

—EDNA W. CHASE (1877–1957). HIRED BY VOGUE IN 1895, CHASE SERVED AS EDITOR OF THAT MAGAZINE FROM 1914 TO 1956. CHASE IS CREDITED WITH MAKING VOGUE THE TOP FASHION MAGAZINE THAT IT IS TODAY.

CHAPTER OBJECTIVES
After reading this chapter, you will be able to:

* List personality traits that are consistent with your behavior.
* Define demographically who you are.
* Discuss values and beliefs that are important to you.
* Categorize findings about yourself into a specific target market.
* Identify clothing stores that match your target market.
* Compare generation clothing characteristics to your own findings.
* Analyze your lifestyle evaluation chart.

FIGURE 2.1

From generation to generation we share many similarities; looks, smiles, and even our taste in clothing. Grandmother, mother, and daughter all exude a sense of belonging.

WHAT IS YOUR PERSONAL STYLE?

What is **personal style?** Personal style is the projection of your total self to others and includes your clothing, your personality, your hair and makeup, the way you walk, talk, and carry yourself. It's the total package. Each of us is unique in each of these characteristics.

You have to know who you are in order to know your own personal style. To evaluate who you are and how this adds up to your own personal style, we will look at several factors:

* Who are you demographically? **Demographic traits** include age, income, marital status, family status, and education.

* Who are you psychographically? **Psychographic traits** include interests, perceptions, attitudes, and lifestyle.

* What consistent **personality traits** do you possess? Friendly, calm, refined, sweet, gregarious, or gracious?

* What **values** and/or beliefs are important to you? Health, spirituality, helping others, money, recognition, love, perfection, and achievement are all examples of individual values.

* What year were you born? We all belong to a **generation** based on when we were born. Generations have similarity not only in age but also in similar buying characteristics. These generations are:

  - G.I. Generation 1900–'24.
  - Silent Generation 1925–'45.
  - Baby Boomers 1946–'64.
  - Generation X 1965–'77.
  - Generation Y 1978–'98.
  - Millennial Generation 1982–2000 (overlaps with Gen Y).

Other generational groups that may be recognized:

- Culture Wars 1980s–present.
- Echo Boom Generation 1986–'93.
- Internet Generation 1994–2001.
- New Silent Generation 1990s or 2000s.
- Generation C–the present (2008) and getting more sophisticated in years to come.

(All of these groups, identified by the year their members were born, have an indirect effect on each of the members' buying patterns of clothing.)

* What are your **goals** with your wardrobe? This last step will help to define why you are choosing the clothing items that you buy.

Identifying each of these factors yourself will help you make clothing choices that are truly in line with achieving your own personal style goals. We will examine each factor further to place you in the style direction that is right for you. Identifying each of these factors will ultimately help you complete your own Personal Style Assessment included in Chapter 12, Tying It All Together…Your Personal Style.

DEMOGRAPHICS

Identifying ourselves demographically is a simple matter of facts and figures. To look your absolute best your choice of clothing should coincide with your age. What is your **age group**? Are you a pre-teen (12–14), teenager (15–17), young adult (18–24 years), adult (25–34), middle age (35–44), mature (45–54), older (55–64), or senior citizen (65 plus)? How has your clothing evolved over the years? Are you stuck in a rut? Are you still wearing the same clothes that you've been wearing for the past 10 years?

Age Group Clothing Choices

Let's consider the age group clothing choice using a lace camisole as our clothing item example. In your twenties, the lace camisole can work in many ways—as a top under a blazer and as a separate worn as a top showing skin and even cleavage. In your thirties, the lace camisole can also work under a blazer and in addition as a separate, but not showing as much skin as in your twenties. In your forties and fifties, the lace camisole becomes an undergarment piece worn under a blazer, jacket, or see-through blouse. The camisole becomes an item worn to express femininity and a little bit of sexuality, but at this age you should be careful not to make this clothing item an eyesore with your total image. Individuals beyond the fifties age group would most likely consider the lace camisole a foundation piece worn only as underwear. No matter what shape you are, in your age group modesty becomes a factor in the style of clothing items you will choose. A good rule of thumb is the younger you are the more skin you can show and forty-somethings and older, less skin. Having respect for your body and who you are is a valuable first step in achieving a tasteful personal style.

The younger you are, the trendier your clothing items can be. The older, more mature individual would look childish in trendy pieces that are not in line with that person's age group and worn by the younger generation. Nevertheless, no matter what your age, you can have trendy items of clothing in your closet. The key is to mix and match the trendy pieces that you own to make your clothing have personal style and individuality.

Another demographic trait we should consider in evaluating our style is **income**. How much money do you have to spend on clothes? Your clothing budget is part of your discretionary income and relates to a direct outcome in how many pieces of clothing you can own. Statistics also reveal that the more **education** one has the higher your income will be which can also lead to more disposable income to spend on clothing.

Family status is a demographic characteristic that makes itself present especially among the elite. Just the mention of the names, Trump, Hilton, or Kennedy and one would expect a certain style of dress. The word **status** evokes rank, position, and class. Clothing is an outward expression of your rank in society. Celebrities are given clothing items to wear because they become the **fashion leaders** with their consistent presence in the media. Some of us become **followers** emulating the looks and styles of the leaders and innovators in the celebrity spotlight and in leading roles in business, government, the sciences, and other professions. Your goal is to be yourself, your own leader, creating your own personal style.

Your family, parents, and siblings all make an impression that forms your clothing choices. As a youngster your parents make your clothing choice decisions. Whether or not your individual style stays in line with your family status is totally an individual choice. Family status in the beginning of your life plays an important part in helping you form an impression of yourself and your clothing decisions. It also plays a major role in why people wear what they wear.

Discretionary Income

Let's consider two individuals, one making $40,000 a year and another making twice that amount, $80,000 per year. If we consider that eight percent of our monthly income may be spent on clothing (to be discussed further in Chapter 9, Shopping Basics), then the person making $40,000 a year would have approximately $267 per month and the $80,000 individual would have $533 to spend on clothing per month. The additional clothing budget on a higher salary allows you more freedom to choose higher price and/or more quality clothing. Your income, or how much money you make, is a demographic fact that cannot be avoided but can be adjusted. How much income and education you choose to obtain is to some extent a personal choice that plays a part in how much and what type of clothing you will wear.

Consider the Amish people who wear a certain style of dress and are limited in their clothing choices. In contrast, Ivanka Trump grew up in a wealthy family where money is not an issue and her clothing choices are many. Ivanka's choices are rumored to be unlimited. Income, education, and status form an integral part of your personal style.

FIGURE 2.2

The simplicity, lack of detail, and style is evident in the clothing of the Amish people. These are people who shun attention, portraying their simple working lifestyle through their choice of clothes.

PSYCHOGRAPHICS

Psychographics include your interests, values, attitudes and your lifestyle. First, let's examine **lifestyle** as it relates to your personal style. Clothing choices may vary from time to time based on your current lifestyle. Completing the lifestyle grid in Chapter 1, Fashion Personality Types, guided you to the type of clothing that is suitable for your current lifestyle. Preview your current life activities. What you do day-to-day determines what you are wearing. You could be a stay-at-home mom, a working executive, a student, or a retail professional, but style remains a part of your image no matter who you are and what you do. When you track your daily events for one week you will be able to notice a pattern that will relate back to your clothing choices. For example, if you spend eight hours a day, five days a week working retail, then 24 percent of your total clothing choices should be work related. Exercise 2.1 will guide you through the process.

Exercise 2.1: Evaluating Your Lifestyle
Directions: You will need to pull out your lifestyle grid completed in Chapter 1, Fashion Personality Types. We will analyze the same activities you have included on your lifestyle grid. These activities are Sleep, Work, School, Exercise, Travel, Dressy, Casual Home, and Casual Away. Table 2.1, Anna's Lifestyle Grid, is an example of how we will calculate what constitutes our weekly lifestyle.

EXAMPLE: To compute the percentage for the week we will divide the total weekly hours by 168 (24 hours in a day x 7 days in a week). We can count the number of boxes colored in for each activity.

- 8 hours a day, 7 days a week at *sleep*—56 total weekly sleep hours. **Sleep weekly—33 percent (56/168)**
- 5 hours a day, 4 days a week *working*—20 total weekly work hours. **Work weekly—12 percent (20/168)**
- 7 hours a day, 2 days a week *school*—14 total weekly school hours. **School weekly—8 percent (14/168)**
- 1 hour a day, 6 days a week *exercise*—6 total weekly exercise hours. **Exercise weekly—4 percent (6/168)**

- 2 hours a day, 7 days a week *travel*—14 total hours traveling.
  Travel weekly—8 percent (14/168)

- 4 hours a day, 1 day a week *dressy*—4 total hours dressy.
  Dressy weekly—2 percent (4/168)

- Average 5 hours a day, 7 days a week *casual home*—35 total casual home hours.
  Casual Home weekly—21 percent (35/168)

- Average 3 hours a day, 7 days a week *casual away*—21 total casual away hours.
  Casual Away weekly—13 percent (21/168)

Analysis

Anna's weekly lifestyle is:

Sleep—33 percent
Work—12 percent
School—8 percent
Casual home—21 percent
Casual away—13 percent
Travel—8 percent
Exercise—4 percent
Dressy—2 percent

TOTAL—101 percent weekly lifestyle (rounding)

Table 2.1 shows the lifestyle of Anna, an individual whose majority of weekly activities includes clothing that is work-related at 12 percent and school at 8 percent. These are the clothes that the majority of individuals will see her wear and use to form a first impression of her. Anna's first impression clothing, work and school, account for 20 percent of her weekly lifestyle. These are the

Table 2.1
ANNA'S LIFESTYLE GRID
A WEEK IN YOUR LIFE LIFESTYLE GRID (EXAMPLE)

clothing items Anna should purchase selectively and consistently. Sleeping and relaxing at 33 percent and casual home at 21 percent account for 54 percent of Anna's home-life wardrobe. Anna's goal is now to figure out what makes her feel comfortable yet still presents a pleasing image. Does Anna have enough clothes to match the percentage of her daily lifestyle? If not, then the next chapter, Closet Evaluation, will help Anna to weed out what is not necessary and to add what is necessary to make her wardrobe match her current lifestyle.

Your lifestyle forms the framework for your clothing choices. Evaluating your lifestyle is an essential step in personal style evaluation. Refer to your Lifestyle Grid on a yearly basis or when there are major changes or upheavals in your life such as a job change that has a totally different dress code. If you have graduated from school and are pursuing other opportunities or entering the workforce, your clothing should change. Analyze the percentages and base your clothing choices on what is needed now and not later. To possess style, one must consider where one is in life.

VALUES AND BELIEFS

Values include your personal beliefs, morals, principles, and ideals. Table 2.2, Value Clothing Implications, shows some examples of how your values relate to your clothing choices.

It's easy to see how your lifestyle and values relate to your clothing choices, but what does attitude and interest have to do with clothing? **Attitude** is a manner of acting, feeling, or thinking that manifests in your opinion and disposition. How you feel on a particular day may determine what you are wearing. **Interest** is very similar to attitude because you're claiming and expressing concern or curiosity about something. We make choices every day in what we put on our bodies. Our clothing speaks volumes about who we are as individuals.

Table 2.2
VALUE CLOTHING IMPLICATIONS

Value	Clothing Implication
Modesty	No low cut tops or see-through clothing. No exposure of skin; more body covering clothes.
Family Life	Possible hand-me-downs from family members. Similarity with parents' style of dress.
Religion	May require a uniform in school, or as a member of the clergy, modest clothing is the attire.
Money	High-priced, name brand, good quality clothing.
Individuality	Choosing clothing that expresses who you are, items that set you apart from others.
Health	Casual, comfortable, workout type clothing. Clothing that is economically friendly.

GENERATION

Generation-based clothing choices can both date you and make you part of a **clothing tribe**. Clothing in this category shows or reveals what was typical at a certain period in time or age. That fact that some dated clothing may still fit you (you've owned these pieces for years!) doesn't mean you should wear it.

The year in which you were born places you into a unique clothing tribe with others your same age. Each generation has certain characteristics that ultimately relate right back to your clothing choice. Refer to Table 2.3, Generation-Based Clothing, for your generation to see if you see yourself within your generational pattern. There may be some of you that differ slightly in your choices from your generation, but for the most part we are all at least partly touched by our generations.

Table 2.3
GENERATION-BASED CLOTHING

Generation	Years	Comments/ Relationship to Clothing
G.I. Generation	1900–1924	Loyalty, duty important, conformist, quality is important, conservative.
Silent Generation	1925–1945	Generous, can't decide clearly, conformist, followers.
Baby Boomers	1946–1964	Idealistic, impatient, money oriented, first divorce generation, ME generation, clothing is important—brand names and status.
Generation X	1965–1977	Some are violent, predominantly single, authentic, and anti-fashion.
Generation Y	1978–1998	Internet, no values, education-oriented, spends money on clothing—enormous impact.
Millennial	1982–2002	Adventurous, impatient, and generally non-committed—individuality and expressing themselves through their clothing choices. Tolerant of racial, gender, and sexual differences; wears what's comfortable and what fits. Those who have leadership status make trends in dress.

Generation C

For years, trend forecasters have been preparing us for the digital creation generation—"Generation C," the C representing "content." This generation uses pictures, movies, blogs, and music as its main form of communication. Included in this category is also the customizing and personalization of any physical goods. You make it yourself and sell it yourself. Clothing as an art form is becoming more widely acceptable; creating, wearing and showcasing one's final project is popular to those who seek uniqueness.

Retail stores and Internet sites are popping up all over allowing individuals to become their own designers. A perfect example of this are the jeans at the website www.makeyourownjeans.com, where you can choose fabric finishes, give your measurements, and complete your order with a pair of jeans made especially for you. Retail store 1154 Lill is another example of customization. Individuals can make their own custom handbag at 1154 Lill. You pick your style and fabric, and your custom handbag will be shipped to you based on your specifications. The Internet allows for you to see the fabric on your style bag without even going into a retail store, which is all part of Generation C—"content" using pictures to make it yourself.

Trendwatching.com believes this is not a trend that just deals with the year you were born. Generation C involves the ever-increasing integration of the Web and the creative juices we all have to make it and do it ourselves. Manufacturers continue to force us to get involved not only for their increasing advertising benefit but also as a benefit to each of us to take an active part in what we like and what we can contribute. As the Web continues to grow, so does this generation.

Identifying your clothing within these five characteristics—demographics, psychographics, personality traits, values/beliefs, and generation—will help you recognize a style pattern within your clothing.

GOALS

What is it that you want your clothing to say about you? What are your **clothing goals**? Your goals will relate back to all the plans, concepts, and existences in your mind about why you choose the clothing you do. Complete Exercise 2.2, Clothing Goals Questionnaire, honestly to see where you stand with your clothing goals.

Exercise 2.2: Clothing Goals Questionnaire

1. I want my clothing to make me:
- **a)** stand out in a crowd.
- **b)** disappear amongst the masses.
- **c)** identify my personality.
- **d)** appear as the unique and different person that I am.

2. My clothing is:
- **a)** artwork—identifying who and what I am.
- **b)** a burden—I would prefer not to wear it.
- **c)** something I can't live without—I keep all clothing pieces that have meaning for me.
- **d)** a variety of choices—mixture of fads, classics, and contemporary pieces.

3. If money were no object, my clothing would be:
- **a)** the brightest, most colorful unique pieces.
- **b)** monotone, boring, and of no significance—the same as if I had no money.
- **c)** carefully selected and chosen with a specific purpose and intention.
- **d)** many, varied, and including the latest styles, classics, and fads.

What Do Your Results Mean?

If you answered mainly a's then your clothing goals lean toward **uniqueness**. You buy clothing mainly for adornment; your body is a work of art expressing who you are. Your clothing becomes an outward expression of yourself and helps society identify who you really are as an individual.

If you answered mainly b's then your clothing goals lean toward the **monotone** look. You look for basic, easy-wearing pieces that are simple and somewhat plain. You tend to purchase the same items in more than one color, and rarely deviate from what you consider normal.

If you answered mainly c's then your clothing goals lean toward **individuality**. You carefully select clothing that expresses who you are. You tend to buy the same brands because you identify with the style and fit. You know who you are and how you want to look.

If you answered mainly d's then your clothing goals lean toward **variety**. You tend to go with the flow and choose clothing based on what is in style at a particular time and how you feel at a particular point in your life. Classics remain the framework of your wardrobe yet you sometimes buy pieces that could be considered a fad.

GETTING ON TRACK

Knowing who you are is the beginning of achieving personal style. Chapter 2, Personal Style Evaluation, covers the steps one must take in order to reveal and evaluate the uniqueness that each of us truly possesses within us. Demographics, psychographics, personality, values, generation, and goals all play a part in our personal style. Continuing to be honest with yourself and evaluate where you are in life is one very important way to make sure you're on the right track.

Completing the Personality Assessment will give you further insight into who you are and how you want others to perceive you.

Personal style may take time for some, and is a *continual process* that may change throughout your lifetime. As you change, so should your clothing choices. Remember, your clothing speaks volumes about who you are, and it's a major factor in the first impression you are exposing to others.

KEY WORDS

age group	generation	personal style
attitude	generation-based clothing	personality traits
clothing goals	goals	psychographic traits
clothing tribe	income	psychographics
demographic traits	individuality	status
education	interest	uniqueness
fashion leaders	lifestyle	values
followers	monotone	

CHAPTER THREE

Closet Evaluation

"A closet full of wire hangers can be the most dangerous place in the world."
—PAUL LYNDE, COMEDIAN AND ACTOR

CHAPTER OBJECTIVES
After reading this chapter, you will be able to:

* Examine your closet from a fashion personality point of view.
* Sort clothing in your closet from the three-part closet evaluation perspective.
* Identify a favorite clothing charity or institution to which you can give away discarded clothing items.
* Prepare clothing items in need of alterations to take to a tailor, and know how to find and what to ask of a tailor that suits your needs.
* Select and analyze items you will wear and place them back in the closet in an orderly fashion (e.g., light to dark, left to right item classifications).
* List ideal closet hardware and extras needed to complete your ideal closet exercise.

TAKING A LOOK INSIDE

Look inside your closet. What you see will reveal valuable information about the person you have become that includes your personal taste, colors, and overall lifestyle. Some people hire professional **closet organizers** to complete this task. Companies like The Container Store specialize in closet organization and organize and design your closet for a fee. Many individuals fear anyone looking inside their closets because of all the information one can assume from their clothing choices. In Chapter 2, Personal Style Evaluation, we discussed our values and clothing choices and what implication a certain value may have on our clothing. If a professional is examining your closet and notices certain items of clothing that reveal another side of you they didn't know you had, then be prepared to explain why you chose that item or items. Even professionals make assumptions that may or may not be correct. You may be wary about what you might find inside your own closet, but rest assured that this is an important step in achieving your own personal style. Your closet is a vital statistic in evaluating *who* you are.

In Chapter 1, Fashion Personality Types, we evaluated our personalities and discovered who we are on the inside. We matched our clothing choices to our personalities, values, beliefs, and lifestyle in Chapter 2, Personal Style Evaluation, and now we need to peer inside our closets to see what impressions our clothing has made to the outside world. Clothing is a **silent language** speaking volumes about ourselves to others before we even open our mouths.

In order to make accurate clothing decisions we need to start with a clean slate. The plan begins with a **three part closet evaluation**. Each part, done simultaneously, will help you to effortlessly achieve your own personal style. The parts consist of what you will:

1. **Wear**—clothing items that stay inside your closet to choose from on a daily basis. These clothing items fit you now and tie into your inner self, your fashion personality. Every single item that remains inside your closet reflects who you are inside and out.

2. Discard—clothing items that are of no use to you and should not be inside your closet. These clothing items will be donated to your favorite charity if still wearable, or simply discarded. This is probably the most difficult part of the closet evaluation process.

3. Alter—these clothing items have some redeemable qualities. Maybe the fabric is of good quality and not out of style. Could it be a dress that will now make an excellent skirt? Are the buttons vintage in style and can be used on another garment?

In this chapter, you will examine all three parts to help you fulfill your dream closet that will allow you to achieve an "easy to choose and wear" lifestyle.

BEGINNING

Where do I begin? Looking inside your closet can be an overwhelming task. Think of an organized closet as the beginning of an extra hour of sleep in the morning. Completing this task will not only help you save time in choosing your wardrobe pieces but also provide you with the opportunity to always look your very best.

Allow yourself ample time to complete this task. Time can vary depending on the number of clothes you own. If you've been hanging onto your clothing since you were a child this process could take all day. You will have to make a decision on each piece of clothing that you own. Your assessment will have an end result in one of the three categories:

1. Is this an item I will wear?
2. Is this a clothing item I need to get rid of?
3. Is this a clothing item I can repair or alter?

It's best to gather boxes and/or containers to begin the process of scrutinizing your clothing. Just as you previously did in evaluating your personality, you will need to complete Exercise 3.1: My Closet Scrutiny, to help you assess what may be needed to begin the closet evaluation process.

Exercise 3.1: My Closet Scrutiny
1. How often do you complete a "spring cleaning" in your closet?
    a) Once a year
    b) Twice a year
    c) Only when necessary

2. How long do you hang on to your clothing?
    a) If it still fits, I keep it.
    b) When I buy a new item, I discard an old item.
    c) I never throw anything away.

3. The closet you currently own is:
    a) big enough to hold all the clothing I own, all seasons.
    b) actually more than one closet; my clothing is separated by current season.
    c) overflowing with clothing items including items that have never been worn.

4. Rank your clothing items by approximate percentage of ownership:
    a) Long-hanging garments (Include coats, dresses, gowns, long skirts and pants) _____ percent.
    b) Short-hanging garments (Include shirts, jackets, suits, and folded pants) _____ percent.
    c) Drawers (Include sweaters, lingerie, socks, and accessories) _____ percent.

d) Shelf Space (Include shoes and boots) _____ percent.
e) Miscellaneous Accessories (Include belts, ties, purses, scarves, hats, and jewelry) _____ percent.

Analysis of Exercise 3.1: My Closet Scrutiny

Analyze your answers to questions 1 through 3. If you answers are mainly the letter A then your closet evaluation will probably take a minimum of a half-day. You are not consistent with completing a thorough closet examination, but are halfway there in sorting out the good from the bad. If you answers are mainly the letter B then your closet may take less than a half-day. You are current with your clothing choices and most of your clothing items are wearable. If you answers are mainly the letter C, then plan on taking a full day or more to analyze your clothing items. You have not begun the process of evaluating your clothing and what you own.

Your answer to the fourth question will help you to decide how your finished closet should look. The categories with the highest percentages will determine the basic look of your closet. More hanging items equal more bar space and more accessories, while foldable items equal more shelf space.

Once you set aside the time you need to complete this task you can begin your three-step closet evaluation by preparing to **pull, sort**, and then **analyze** each piece. Depending on the number of clothing items you own, you will need a minimum of three boxes. One box will say *wear* and will eventually be empty because these are the items that will return to your closet. Another box will say *discard* and will eventually be taken to your favorite charity. Some of the clothing items in this box may truly be thrown away and discarded. These items are simply of no use to anyone. The third box will say *alter*. These items will be taken to a tailor to make new and eventually end up back in your closet as a wearable item.

Let's look at each category separately to allow you, the clothing owner, to know what it is you should be looking for when beginning this tremendous task.

WEAR

All items that end up in your *wear* box are current, in style, and need no alteration. A further examination of the clothing items that should appear in this category will be reviewed in Chapter 6, Cluster Concept. At this time, you only need to examine what you have currently.

The steps you need to take to complete the *wear process* are:

1. **Remain**—first step taken when analyzing your current clothing. What items will remain inside your closet that you will wear? These items *fit your body now*, are current and in style, and need no alterations or repair.

2. **Organize**—keep like items together by categorizing your clothing by type—all jackets, all skirts, all pants, etc. Separate items that should not be on hangers from the closet items. These shelf-clothing items include sweaters, active wear, t-shirts, and some nightwear.

3. **Color**—within each category, colorize your clothing from light to dark, going from the left side to the right side of your closet. It's helpful to have a color wheel inside your closet to refer to when needed. Categorizing clothing from light to dark can be confusing with the myriad of colors that are available today. If you are stuck on which color to place first, refer to the color wheel to see where it fits in. Because you will probably notice similarities in color with your clothing choices, it may be difficult to colorize correctly. A color wheel helps you organize your closet and stay on track when deciding what goes with what when choosing what to wear. If you decide to wear all one color, **monotone**, then use the color wheel to analyze shades of the same color. If you decide to be **complementary**, then choose colors that are opposite each other on the color wheel. If you want to be distinctive then choose **analogous** colors, or colors that are related and have at least one color in common. Further analysis of color and clothing selection will be discussed in Chapter 5, Wardrobe Selection Factors.

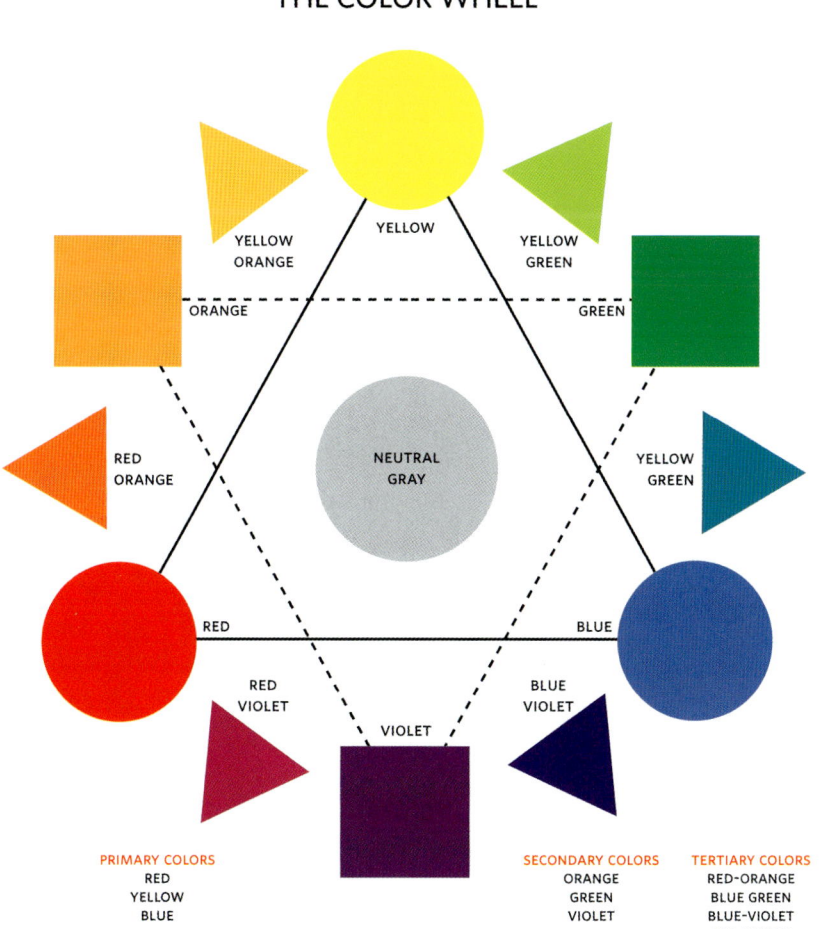

FIGURE 3.1
The basic color wheel consists of three sets of colors—primary, secondary, and tertiary. The clothing in your closet should be colorized just like the colors on a color wheel.

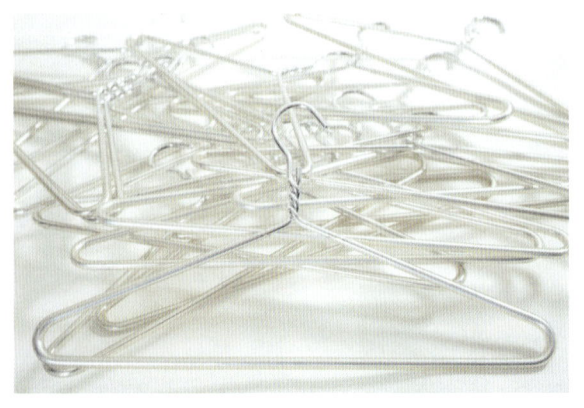
(A)

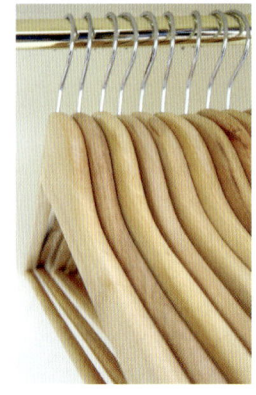
(B)

FIGURE 3.2
Common in most closets, **(a) chrome** and **(b) wood** hangers are used for a variety of clothing types such as shirts, jackets, and coats. Specialty hangers—**(c) Euro, (d) tubular**, and **(e) grippy**—help your clothing last longer by allowing for easy visibility and easy access in your closet.

(C)

(D)

(E)

4. Hangers—Utilize various hangers for each type of clothing.

- **Chrome hangers**—steel, strong, chrome finish. Good for hanging coats and jackets.
- **Natural wood hangers**—durable, versatile, flat profile. Suitable for a wide variety of garments, including shirts, blouses, coats, and jackets.
- **Euro Hanger**—thick, sculpted arms made of smooth plastic. Premium hanger for clothing in the laundry room.
- **Tubular hangers**—plastic, available in a rainbow of colors. Clothing can be organized by season or category by choosing a color. Useful for a variety of clothing from denim to blouses.
- **Grippy Hangers**—core of the hanger is usually made of chrome and the hanger grips have foam which help to cushion your garment. These hangers are suitable for skirts, slacks, and strapless dresses.

Various hangers are available for a variety of clothing types. Websites like www.containerstore.com detail the various types of hangers available and their uses. There are five major categories of hangers: **wood, metal, plastic, specialty, and children's**. Within each of these categories are a multitude of variations. Examine your clothes to see which type of hanger is best for your clothing. An inexpensive way to organize your closet is to decide on using plastic hangers. You can color code each category of clothing by the color of your hangers. For example, blue hangers for shirts and blouses, white hangers for jackets and blazers, green hangers for pants, and black hangers for skirts. Your closet will look organized, neat, and made easy for you to find what you need. The wear items are now in your closet, organized, colorized, and on the proper hangers.

Exercise 3.2: My Before and After Closet
Complete a Before-and-After Closet within your home by following these steps:

1. Take a picture of your closet as it is right now.

2. Mount the picture on construction board or paper highlighting and identifying areas that need to be changed with the use of arrows.

3. Make a list of items needed to complete the ideal closet. Note shopping items and construction needed that may require a professional or carpenter to complete. Cut out photographs of supply items needed for your ideal closet and post them on the board.

4. Cut swatches of fabric, if needed, and post on poster board. Glue paint chips of color used in the closet. Fabric may be used to line your clothing baskets or drawers.

5. Cut out photographs of lighting to be used in the closet.

6. Note improvements made in writing and with a picture.

7. Draw a picture of your ideal closet utilizing the additional materials chosen.

     Once your closet is complete with only wearable items inside, you are then ready to move on to adding items to your current assortment.

FIGURE 3.3 (OPPOSITE)
A dream closet is within reach utilizing a storage system like this one by elfa®.

DISCARD

The second part of closet analysis is *discarding*. This category may be sentimental to some and may require outside help to analyze those clothing items you really need to throw out. There are certain guidelines to follow when considering what clothing to discard. These guidelines are:

1. If you haven't worn the item in the past two years discard it.

2. If you still have price tags on the clothing item and have never worn the item, get rid of it.

3. If you wore the clothing item in high school, or if it is at least 10 years old, then it's time to discard it. Unless it's **vintage,** which is another subject altogether, dated clothing will date you faster than your looks.

4. If the clothing item is not part of your color scheme then it's time to discard it. You will know what colors, neutrals, and accents work within your clothing assortment upon completing the section on color in Chapter 5, Wardrobe Selection Factors.

5. If the clothing item is not in line with your body type then it needs to be discarded. Just because an item of clothing is popular doesn't mean you should wear it. Chapter 4, Body Type Evaluation, examines this further, but if you look in the mirror upon first examination and sense it doesn't feel right or look right then it's time to get rid of it.

These guidelines will help you decide what you need to do with your clothing. You can (1) throw them away, (2) give them to a charity, (3) give them to a friend or a relative, or (4) place them in a thrift shop or consignment store. Keep in mind that few items require the first option. An example of a clothing

VINTAGE CLOTHING AND YOUR PERSONAL STYLE

Vintage clothing refers to garments that come from another era. Most individuals say clothing that is 25 years old or more is considered vintage. Some clothing historians clarify vintage clothing by referring to the year the clothing was manufactured. I have found that clothing from the years 1920 to 1975 would be considered vintage. Anything older than 1920 would be considered **antique** clothing, and any clothing from 1975 to approximately 20 years later would be considered **retro**.

"A vintage purist will tell you that anything within the past 15 years should be referred to as contemporary, and I have to agree," says vintage buyer and seller Paula Weston Thomas. Vintage clothing that is still in excellent shape and doesn't look too much like a *costume* from another era can be worn beautifully, doesn't look dated, and looks exactly like what it is—quality clothing.

Popular designer vintage clothing worn by celebrities and others include Valentino, Bill Blass, Emilio Pucci, Oscar de la Renta, Pauline Trigere, and Alfred Shaheen. Their clothing is timeless and the quality is everlasting. Their pieces can be bought from various vintage sellers online and in vintage boutiques. One way to check the merits of a vintage seller is to contact The Vintage Fashion Guild (VFG) (www.vintagefashionguild.org) VFG is an international guild founded in 2002 by vintage sellers willing to share their knowledge and passion of vintage clothing. Part of their mission is to position vintage clothing as a viable alternative to conventional fashion.

QUICK VINTAGE LABEL TIPS BY THE VFG

If vintage clothing is of interest to you and it's something you would like to invest in, then be sure to refer to the VFG for some quick tips on what to look for in vintage fashion labels; these include:

* Look for labels in the side seams and even in the hems of older garments.
* The U.S. National Labor Relations Act was passed in 1935 and labels recognizing this act would appear after this date.

- Union labels would reflect the year and union affiliation. According to the Fashion Guild website: "The ILGWU (International Ladies' Garment Workers' Union) was formed in 1900. It joined the CIO (Congress of Industrial Organizations) briefly in 1937. Rejoined the AFL (American Federation of Labor) in 1940. AFL-CIO merged in 1955. In 1995 ILGWU reformed as UNITE."

- Country of origin labels originated in the United States in 1891 following the McKinley Act.

- Garment care labels began in 1971 in the United States. The current labels on clothing were introduced in 1983.

- International care symbols were developed in 1971.

- In 1960 the USA Textile Products Identifications Act mandated the use of fabric content labels.

- The Fur Products labeling act of 1952 required an accurate description of fur (e.g., "Hudson Seal" became "sheared muskrat").

- A small "e" on the label of a pair of Levi's denims means they were manufactured after 1971 and a capital "E" if pre-1971.

IS VINTAGE FOR YOU?

No matter how you look at it, vintage means old can be new again, and most certainly it offers a unique and exciting alternative for those who find it fits their personal style. Indeed, a viable alternative clothing choice is vintage clothing. Remember to apply all the principles learned in this book when purchasing vintage clothing. Your personal style will look its absolute best when uniqueness and all other factors form a cohesive total look.

item that should be thrown away is one whose fabric has no redeemable qualities. The fabric is torn and cannot be repaired or used to make another garment. Discarding an article of clothing may mean that you don't need or want it, but others might. You know the old saying, "one man's trash is another man's treasure." The trend now is to wear old clothing that has been re-made or re-purposed into something else. The millennial generation, (1982–2002), discussed in Chapter 2, Personal Style Evaluation, is big on creativity and re-use anything to make what they wear. Individuality and expressing themselves through their clothing choices are characteristics of this generation. Materials such as old shower curtains, bubble wrap, umbrellas, egg cartons, cell phones, and plastic garbage bags are used to make unique clothing items. Chapter 12, Going Green and Your Personal Style, will discuss this re-purposing topic further.

Throwing the item away is simply that, putting it in the trash. There are no redeemable qualities at all to the clothing. Giving clothing to charity is best when the items are still in fairly good condition and these clothing items will clothe someone in need. Depending on the clothing items to be given away there are plenty of charities to choose from that are willing to take your items. To find a list of charities that you can review and connect with to possibly make a donation refer to table 3.1 for charity information, tips and resources.

ALTER

Everyone should have a tailor that knows their body and are able to assist them when alterations are needed. Alterations may require time, especially when you have to practically make something new again, or a small job when you are just in need of a repair. Locate and use a good tailor to keep your clothing in tip-top shape. The tailor may be your local dry cleaner or someone you know that sews well. In the long run, it will lengthen the life of your clothing and make you not only look good but feel good also.

Table 3.1
CHARITIES: WHERE SHOULD I GIVE MY CLOTHING?

One way to find a charity to which you can feel good about contributing your clothing is through websites such as Charity Navigator (www.charitynavigator.org). The mission of Charity Navigator is to "help givers and celebrate the work of charities." Charity Navigator strives to achieve this goal by monitoring the performance of charities, ranking them according to its findings, and providing contact information. (www.charitynavigator.com, 2006).

But do they accept clothing contributions? It's always worth contacting them to find out. Many organizations, not generally considered in the business of distributing used clothing, can raise good money by collecting them and selling them on the used clothing market or to "rag pickers," who pay by the pound.

Table 3.1a
TEN SUPER-SIZED CHARITIES

Below are 10 of the biggest charities in the United States that Charity Navigator scored well.

Rank	Charity	Website (contact)
1	American Red Cross	www.redcross.org
2	AmeriCares	www.americares.org
3	World Vision	www.worldvision.org
4	American Cancer Society	www.cancer.org
5	Feed the Children	www.feedthechildren.org
6	Food for the Poor	www.foodforthepoor.org
7	Volunteers of America	www.voa.org
8	CARE	www.care.org
9	America's Second Harvest	www.secondharvest.org
10	The Nature Conservancy	www.nature.org

Table 3.1b
TEN SLAM-DUNK CHARITIES

Charity Navigator monitors the performance of more than 5,300 of the largest charities in the United States. It then ranks them according to its findings. Visit its website for more on the methodology of its rankings. Basically, any score over 60 means that the organization has been ranked at the highest level. Below are the top 10 from 2006. (www.charitynavigator.com, 2006).

Rank	Charity	Website (contact)	Overall Score
1	Mayor's Fund to Advance New York City	www.nyc.gov/fund	69.86
2	Asha for Education	www.ashanet.org	69.69
3	Fund for Public Schools	www.schools.nyc.gov/fundforpublicschools	69.65
4	Food Gatherers	www.foodgatherers.org	69.58
5	Louisville Zoo Foundation	www.louisvillezoo.org	69.57
6	Fisher House Foundation	www.fisherhouse.org	69.56
7	Scholarship America	www.scholarshipamerica.org	69.55
8	Catholic Charities USA	www.catholiccharitiesusa.org	69.51
9	Partners In Health	www.pih.org	69.49
10	California Community Foundation	www.califund.org	69.47

Source: www.charitynavigator.org/index.cfm?bay=topten.detail&listid=17, 2006

Tips on Finding a Good Tailor
So how do you go about finding a good tailor? Tailoring is an art form and there are certain pointers one should look for when inquiring about and finding the best person for your needs; these include:

1. Ask questions: how long has the person been in business?

2. Ask for references: can the tailor show photos or samples of his or her work?

3. Communication: does the tailor listen to your needs and wants and understand how to make them come to fruition? Is the tailor honest in what he can and cannot do?

4. Is the tailor a member of any professional clothing organization? **The Custom Tailors and Designers Association of America (CTDA)** or **The Professional Association of Custom Clothiers (PACC)** are two examples.

5. Does the tailor specialize in any type of work such as bridal gowns or men's clothing?

6. Check for length of time and turnaround time, reasonable or too long?

7. Are the rates acceptable for the amount of work being done on your clothing?

What Are the Normal Rates for Tailoring?
Rates to alter garments depend on where you take your garments, i.e., to a local dry cleaner, a fashion student, or a professional who has been in the business for years. A tailor that has been in business for quite some time and is a member of a professional tailoring organization will be able to charge more

money than someone who has less experience. Rates vary by individual and company but most charge by the garment and service needed. For example, costs for hemming a pair of pants could range by several dollars depending on fabrication and garment details. In addition, other than hemming, other alteration categories that can be done are relining, patches, zipper replacement, waist-in/out, tapering, buttons, and miscellaneous services such as repairing seams and holes, and re-sewing belt loops.

You will ultimately look and feel better in your clothing when they fit you comfortably and correctly. Take the time to invest in finding the best tailor that will match your needs and budget.

OTHER USES FOR OLD CLOTHING

There are also alternative uses for your clothing that is ripped, torn, and in need of repair. You can use the fabric from the clothing as a duster for furniture or shoes. And, if in style, you can use pieces of the fabric as patchwork on denim to create a trendy look. You might have your tailor, or even try your own hand at creating unique fashion pieces, especially if your fashion personality tends toward the artsy or eclectic. You could change old denim pants to a skirt by cutting the legs and creating a patchwork motif in the v-section that remains open, or cut out squares or other shapes from old clothing fabric to use as patches on jackets for an eclectic look. Let your imagination run wild when reusing old fabric. The end result will definitely be unique and the style individually yours.

PRACTICAL BEAUTY

Analyzing your closet is the beginning of seeing what you own and what you need to clean out. Completing the wear, discard, and alter steps will guide you to a well-organized closet suitable for the style maven that you are becoming.

Once you complete your ideal closet exercise, take a photograph of your dream closet. You will begin to notice colors, styles, and categories that you like by examining your closet. As you begin to expand the wearable clothing items in your closet, make note of additional improvements that may be needed. You may decide to add specialty hangers, additional shelving, baskets, and hooks or hang bars. Whatever you decide to do, make sure these additions allow your clothing to be visible and within easy reach. A closet should not only be beautiful but practical.

KEY WORDS

alter	discard	retro
analogous	Euro hangers	silent language
analyze	grippy hangers	sort
antique	metal category of hangers	specialty category of hangers
children's category of hangers	monotone	three part closet evaluation
chrome hangers	natural wood hangers	tubular hangers
closet organizers	plastic category of hangers	vintage
complementary	Professional Association of Custom Clothiers (PACC)	wear
Custom Tailors and Designers Association of America (CTDA)	pull	wood category of hangers

RESOURCES

Charity Navigator. (2006). *10 Super-Sized Charities*. Retrieved on March 30, 2008 from www.charitynavigator.org.

Charity Navigator. (2006). *10 Slam-Dunk Charities*. Retrieved March 30, 2008 from www.charitynavigator.com.

The Container Store. (2008). *Closet*. Retrieved on March 29, 2008 from www.thecontainerstore.com.

E-How, Inc. (2008). *How to Hire a Tailor*. Retrieved on March 31, 2008 from www.ehow.com/how_108138_hire-tailor.html?ref=fuel.

Femminastyle Vintage. (2008). *Vintage Clothing*. Retrieved on March 29, 2008 from www.femminastyle.com/index.php?main_page=page&id=23.

Green Earth® Cleaning. (2008). *Alterations Price List*. Retrieved on March 31, 2008 from www.naturalcleaners.com/pricelistalt.html.

Gordon, M. (2007). *New Moon Vintage*. Retrieved on March 29, 2008 from www.newmoonvintage.com/index.php?cPath=28.

Weston Thomas, P. (2006). *What is Vintage Fashion Today on the Internet?* Retrieved on March 29, 2008 from www.fashion-era.com/Vintage_fashion/1_what_is_vintage_fashion.htm.

Vintage Fashion Guild. (2008). *Quick Tip—Material World*. Retrieved on March 29, 2008 from www.vintagefashionguild.org/content/blogcategory/50/86/.

PART II

Wardrobe Evaluation: *What* Should You Wear?

CHAPTER FOUR

Body Type Evaluation

"But those aren't the flavors. That'd make too much sense. Apple and pear, according to Dr. Phil, are body types the bars are made for. Hey, I've got some advice. If you look like an apple or a pear, eat an apple or a pear!"

—DR. PHILLIP MCGRAW. BEST KNOWN AS "DR. PHIL," THE PSYCHOLOGIST, AUTHOR, AND TALK SHOW HOST'S POPULAR TELEVISION SHOW DEALS WITH PSYCHOLOGY-THEMED ISSUES.

CHAPTER OBJECTIVES
After reading this chapter, you will be able to:

* Identify and define the four major body types for women.
* List three additional body types for women identified by body measurements.
* Carry out the body type tracing exercise to identify body type.
* Define proportion and its relationship to body types.
* Carry out the body length proportion exercise.
* List the characteristics of an ideal proportion body type using the **Golden Mean Ratio of 3:5:8.**

* Identify pear, apple, and other body types outside of the norm.
* Identify clothing choices suitable for each body type.

LET'S GET PHYSICAL

We are all different human beings with unique body types that are specific to each of us. Knowing our bodies from tip to toe—indentations, curves, roundness, flatness, flab, lumps, bumps, and humps—helps us identify the right type of clothing that will not only flatter us, but also help us feel good about ourselves.

This chapter will allow you to examine your body from a physical point of view. The exercises will give you clues to what is right and not right (according to the norm) about your body. The goal is to allow your clothing to be a valuable tool in helping you to achieve a look that is not only suitable to you, but to your body. This chapter is essential in realizing what your body type is and how it relates to your clothing choices that will ultimately make you a style maven.

BODY NORMAL IN THE FASHION INDUSTRY

The word "ideal" can mean different things to different people, but the dictionary defines **ideal** as perfect, tops, supreme, ultimate, and the best. In the fashion industry ideal is hard to reach for anyone, but the **norm** is plausible and is expected from the viewpoint of fashion designers in order for one to look good in their clothing. Norm is what is considered to be the standard, the average, and what is considered customary to most. It is rumored that Italian fashion designer **Valentino** would only allow talk show host **Oprah Winfrey** to wear his clothing after she lost the weight and was considered "normal" in his eyes. Valentino has said "the key to elegance is not just wearing beautiful things but making what you're wearing come alive." Designers want their clothing to sell and stand out against the human body frame. In order for this to occur the model has to be shaped almost like a hanger for the clothes to hang well on the body.

Throughout history the "ideal" body frame size has changed. As far back as the year 1639, **The Three Graces** sculpture in Greek mythology (which represents beauty, charm, and joy), depicts three nude, slender, female figures. In his 1887 painting "**The Bathers** ," Pierre-Auguste Renoir depicted a more curvy female body. Along came the 1920s and the era of the flapper dress and women were yet again slender. Actress and movie star **Marilyn Monroe** in the 1950s depicted a more curvy female body frame that women wanted to emulate. Then in the 1960s English supermodel **Twiggy** came on the fashion scene, and for the first time in fashion history a very thin, slightly underweight woman became the ideal body image. At the age of 16, Twiggy signed her modeling contract and weighed only 90 pounds. The rise of the disease **anorexia nervosa** began in the 1970s with females striving to be super-thin and having intense fears of gaining weight. American singer **Karen Carpenter** died from complications of the disease in 1983 and heightened the fear of what it means to be too thin.

From 1988 to 2002, fashion magazines *Vogue*, *Cosmopolitan*, and *Harper's Bazaar* have shown models on their front covers showcasing the latest fashion. Thin, slender supermodels Paulina Porizkova, Cindy Crawford, and Naomi Campbell are a few that have graced the covers, but according to Media Empire Forbes, in 2007 Brazilian model **Gisele Bündchen** ranks as the highest-paid supermodel. Bündchen's measurements at 5 feet 7.7 inches tall, 130 pounds are 38-27-37. Designers love the way their clothes grace her body and how the clothes drape her slender frame. We all know not everyone is as tall and thin as a supermodel.

According to the U.S. Department of Health and Human Services, from 1999–2002, the average U.S. woman was 5 feet 3.8 inches tall and weighed 163 pounds. This is a far cry from the average model height and weight of the example cited above of supermodel Gisele Bündchen. So, what is considered normal? Is it supermodel size or the average American woman size? Consider the uproar at Madrid's fashion week in 2006 when 30 percent of the models were banned from walking the catwalk because they were considered too thin. According to Regional Official Concha Guerra, "fashion is a mirror and many teenagers imitate what they see on the catwalk." The rise of health concerns that may occur with being too thin is reason enough for more attention to be drawn to this subject.

Are we becoming a society of "curves rule" again, or is thin still in? The debate will forever go on and everyone has an opinion. In May, 2006, research—conducted by the Maternal and Child Health Research Program, the U.S. Department of Health and Human Services, the University of Maryland General Clinical Research Center, the General Clinical Research Centers Program, and the National Center for Research Resources of the National Institutes of Health—attempted to try to understand body size satisfaction among female adolescents The results showed that although most adolescents (55 percent) were satisfied with their current body weight, those that were not satisfied desired to be thinner. Are we ever satisfied?

Demographics and psychographics play a part in how you view yourself and your body image, as we discussed in Chapter 2, Personal Style Evaluation. What is normal to you may not be considered normal to someone else. What are your values and beliefs and how does race and age affect how you feel about your body? The norm is not the same for everyone. A healthy confident woman weighing over 200 pounds with a small body frame may consider herself beautiful while others may consider her obese. Actress and comedian **Monique** is a perfect example of "big is beautiful" and has made a successful career speaking openly about her size. She has a bestselling book *Skinny Women are Evil,* and a loyal fan following. She has also introduced a clothing line titled BBLI, which stands for big, beautiful, and loving it.

The topic of what is considered ideal and normal in female body size is vast, but as time and society continue to evolve, so do our viewpoints. There will continue to be a variety of studies on the subject, and thin models will continue to rule the runway. Love your body as it is today, and continue to dress appropriately for your size. You will feel good about who you are, and others will notice that positive image in you also.

Complete Exercise 4.1, Body Scrutiny, to further analyze what type of body you possess.

Exercise 4.1: Body Scrutiny

What's needed? A full-length three-way mirror; a body suit, unitard, or very close-fitting clothing; a tape measure; a **learning partner** and an open mind!

1. Stand in front of the mirror with your hands to your sides.

2. Take a look at yourself from the front, back, and sides.

3. Answer the following questions:

- What parts of your body do you like the most? List three assets. Why?
- How often do you show off this favorite part of your body through your clothing choices?
- What clothing would you wear to emphasize these assets?
- What parts of your body do you like the least? List three examples. Why?
- How do you camouflage this least favorite part of your body? What clothing would you wear to de-emphasize these parts of your body?
- Is your body more round or angular?
- What shape would you assign your body—square, rectangle, tubular,

FIGURE 4.1
Legendary actress Marilyn Monroe looks stunning in this gold dress. Her clothing fits her body and accentuates her assets. An ideal body type is in the eye of the beholder.

circle, diamond, triangle, or inverted triangle? (See a discussion on The Four Major Body Types below.)

* What adjectives have others used to describe your physical shape?

4. Describe the physical features of your body you aspire to have. You may already possess these features or you may be striving to attain what is considered normal to you.

Your goal in this exercise is to match the physical features of your body with the ideal features to which you aspire. List the ways you can do this with your clothing choices.

THE FOUR MAJOR BODY TYPES

To look at ourselves objectively we need to be able to view our naked bodies from all angles; front, back, right side and left side. To draw our bodies on a piece of paper in a simple manner we would all be stick figures with a circle for a head. Individuality is achieved when we see how each of us fills out the stick figures.

What line shape does our body form? Is it a **rectangle**—boxy and tubular, **triangle**—small on top and larger on the bottom, **inverted triangle**—large on top and small on the bottom, **hourglass**—bottom and top equal measurements and waist 9 to 11 inches smaller? The only way to truly see what body shape we are is to outline our bodies on a piece of paper. Complete Exercise 4.2, Body Tracing.

ACHIEVING AN IDEAL BODY FIT TYPE

In the 1950s and well into the Sixties, celebrity figure Marilyn Monroe's body type was considered ideal. She had an hourglass shape where her bust and hips were equal in size and her waist measurement was anywhere from 9 to 11 inches smaller than her bust. Marilyn wore a size two during this time period but if she wore alive today and had the same measurements she would be considered a size 12. Don't get hung up on the numbers, cut the numbers out of your clothing if you have to. A proper fit of your garment is what will make you look your very best. *Emphasize the positive and de-emphasize the negative parts of your body.* You will always look your best when we see the most pleasing parts of who and what you are.

Exercise 4.2: Body Tracing

What's needed? You will need body tracing paper like **Hecto brand** paper, different color dry erase markers, tape measure, yardstick, and a learning partner. Similar to the body scrutiny exercise you should wear a body suit or close fitting clothing. No shoes should be worn when completing this exercise.

Steps to take to complete your body tracing:

1. Cut enough paper to accommodate your body height and add four to six inches.

2. Tape the paper against the wall, making sure the paper drapes the floor to achieve the most accurate height measurement.

3. Working with your learning partner each of you will take turns standing with your back against the wall, legs apart, arms outstretched, and fingers spread apart.

FIGURE 4.2

It can be useful to look at our bodies as stick figures. Each of us are different individuals who fill out our "stick" outlines in various ways, ultimately forming a shape all our own.

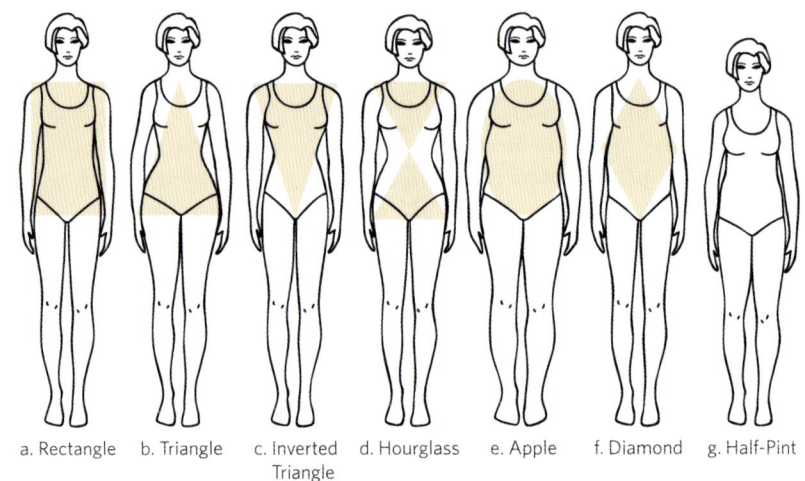

a. Rectangle   b. Triangle   c. Inverted Triangle   d. Hourglass   e. Apple   f. Diamond   g. Half-Pint

4. Trace your entire body being careful to get all the curves your body possesses.

5. Place a horizontal line across from the top of your head and a horizontal line to your natural waistline, approximately where your belly button is and body shape indents.

6. Using a different color marker, draw a dotted line from the top of your head to your neckline and continue to your waist, hips, and down to the bottom of the floor. Allow the line to flow the way your body flows.

7. Can you see a shape forming with the dotted line? Which shape is your body closest too?

Table 4.1
FOUR MAJOR BODY TYPE IDENTIFIERS

Body Type	Key identifiers	Weight gain
Rectangle	Very few curves, body is straight up and down, head appears large for body.	Weight gain occurs evenly over entire body.
Triangle	Can be two sizes, smaller on top than the bottom; pear shaped.	Weight gain occurs in outer thighs and rear.
Inverted Triangle	Shoulders broader than hips, flat rear.	Weight gain occurs in breast, midriff, and stomach.
Hourglass	Hourglass curves with a definite waist.	Weight gain occurs around the waist, stomach, thighs, and rear.

Seeing the outline of your body on a piece of paper may be an eye opener for some, but it's one of the keys to learning how to dress your best. Identifying which body type you are involves not only a visual means of looking at yourself (ideally you and your learning partner will accurately evaluate each other), but also requires the use of a tape measure. You will use the tape measure to measure your bust, waist, and hips **circumference**. The measurement of these three parts of your body gives you specific clues or identifiers to which body type is yours. The body type identifying list above is based on an individual's metabolism and where you gain weight. Refer to the list when evaluating your answers to the questions in Exercise 4.2, Body Tracing.

Now that you have examined your body on paper and reviewed the key identifiers, you should have an idea of which body type is yours. Some of us may not fall neatly into any of the four categories but instead fall somewhere in between

THREAD 4.2

WAISTS AND WAIST NOTS

"I have found that most people know where their challenging areas are and a lot of the challenges come in the form of do I have a tummy or don't I? I call these the WAISTS—hourglass and inverted triangles, and the WAIST NOTS—rectangle and triangle," says Catherine Schuller of Figure & Fit, an in-store retail program at Sak's Fifth Aveneue New York. This retail program created by Schuller helps women figure out their body type and what clothing best suits them.

Schueller has created a simple way to look at your body; do you or don't you have a waist? I believe everyone has a waistline but we tend to look at proportion and the total figure. How many inches is your waistline compared to your bust and hip measurement? Your shape is determined by the inches of your bust, waist, and hip. Visually, looking at your body, if you see a definite waistline then, according to Schueller, you are an inverted triangle or hourglass figure. And no waist is a rectangle or triangle shape. Either way, a clothing technique that will draw your eye towards your face is for any shape woman to create a waist right under her bustline. This part of the woman's body is considered the smallest for any woman, so whether you are a "waist" or a "waist-not" you will still look your very best.

or totally outside the so-called norm. As stated previously, what is considered normal to you may not be normal to others when it comes to body shapes and sizes.

Stylist Sam Sambora in his book *Real Style* has identified three additional body types also based on visual identifiers such as where you usually gain weight. These three additional types are:

1. **Apple body type**—full bust and midsection; great breasts and lower legs.

2. **Diamond body type**—wide shoulders, narrow hips, large bust; great legs.

3. **Half-pint body type**—based more on *stature* than weight gain. This body type is a short stature with a petite frame and can be found in any body type.

92   BODY TYPE EVALUATION

To go over the main points, the clues you are using to make your body type decision are related to:

- **appearance**—your evaluation from just looking at yourself in a three-way mirror and on paper.

- **weight gain**—the part or parts of your body where you usually gain weight based on your actual measurements.

- **height**—knowing your stature: short—less than 5 feet, 4 inches tall, average—5 feet, 5 inches to 5 feet 6 inches; and tall—5 feet, 7 and above.

These three factors will give you the clues you'll need to know how you are shaped.

Exercise 4.3: True Fit Sizing

To realize your true fit you will need to take your body measurements—bust, waist, and hips—and compare them to the sizing on the back of a **pattern**. Pattern sizing is definitely a true body size test and different than ready-to-wear sizing. You will need to take ten measurements, the first four of which will determine pattern size and the last six, any length adjustments that may be needed.

You will need a tape measure, comfortable close-fitting clothing or a unitard, proper fitting undergarments, a piece of narrow elastic, and a full length mirror. You will also need a learning partner to help you take the measurements.

Begin by tying the elastic around your waist and bend from side to side until the elastic settles in at your natural waistline. You are now ready to take the measurements.

The measurements are:

   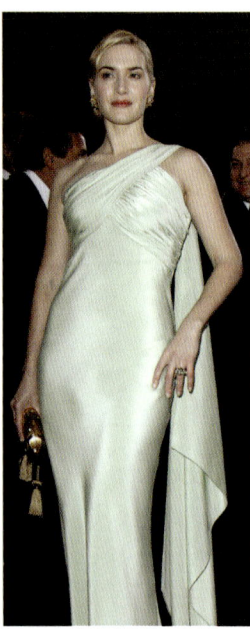

FIGURE 4.3

These celebrities (referenced from left to right) exhibit different body types yet look their absolute best in clothing that shows off their assets. Embodying the hourglass is Halle Berry, while Garcelle Beauvais is a half-pint. Displaying her inverted triangle is Nicolette Sheridan, while Kate Winslet possesses a triangle shape.

1. Bust—around the fullest part.
2. Waist—around the body at the elastic.
3. Hips—around the fullest part.
4. Thighs—around the thighs if fuller than the hip.
5. Back/waist length—from the bone at center back down to the elastic at your waistline.
6. Arm length—from your shoulder joint bone to the elbow.
7. Elbow to wrist measurement—from your elbow to the wrist bone.
8. Add measurements from numbers 6 and 7 to determine shoulder-to-wrist measurement.
9. Arm measurement—your total arm length.
10. Total height—from the top of your head to the floor, using a flat ruler placed against the wall. Stand naturally with your back to the wall and mark the point where the top of your head is; take this measurement from top to bottom.

These ten measurements will help you determine your pattern size and true fit. Use these measurements as a guide when choosing clothing for a proper fit. Ready-to-wear and sewing garments are entirely different sizing, so choose wisely.

PROPORTION

Your height or stature identifiers can be recognized by knowing if your body is in **proportion** or not. Proportion is a means of identifying how our body parts are in relationship to one another. Our body can be divided into eight parts with the measurement of our head as the basis of ideal body proportion. Our head size provides clues to the harmony and balance of our total body. Everyone's body is divided into five sections composed of eight parts. The parts are the head (one head-size), neck to waist (two head-sizes), crotch or midsection (one head size), crotch to knees (two head sizes), and knees to soles of feet (two head sizes) for a total of eight heads tall.

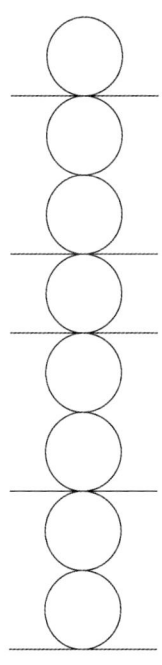

FIGURE 4.4
As an artist accurately draws a human figure, so can we evaluate our bodies in head parts. This numerical look at our bodies simplifies the term proportion, utilizing our head size as the measurement to guide us.

When we look at our body unclothed we all have a top half—our **upper torso**, head to waist—and a bottom half—waist to soles of feet. Using the heads tall proportion as our guide, we will identify a ratio, 3:5:8, as the **Golden Mean**. This ratio allows us to separate our body into sections that are easy to dress. The top part of our body (head to waist), or three heads, is in proportion to the bottom half of our body (waist to soles of feet), or five heads, and therefore is in proportion to our total body, or eight heads. The Golden Mean is a *visual* means of looking at our body proportionately. The actual measurement of these proportions comes from ancient architecture and sculpture and applied to the body. Simply put, the Golden Mean involves proportion and looking at the relationship of the size of two things. We are comparing the top of our body (three heads) to the bottom of our body (five heads).

INTERESTING BODY SHAPES

A body always looks more interesting when clothed in unequal parts. So, what does this mean? If we refer to Figure 4.5, we can make a decision on what shape is most interesting to us. What part of our body is our eye drawn to? If we draw a body as a rectangle and divide up the rectangle in sections symbolizing the clothes we wear we will see interesting relationships.

Reviewing the five rectangles in Figure 4.5 you can visually identify the shape of each of the garments. See Figure:

A. No waistline; like a shift dress. In this drawing there is no clothing divider and the look is simple and the eye is not drawn to any specific part of the body.

B. High waistline; like an empire dress. In this drawing the eye is drawn to the top of the body towards the face. The top part of the body is smaller than the bottom part of the body.

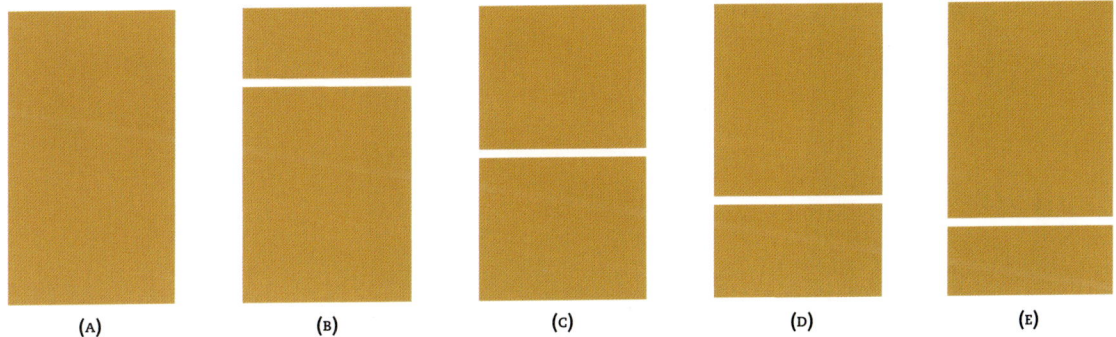

(A) (B) (C) (D) (E)

FIGURES 4.5
What if we all considered our bodies like rectangles? How would you clothe a rectangle to look less boxy?

C. Natural waistline; like a top and skirt or shirtdress. The look in this drawing is even, with top and bottom cutting the body in half. The upper and bottom parts of the body are emphasized.

D. Drop waist; long jacket or tunic top at hip level. The bottom part of the body is smaller than the top part of the body. The eye is drawn towards the bottom portion of the body away from the face.

E. Longer than your waistline, three quarter length coat over skirt or pants. This drawing is the opposite of the high waistline drawing the eye away from the face and towards the bottom of the body.

Using what you know about body shapes, identify which of the women pictured in Figure 4.6 is the longest, the broadest, the shortest, the most slender, and why?

CLOTHING CHOICES AS THEY RELATE TO PROPORTION

Why do we need to know if our body is in proportion or not? We need to know because we visually want to present a pleasing view to the world. The ultimate

FIGURE 4.6

Clothing retailer Madewell showcases a variety of clothing styles to choose from in tops, separates, and dresses. Proportion is shown in all three of these uneven and even looks, yet all are interesting.

goal of knowing who and what we are proportionately is to place the emphasis on that part of our body that is visually pleasing to the eye. Our face, or **personality area** as it is called, plays a leading role in what makes each of us unique and special.

We can achieve the look we want through our clothing choices and through the use of color, fabrics and texture, line, and shape. These principles will be discussed further in Chapter 5, Wardrobe Selection Factors.

Suppose we are thick in the middle section of our body. We can focus the attention to the top part of our body by wearing empire waist clothing, focusing the attention upwards toward the face. Vertical lines can lengthen our body and take the focus away from the top part of our body if we have a large bust. A body with no shape or waistline can be camouflaged by choosing garments with interesting designs and/or patterns.

Exercise 4.4: Garments That Camouflage
From magazines, cut out pictures of garments that identify and emphasize the following body parts: 1) waistline, 2) bust, 3) legs, 4) arms, 5) hips or buttocks, 6) back, 7) neck, 8) shoulders, 9) wrists, and 10) ankles. While emphasizing one part of the body, which part of the body is therefore de-emphasized? Why?

BODY TYPE RECOGNITION

At the beginning of this chapter we identified four major body types. Most likely, yours will fall somewhere within one of these types. At this point it is easy to recognize which is the key feature of each body type and what needs to get noticed.

The rectangle body type needs to draw the viewer's attention up to the face. In addition, you can emphasize this up and down figure-type by adding a belt or other accessories to create interest. The triangle body type emphasis should be on the top section of your body calling attention to your

FIGURE 4.7
The New Look epitomizes an ideal look for all. The balance of a tight fit and a full fit visually creates interest and emphasizes the waistline.

The New Look
The phrase "New Look" was coined by Carmel Snow, the powerful editor-in-chief of *Harpers Bazaar*. Dior's debut collection, Corolle line, was first presented on February 12, 1947. The look is described as having very small tucked-in waists, sloped, easy shoulders, and having a full skirt. Dior is quoted as saying "I have designed flower women." Dior's look employed fabrics whose tops were mostly boned, bustier-style bodices, the skirt hip section had padding, and petticoats that made his dresses flare out from the waist giving his models a very curvaceous form. The hem of the skirt was very flattering on the calves and ankles, giving a beautiful silhouette. To create this look Dior used a tremendous amount of fabric. Backlash arose because of the amount of fabrics that was used in a single dress or suit, but as soon as the War Time Shortages came to an end, opposition ceased. To this day Dior's design represents consistent classic elegance, stressing the feminine look. The New Look revolutionized women's dress and reestablished Paris as the center of the fashion world after World War II.

neck, shoulders, and bust line. Drawing attention to the upper torso allows the triangle silhouette to be in proportion. The inverted triangle needs to add fullness to the lower half of the body, creating the illusion of an hourglass. Full skirts and pleated pants help to draw attention to the lower half. Be careful when adding fullness to one half of the body—one should then tighten up the other half. Otherwise, total fullness makes for complete roundness and a look that will overwhelm your entire body. In the case of the inverted triangle one would wear tops that are fitted just like the **New Look** created by Christian Dior.

Emphasis for the hourglass figure should be placed on the waist line. The waist in this figure type is small and should be noticed. People who have this figure type, which is considered ideal by most people, can wear most clothing simply because they are in proportion; that is to say that their bodies are sectioned evenly as close as possible to the Golden Mean.

BODY NORMAL

Knowing your body type is crucial in choosing and selecting the right clothing. The steps taken to knowing how you look and what looks best on you is vital in achieving your own personal style. Look in the mirror on a daily basis and be honest with yourself. Are you showing to the world what you consider is the best you can be? Are you being consistent with this message? If not, make it a habit to choose only those items that will emphasize what you consider body normal for you.

KEY WORDS

anorexia nervosa	ideal	proportion
apple body type	inverted triangle body type	rectangle body type
circumference	Karen Carpenter	The Bathers
diamond body type	learning partner	The Three Graces
Dior's New Look	Marilyn Monroe	triangle body type
Gisele Bündchen	Monique	Twiggy
golden mean ratio	norm	upper torso
half-pint body type	Oprah Winfrey	Valentino
Hecto brand paper	pattern	
hourglass body type	personality area	

RESOURCES

Healthbolt. (2006). A short history of the "ideal" female body. Retrieved on April 1, 2008 from www.healthbolt.net/2006/12/27/a-short-history-of-the-ideal-female-body/.

Mitola, A., Papas, M., Le, K., Fusillo, L., and Black, M. (2008). Agreement with satisfaction in adolescent body size between female caregivers and teens from a low-income African-American community, *Journal of Pediatric Psychology*. Retrieved on April 1, 2008 from http://jpepsy.oxfordjournals.org/cgi/content/full/32/1/42.

Celebrity Artist Entertainment. (2008). Monique fat chance. Retrieved on April 1, 2008 from www.caentertainment.com/bios/MoNiquebio2.htm.

Seleshanko, K. (2006). Inside Christian Dior's new look, The Vintage Connection. Retrieved on April 1, 2008 from www.vintageconnection.net/NewLook.htm.

Vashti.net. (2008). The golden mean. Retrieved on April 1, 2008 from www.vashti.net/mceinc/golden.htm.

Wonderquest. (2007). Women Sizes: British, USA, Canadian and Mexican, the age group with the best memory. Retrieved on April 1, 2008 from www.wonderquest.com/size-women-memory.htm.

CHAPTER FIVE

Wardrobe Selection Factors

"But great style, and a great career, can come only from being true to one's self, one's taste, and one's values."

—MARC JACOBS, AMERICAN FASHION DESIGNER WHOSE FASHION LINES MARC JACOBS AND MARC BY MARC JACOBS ARE SOUGHT AFTER BY MANY CELEBRITIES. JACOBS IS ALSO CREATIVE DIRECTOR OF LOUIS VUITTON, THE FRENCH LUXURY FASHION AND LEATHER GOODS BRAND.

CHAPTER OBJECTIVES
After reading this chapter, you will be able to:

* *Regarding fit:*
  - Define the word *style*.
  - Define the word *fit*.
  - List the tips to accurate clothing fit.
  - Identify the bust, waist and hip measurements for women's, women's petite, and women's plus sizes.

* *Regarding color:*
  - List the color seasons and its relationship to clothing choices.
  - Recognize the colors on the color wheel and the terminology associated with the colors on the wheel.
  - Demonstrate the color draping technique.

* *Regarding fabric:*
  - Compare and contrast the differences between natural and man-made fabrics.
  - List the basic fabric characteristics and its relationship to individual clothing choices.
* *Regarding quality:*
  - Comprehend the difference between excellent, good, and poor quality clothing.
  - Compute the cost per wearing formula.
* *Regarding style:*
  - Be aware of the variety of clothing styles available and how it relates to each individual body type.
  - Define the word *emphasis* and understand its relationship with style.
* *Care:*
  - Recognize care labels and the requirements for proper clothing care.

WHAT IS STYLE?

We all know individuals who we think have great style. There's that special something that sets them apart from other people and makes them unique. The word **style** means the current fashionable way of dressing. Fashion experts consider individuals who have style to be those who wear garments of a current and smart design. Fashion styles come and go and constantly change, but those individuals who stand out and who make a stylish first impression are those who are in the know with what is hot at a given point in time.

Style mavens are individuals who dress for their body types and very rarely have fashion faux pas. Celebrities in this category are Gwyneth Paltrow,

FIGURE 5.1

In the television series *Sex and the City*, stars (from left) Kim Cattrall, Cynthia Nixon, Kristin Davis, and Sarah Jessica Parker exemplified different styles suitable to match personalities of their characters. Their styles were always current, trendy, fashionable, and appealing to most individuals.

who is very consistent with classic styles and high-quality looks; Reese Witherspoon, whose Southern charm and bright colors usually make her a stand-out in any crowd; and Gwen Stefani, who is dramatic, eclectic, and in her own words someone who "enjoys being a girl." Sarah Jessica Parker's style is most often recognized as her character Carrie Bradshaw's kooky, trendy looks from the popular HBO television show *Sex and the City*. Patricia Fields, stylist for the show, achieved notoriety for the one-of-a-kind looks she created on the show; loyal fans of the show would watch weekly to see the creative fashions. Model-turned-actress Charlize Theron's style has evolved from her beginnings, dressing casually on her family's farm, to the red carpet styles she exhibits today. All of these individuals express a unique fashion personality yet stay within the realm of the current and fashionable.

WARDROBE SELECTION FACTORS

To help you achieve your own personal style, six factors need to be continually kept in unison; these are **fit**, **color**, fabric, **quality**, **style**, and care. Let's take a look at each of these factors individually to see how each affects your personal style.

FIT

Achieving personal style means knowing what works for your body type. In Chapter 4, Body Type Evaluation, we examined our bodies and identified our body types as hourglass, triangle, inverted triangle, and rectangle. Understanding our bodies helps us to identify our assets and to focus our attention on these assets with our clothing. Emphasizing our assets with correct fit is a visual means of presentation and a great start to achieving personal style. Clothing that fits your body well enhances your total image. Examine the chart in Table 5.1 and review the celebrities and their body types. A look at the celebrity photographs will reveal visually how they complement their body assets through their clothing choices.

Table 5.1
CELEBRITY FIGURE TYPES

Body Type	Hourglass	Inverted Triangle	Triangle	Rectangle
	Jessica Simpson	Elizabeth Hurley	Mischa Barton	Kate Hudson
	Drew Barrymore	Nicolette Sheridan	Alicia Keys	Sarah Jessica Parker
	Salma Hayek	Julia Louis-Dreyfus	Kelly Clarkson	Reese Witherspoon
	Eva Mendes	Diane Lane	Jennifer Lopez	Liv Tyler

Source: *In Style* magazine, January 2007.

Fit is defined as the state of an article of clothing having the proper size or shape for a particular figure. Reviewing your body type assets reveal which part of the body should be highlighted. Those with:

* **hourglass figures** should emphasize their waistlines and make sure their clothing hugs their curves, but not too tightly.

* **inverted triangle figures** should highlight the bottom portion of their bodies to match their broad tops. Full skirts or pants with pockets will help balance the bottom half to allow a more proportioned visual presentation.

* **triangle body types** should emphasize their shoulders to visually proportion the top half with the bottom half. Jackets with shoulder emphasis or strapless dresses will help to achieve this visual presentation.

* **Rectangle body types** should emphasize their arms and legs. This body type is "boyish" in appearance, and your goal is to show off your

great arms and/or legs. Adding belts, fitted tops, or jackets can create a waistline.

Again, the key is to emphasize the positive and de-emphasize the negative aspects of your body.

Additional Body Types

Suppose your body type is not close to any of the four previous categories of hourglass, triangle, inverted triangle, or rectangle. The three additional body types, **pear**, **oval**, or apple, and diamond shapes also alter clothing fit. Very similar to the triangle shape, the pear shape, or small on top and wide on the bottom, has clothing choices that fall in line with the triangle body type. The oval or apple shape bears a resemblance to the rectangle with two exceptions: full midsection and overall shape is rounded instead of rectangular. Clothing choices for this shape should highlight lower legs, similar to the rectangle. The diamond shape is similar to the oval, but narrow shoulders and a full midsection identify the overall silhouette. Once again, this silhouette should focus on emphasizing your legs.

It's worth repeating, the goal is to emphasize the positive and de-emphasize the negative parts of your body. If you know your body, then you know your fit.

Fit Style Rules

Garments should:

* fit *comfortably* but not confine the body.
* allow for *ease of movement* and not be restrictive.
* not show *wrinkles,* an indicator of too tight or too loose clothing.
* not *gather* around zippers or waistbands.

FIGURE 5.2

Fit is the most important wardrobe selection factor. Seek the advice of an honest friend to give you advice on how the garment *really* looks on you. Too tight? Too loose? Neither is stylish. Get it right to fit *your* body.

* not *gap* at the bust line.

* be able to *button or close without pulls or strains* even if garment is worn open.

* when a jacket, have a *horizontal shoulder length* that ends at the arm socket.

* when trousers, have a waist that does not have *flesh overflow*. If the waistline is too small, then your body flesh will hang over the top of the trouser.

* when trousers, not have *pocket* or *zipper spread*. The trousers are too small if the pocket does not lie flat against the body or zipper is wide open.

Table 5.2
WOMEN'S MEASUREMENT CHARTS

A. WOMEN'S APPROXIMATE SIZING

European Size	US Size	Standard	Bust	Waist	Hips
30	0	XS	31-32	23-24	33.5-34.5
32	2	XS	32-33	24-25	34.5-35.5
34	4	S	33-34	25-26	35.5-36.5
36	6	S	34-35	26-27	36.5-37.5
38	8	M	35-36	27-28	37.5-38.5
40	10	M	36-37	28-29	38.5-39.5
42	12	L	37.5-38.5	30-31	40-41
44	14	L	39-40	31-32	41.5-42.5
46	16	XL	40.5-41.5	32.5-33.5	43-44
48	18	XL	41.5-42.5	33.5-34.5	43.5-44.5

B. WOMEN'S PETITE APPROXIMATE SIZING

Size	Standard	Bust	Waist	Hip
2P	XS	31.5-32.5	23.5-24.5	33.5-34.5
4P	S	32.5-33.5	24.5-25.5	34.5-35.5
6P	S	33.5-34.5	25.5-26.5	35.5-36.5
8P	M	34.5-35.5	26.5-27.5	36.5-37.5
10P	M	35.5-36.5	27.5-28.5	37.5-38.5
12P	L	37-38	29-30	39-40
14P	L	38-40	31.5-31.5	40.5-41.5
16P	XL	40-41	32-33	42-43
18P	XL	41-43	33.5-34.5	43-44

C. Women's Plus Approximate Sizing

Size	Standard	Bust	Waist	Hip
14W	1X	40-42	41.5-43.5	41-43
16W	1X	42-44	43.5-45.5	43-45
18W	2X	44-46	45.5-47.5	45-47
20W	2X	46-48	47.5-49.5	47-49
22W	3X	48-50	49.5-51.5	49-51
24W	3X	51-52	51.5-53.5	51-53

Source: Ebay apparel guides. Retreived on March 3, 2008 from http://pages.ebay.com/buy/guides/apparel-accessories-buying-guide/sizingcharts.

* not have *incorrect length* (i.e., shirtsleeves or trousers are too long or too short). Garment sleeve and trouser length is critical to a proper fit.

Observing these rules, you can begin to see what is important to an accurate fit. No matter what size you are currently, great style is not achieved unless your clothing fits well. **Sizing**, or graded classifications of measure, varies per manufacturer. Trying on clothes is the best way to know what works for you. United States and European clothing sizings are different. Table 5.2 illustrates typical measurement charts for women's, women's petite, and women's plus sizes.

Fit Summary
Following the fit style rules will keep you on track to achieving great style. Fit is the most important wardrobe selection factor. You can have on the most expensive outfit but if it doesn't fit you well the appeal is totally lost. Make an effort to achieve excellent clothing fit. How can this be done?

PERFECT FIT JEANS

We all wear and own jeans, and according to Cotton, Inc. women wear jeans 3.94 days a week. This universal clothing item has become the dress up or down staple in a woman's wardrobe. There are a variety of styles, shapes, and sizes available from which to choose; trying on plenty of jeans is essential to get the perfect fit.

To find the perfect-fitting jeans requires not only time, but patience. What should you look for and what is necessary to get the right pair of jeans?

1. Body type—do you know your shape? In Chapter 4, Body Type Evaluation, you discovered whether you have an hourglass, triangle, inverted triangle, or rectangle shape. Denim manufacturers make their jeans to fit certain body types. If you know what to look for the process is much easier. For example the following jeans are best for…

* long legs—Lucky Brand Jeans, Rock & Republic, Notify, and Habitual.
* rectangle, straight figure—Yanuk, Paige Denim, and Lucky Brand.
* thick middle—Paper Denim & Cloth, Seven, GAP, and Calvin Klein.
* large hips—Seven, Levi's, Banana Republic, and Joe's Jeans.
* big butts—James, Seven, Citizens of Humanity, and Earnest Sewn.

2. Retail store—where do you go? Visit a multitude and variety of stores. Department stores, boutiques, thrift shops, and even consignment shops carry denim. Brands vary per store.

3. Fit—try on at least 10 pairs to compare the fit. The more jeans you try on the better chance you will have of finding the perfect-fitting jeans. Compare the fits of each pair and note which ones make you look and feel your best. Sit, stand, and move around in each pair to see which pair feels the best and is the most comfortable.

4. Tailor—remember, a good tailor is invaluable for a perfect fit and that includes jeans. If the length is too long but everything else is okay, then shortening the jeans requires just a trip to the tailor.

5. Friends and family—ask your friends and family members how the jeans look on you. You will know if they are being honest with you, especially if they are wearing a great-fitting pair of jeans!

Buying Jeans Online
Buying jeans online can be challenging even though this is an option. The online website www.zafu.com is devoted to helping women find the best fit, style, and size jeans. After completing a short questionnaire noting fit problems, and favorite, if any, brands, the website will select brands for your choosing. In a survey conducted by Zafu.com, 73 percent of women noted "making their bottoms look good" as the most important thing a jean can do for them (Zafu, 2008). Other factors that are important are dark denim for the long and lean look, and a lower waistband to elongate the upper torso.

Invest in several, at least three pairs, of high quality, great-fitting jeans to have an essential denim wardrobe. One pair can be tailored for casual events for a low heel shoe, another for those dressy events and high heels, and the third pair for flats and sandals everyday. You will always be in style with a great fitting pair of jeans.

* Find a brand of clothing that fits you well and requires very little tailoring.
* Buy your right size—for the size you are currently, not what you wish to be.
* Find a good tailor who can alter your clothing to your body.
* Trust your instinct. If it doesn't feel comfortable, most likely the fit is not right.

THE COLOR WHEEL

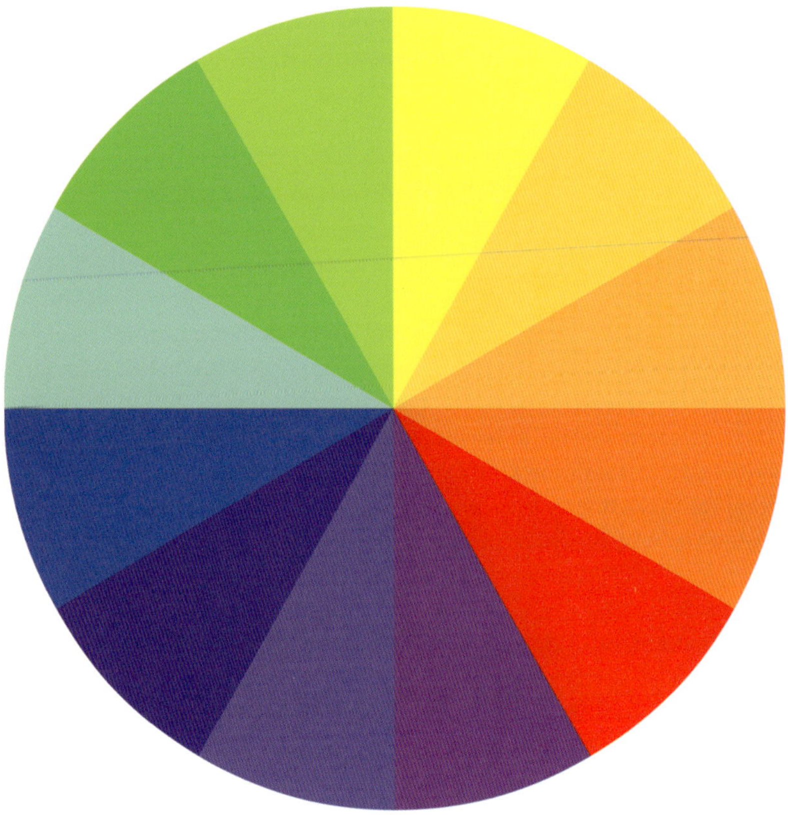

FIGURE 5.3
Sir Isaac Newton (1643–1727) developed the first circular diagram of colors now known as the color wheel. The color wheel will be used to help you look your very best.

Color
One of the first things you notice about clothing is its color. When shopping for a garment you are naturally drawn to the color first. Color is the essence of light, varying in wavelengths and enabling our eyes to see different colors. Color is also a psychological as well as a visual selection factor. Psychologically, black reminds some of death, a funeral, whereas white is pure and heavenly. Visually, black, because of its dark shade, is slenderizing while white, because of its bright shade, adds additional volume. Color becomes an important way to add visual presence to your personal style.

THE TWELVE-HUE COLOR WHEEL

In order to analyze what colors look best on you, we begin by looking at the color wheel and the terminology associated with its use.

The 12-hue color wheel in Figure 5.3 shows a variety of color relationships. The word **hue** refers to the name of the color family—for example, the hues of red, blue, or green. In clothing, color names can be very descriptive; they may relate to a food, as in the color salmon, or to a bird, as in canary yellow. If you are not familiar with these items then you may not be able to relate the hue to the clothing item. Clothing color names attract your attention and arouse your interest in pursuing the item.

You can have either **warm hues** or **cool hues**. The warm hues on the color wheel are more yellow like the sun, blazing like fire, and appear on the left side of the color wheel. They are intense, bright colors and in clothing make you appear larger and increase your body size. Warm hues can make you appear shorter and heavier. Cool hues are like the sky and water and appear on the right side of the color wheel. These colors recede in the background and are darker in shade and therefore decrease body size and make you appear tall and slim.

Primary colors—red, yellow, and blue—are colors that are not mixed with any other color and are placed equidistant from each other on the color wheel.

Additional terminology associated with color in clothing is **value**, which describes the lightness or darkness of a color, and **chroma,** the purity of a color. **Harmony**, the combinations of hues, is important to achieve a certain look and style. Refer to the color wheel to see the color harmonies.

Types of color harmonies are:

* **Monochromatic**, all one color, using one hue (e.g., all black).
* **Contrasting** color harmony, no hue in common (e.g., red and blue).
* **Analogous**, colors that appear next to each other on the color wheel (e.g., yellow-orange, yellow, and yellow-green).
* **Complementary**, colors that appear opposite each other on the color wheel (e.g., blue and orange).

A variety of other color harmonies are associated with the color wheel. This textbook focuses on the previous four harmonies and their relationship to clothing and personal style. The following chart shows the link between hue, value, chroma, and harmony as it relates to clothing choices.

Color, and its relationship to personal style, allows you to experiment visually with your clothing choices. Fashion personalities and body types are interchangeable with hues, values, chroma, and harmony. You can be elegant in style, prefer warm hues, and have an hourglass shape, or prefer cool hues and have an inverted triangle shape. What's most important is using color to highlight your body assets as identified in Chapter 4, Body Type Evaluation.

Seasonal Color Theory

The **color seasons**—autumn, spring, winter and summer—are related to the colors on the color wheel. Autumn and spring seasons are warm hues and winter and summer are cool hues. Seasons represent an easy identifiable way for

Table 5.3
COLOR HARMONIES AND CLOTHING

Clothing Choice	Hue	Value	Chroma	Harmony	Fashion Personality
Appear larger, increase size	Warm hues	Light	Pure	Contrasting Complementary	Dramatic Romantic Elegant
Appear smaller, decrease size	Cool hues	Dark	Weak	Monochromatic Analogous	Classic Sporty Elegant

you to examine which colors look best against your skin tone. Artist, colorist, and writer Kathryn Kalisz, has established the 12-tone color process based on her beliefs that there are more than 12 descriptive way to describe our skin tones and color. In order to provide a more accurate analysis of color, Kalisz has identified the 12 tones of color. The twelve tones fall within the four seasonal categories. These color categories are winter dark, winter true, winter bright, spring bright, spring true, spring light, summer light, summer true, summer soft, autumn soft, autumn true, and autumn dark. We will examine the four seasons in further detail, and when you begin the color draping process you will be able to justify if you need to go beyond the four seasons. For further explanation on the 12 tones, refer to the Sci-Art website for color analysis details: www.sci-art-global.com, and personal color analysis section.

AUTUMN COLOR SEASON Autumn season colors relate back to the foliage of the season; warm olives, deep, rich golden browns, and warm grays. Neutral color beige, ecru, or oyster works well against your skin tone since you have

FIGURE 5.4 (TOP LEFT) Actress and singer Jennifer Lopez exemplifies the autumn color season.

FIGURE 5.5 (TOP RIGHT) Actress Kate Hudson exemplifies the spring color season.

FIGURE 5.6 (BOTTOM LEFT) Actresses Courtney Cox and Eva Longoria (left to right) exemplify the winter color season.

FIGURE 5.7 (BOTTOM RIGHT) Actress Jennifer Aniston exemplifies the summer color season.

more green tones in your veins. Upon completing the color draping exercise you will be able to further your discussion of skin tones and color. Color adjectives that work well for the autumn individual are *warm, rich, spicy, golden,* and *exotic*. Celebrities that exhibit this color season are Eva Mendes, Marcia Cross, and Jennifer Lopez.

SPRING COLOR SEASON The spring season is characterized as sunny and bright and so are the individuals that characterize this season. Celebrities that fall within this category are Kate Hudson, Cameron Diaz, and Meg Ryan. Dusty, muted colors work best against the spring skin tone so as not to overwhelm the soft, serene coloring of the individuals' skin and eyes. Colors that work well for the spring season are dusty blues and pinks, and soft white colors. Spring season individuals should avoid very bright, vibrant colors. Color adjectives that work well for the spring individual are *serene* and *soft*.

WINTER COLOR SEASON A winter individual has a lot of visual contrast in their coloring and therefore can wear very intense, bright, deep colors. In addition neutral colors that work well are black, navy, charcoal, and even bright white. Celebrities that fall within this season category are Courtney Cox, Eva Longoria, and Catherine Zeta Jones. Accessories and accents for the winter individual should also be vibrant and intense; deep gold jewel tones are a good example for this season. Winter individuals should avoid any muted, or earth tone colors that will make the winter individual look very sallow and shadowed. Color adjectives that work for the winter individual are *intense* and *vibrant*.

SUMMER COLOR SEASON The summer individual coloring is described as serene and calm. The summer person should avoid very intense colors that will drown them out yet should choose colors like rose, soft pink, and other soft, dusted, muted colors. Celebrities that fall within this season are Jennifer Aniston, Michelle Pfeiffer, and Diane Sawyer. Delicate and serene describe the color palette for a summer individual. Similar yet different to the spring individual, the summer individual has more cool (blue) undertones to their skin coloring while the spring individual has more warm (green) undertones to their skin. Color adjectives that work for the summer individual include *serene* and *calm*.

Color Draping
Color draping is the process whereby color analysis is achieved to identify your correct color choices. Three principles are involved in choosing the right colors for you, skin tone, hair color, and eye color. Once you have identified these three principles, then relating them to the color seasons becomes the next priority. A quick identifier to a warm or cool skin tone is to look at the color of your veins. Are your veins green (warm) or blue (cool) in color? Is your hair color one solid color and pure (cool), or multicolored (warm)? Are your eyes dark and clear (cool) or grayer and muted (warm)? Knowing your personal coloring will help you achieve a personal style that is worthy of distinction.

Color Draping Process
To begin the color draping process, students should have a gray sheet or cape draped over their body. No makeup should be worn to assess a true color test. In addition, lighting that resembles the true outdoors should be used. The **Ott light bulb** is a good indicator of natural light and is used often in color draping to identify a realistic color season. The Ott light technology is considered to be natural lighting because it is low heat and low glare thereby duplicating natural lighting, which also helps to make the bulb energy efficient. This science-based natural based daylight formula bulb reduces eyestrain and makes reading small print easier. Observing fine details and recognizing colors become much easier

with the use of this bulb. Exercise 5.1 will take you and your learning partner through the color draping process. Upon completion of your color analysis, validate the color choices of your season with clothing. You should not only *look* good in your colors but also *feel* good. Use color to accentuate and highlight the positive parts of your body.

Exercise 5.1: Color Draping

SUPPLIES To begin the color draping process the minimum supplies you will need are:

- Proper lighting; the Ott light bulb placed in a floor lamp for maximum exposure.
- Three-way mirror for optimal viewing of the draping process.
- Set of 4 seasonal color drapes.

ADDITIONAL SUPPLIES The following supplies may also come in handy for color analysis:

- Hand test boards used to help the client identify the color season before the draping process begins.
- Set of 12-tone seasonal color drapes (to be used instead of the 4 season drapes).
- Set of 4 fabric scarves for seasonal placement, gold, silver, black, or brown (to be used instead of the vein test).

SURROUNDINGS To perform an optimum color analysis you will need to have the proper surroundings; to achieve this:

* You will need to work in pairs, so team up with another individual to perform the analysis. One person will be the color analyst and the other will be the client. The client should sit in a comfortable chair facing the 3-way mirror.

* All color viewing should be done against a neutral gray background. Your wall coloring and any backdrop should be in a light neutral shade of gray.

* The client's hair should be covered with a neutral gray cap and clothing should be covered with a neutral gray robe or draped with a neutral gray sheet.

* The analyst, or person performing the draping, should also be wearing a neutral gray robe or covered with a gray cloth.

TESTING The color analyst will begin the draping process by beginning with the seasonal drapes that best match the client's skin and eye color:

* The client, while looking in the mirror, will note which colors feel best as the analyst drapes the seasonal color drapes around the shoulder and under the neckline.

* The analyst will note any differences in facial appearance of the client as each color drape is placed. Do the eyes look drawn; are the cheeks sallow, and does the client's face light up?

* The color analyst will continue this process with each of the seasonal drapes until the proper connection of skin and eye color are in effect.

- Once the season is chosen the client will remove the gray cap to see if the hair color would make any drastic changes to the season chosen. If the hair is colored, dyed, or streaked, the chosen season will remain the same just not all colors may be worn.
- The most important factor in color analysis is the client's skin tone and what looks best against the skin.

Benefits of Color Analysis

The benefits of color analysis are many. According to colorist Kalisz, the benefits of a successful color analysis are beauty, harmony, balance, and wellness. Color makes you feel good because you look good. You will find harmony within your environment whose coloring is a match to your own personal coloring. Personality and coloring is a beneficial process where you match who you are with the correct coloring. Extensive studies have been done on the topic of personality and color, and one option is to take a Personal Traits Survey to see which colors are best for your personality type. This personality test is offered through Sci-Art Co, LLC, and is one of many that are available. You can refer to the fashion personality analysis test you completed in Chapter 1, Fashion Personality Types, to see how your personal coloring and personality are interrelated. In Table 5.4, Psychology of Color, you will be able to match a color with the suggested adjective the color evokes. Reviewing the chart may help to clarify why you choose to wear certain colors.

Lastly, wellness and color are interrelated because color is energy. Utilizing the process of **chromotherapy,** or color therapy, a therapist will use the color and light to balance energy and allow the vibrations of the body to be in a frequency that will result in health, welfare and harmony.

Table 5.4
PSYCHOLOGY OF COLOR

Color	Suggestion
Black	Wealth, power, confidence, sophistication
Purple	Royalty, creativity, dignity, mystery
Green	Growth, stability, wealth, calming
Red	Hot, intense, strength, exciting
Yellow	Optimism, vitality, happy, new
Blue	Intellectual, tradition, trust, conservative
White	Clean, pure, innocent, truth
Orange	Activity, motion, energy, affordable
Pink	Romance, passive, stress-reducer, compliant

Color Association of the United States

Color Association of the United States (CAUS), founded in 1915, issues four color forecast cards a year to subscribers in the apparel industry. Color experts identify the colors of the seasons and manufacturers and designers produce their clothing based on these color selections. As a member of the CAUS, you will have access to color trends 22 months ahead of the selling season. These color trends have been chosen by a committee of eight working professionals who base their results by studying past trends, the political and social climate, current technologies and consumers. CAUS has been a valuable resource to those businesses that want to be successful.

UNIVERSALLY FLATTERING COLORS

Are there any colors that flatter everyone no matter what their hair, eye, or skin color? **Pantone Color Institute,** known as the international authority on color, believes there are four flattering colors that work for everyone. These colors fall into the middle of the color spectrum and are therefore not too warm or not too cool. Pantone's Fashion and Color System is a vital tool for designers to select colors to use in their apparel lines. The four colors are:

1. **Eggplant**—this color is a deep purple and deep enough to be considered by some to be a neutral, like a black, brown or navy.

3. **Indian Teal**—a great combination of green and blue that flatters everyone. The richness of this color brings out the brightness in everyone's eyes.

2. **Mellow Rose**—another color that could be considered a neutral because it falls somewhere in between a light pink and a peach.

4. **True Red**—red is considered a powerful, strong color in fashion and also represents love. The "true" color red is not too cool, like a cherry, and not too warm, like a tomato, yet falls somewhere in between.

Consider broadening your neutral color palette with these universal colors. Not only will it add color to your wardrobe but it will expand your clothing options. (Wikiel, 2005)

Color Summary

Color, used wisely, can enhance any wardrobe and become a significant part of your personal style. Use color both psychologically and visually—to make you feel good and to make you look good. Remember to consider whether or not you are warm or cool, and use the color wheel as your guide.

Fabric

There is a multitude of fabrics available in various weights and textures. There are **natural fiber fabrics** such as cotton, linen, wool, and silk, and **manmade fabrics** such as rayon, polyester, and acetate. Natural fibers originate from animals or plants, and manmade fibers are processed with the use of chemicals. Every fabric has **texture**, the surface feeling that results when touched. Examples of textures are smooth, rough, crisp, course, nubby, fine, clingy, shiny and heavy. The chart below identifies common fabrics, textures, and clothing indicators and their relationship to personal style.

FIGURE 5.8
This pile of yellow fabric shows its course, rough texture. Choose your fabric wisely because it may add pounds to your body frame.

Fabric Design

A fashionable garment may be considered fashionable because of the fabric design. The design of the fabric includes the motif or pattern on the fabric. There are several designs that you could choose from that will suit your personal style, and these designs are one of four major types:

1. **Batik fabric design**—The word batik comes from the word "ambatik" meaning "a cloth with little dots." It is also believed the word comes from the Japanese word "tritik," which means a dying process where the patterns are done after the fabric is tied and sewed, similar to tie-dying techniques. In the

Table 5.5
FABRIC TEXTURES

Fabric Names	Texture	Clothing indicator
Linen	Crisp, fine, hard	No significant bulk added to body frame
Wool	Rough, heavy	Adds weight to body frame
Silk	Shiny, smooth	Adds weight to body frame
Cotton	Dull, soft	Subtracts weight
Tweed	Nubby, rough	Adds weight
Flannel	Dull, rough	Adds weight
Crepe	Soft, lightweight	Subtracts weight
Jersey	Clingy, soft	Subtracts weight

batik process wax is applied to the area that will remain patternless. After the fabric is dyed the wax is removed through a boiling process. Common fabrics that are used in this process are cotton and silk. Java, Indonesia is known as the country making the finest batik cloth.

The most common uses of batik fabrication are for Indian sarees, scarves, and other apparel items. Popular batik patterns consist of flowers, plants, birds, insects, and even some geometric shapes. Because of the beauty of the patterns on batik fabric this fabric is often used as a wall hanging and artwork. All body shapes should be careful not to have too much batik fabric design in their garment. A little goes a long way and will add just the touch you will need to make your outfit special. Any fashion personality can utilize wearing batik fabric design but the natural or eclectic fashion personality will work best allowing the beauty of the fabric to shine.

2. **Dyed fabric design**—dyed fabric is made from colored fibers. The dye used to color the fibers is from animal, vegetable, or mineral origin. In 1856 William Henry Perkin discovered **mauveiene**, the first manmade organic dye. Since that time there have been many fabric dyeing processes including acid dye—usually using fibers of silk, wool, or nylon; basic dye—wool and silk fibers; direct (substantive) dye—leather, wool, silk, or nylon fibers. Mordent is a dyeing substance that improves the fastness of the dye on the fibers. Vat, reactive, and azoic dyes uses chemicals to bind the dyes to the fibers. Cellulose acetate fibers such as nylon, triacetate, polyester, and acrylic use water-soluble disperse dye.

   Dyeing the fabric definitely can make the fabric more beautiful and help to create a fashionable garment. When choosing a dyed fabric for your garments consider your color season as a basis for choosing the fabric. Any fashion personality can wear dyed fabric when choosing the color wisely.

3. **Embroidered fabric design**—as early as 3000 B.C. embroidered fabric has been in use. Fabric may be embroidered by hand or machine and practically any fabric may be embroidered. To **embroider** means to decorate or embellish the fabric by sewing strands of material on another material layer to form a decorative design or pattern. Embroidered fabric may also be used as wall hangings because of its intricate design and beauty. Any fashion personality may wear embroidered fabric, but it works best with the dramatic fashion personality. Both the fashion personality and the fabric design are usually bold, interesting, and beautiful.

4. **Printed fabric design**—the pattern on printed fabric design is done with ink or dye. Thin and delicate fabrics are usually associated with printed fabric design. Types of printing can range from block printing where the pattern is arranged on a wooden block to direct printing where, similar to an inkjet printer, the fabric accepts the ink from a digital printer.

   The printed fabric design is compatible with the sporty and dramatic personalities. The bold colors and patterns will not be hidden with these fashion personalities.

5. **Painted Fabric**—painting the fabric by hand to create patterns. The patterns are floral, geometric, or religious. Painted fabrics are commonly used for wall hangings, tablecloths, or even in upholstery. Any fashion personality can wear painted fabric in limited quantity. Most painted fabric is not used in large amounts for apparel because the pattern can be overwhelming for any body type.

Fabric Design Principles

In the apparel industry there are design principles that help to unite and form the fabric. These design principles are **rhythm**, **emphasis**, **proportion**, **balance**, and **unity**. Let's examine each of these principles separately and their relationship to fabric.

RHYTHM   Rhythm refers to the progression of a pattern or a color. In fabric design rhythm creates movement and moves the eye back and forth. The fabric swatch shown in Figure 5.9 creates movement within the design and pattern. This fabric, when used in any apparel item, will draw the eye in a continuous movement and create focus and attention.

EMPHASIS   Emphasis is the quality that draws your attention directly to it, like a logo or stripe. To emphasize means to highlight and point out. In fabric design

FIGURE 5.9
This fabric swatch displays rhythm.

we create emphasis to call attention to a certain part of our body. In the fabric swatches in Figure 5.10, emphasis is created through color and design.

PROPORTION In fabric design, proportion refers to the relationship between the parts of the design. Is the design in proportion to the entire garment? The example in Figure 5.11 shows a design on a garment and its relationship to the entire garment. The size of the design on the garment remains in proportion to the entire T-shirt.

BALANCE Balance refers to both sides of a garment design being equal or totally in sync. If you fold a garment in half and each half is exactly the same then you have **symmetrical balance.** If the two sides are different yet remain equal in weight then you have **asymmetrical balance.** The two photographs in Figure 5.12 illustrate the principle of balance. Visually looking at a garment you will notice if the garment appears to be equal. There is no right or wrong in achieving balance. It's up to the designer to decide.

(A)

(B)

FIGURE 5.10
Fabric swatch (a) emphasizes color, fabric swatch (b) emphasizes design.

UNITY A unified garment is in harmony and creates agreement with all of the other parts of the design. Lines, shapes, and colors can all create unity within a garment. For example, curved lines can all create unity within a design; diamond shapes can do the same. Colors that are similar can also create unity by creating a mood and forming an overall unified look. All of the design principles create unity by expressing a theme or mood of the garment.

Fabric 101

How do you choose the right fabric? Fabric characteristics have weight and texture, and the fibers that make up the fabric can be either manmade or natural. With so many choices, how do you choose the right fabric for your garment?

One of the best ways to analyze fabric is to preview the fabric from a designer's viewpoint. Why do designers choose the fabrics they do for the garments they make? In Exercise 5.2 you will examine how to choose fabric for a skirt.

FIGURE 5.11
Top with design in proportion to the top.

Exercise 5.2: Pattern Fabric Choices

You are a designer for a women's clothing store. Your job is to design three skirts for your next season's collection. You goal is to make all three designs be unique and different. Follow the steps in completing your fabric design board:

* Go to a fabric store and choose three different skirt patterns. Remember, each skirt should be unique and different yet have unity.

* You will need the front and back information from the pattern envelope to complete your fabric design board. Highlight your skirt choice and

FIGURE 5.12 Symmetrical (left) and asymmetrical balance (right).

FIGURE 15.13
Unity Sweaters

make note of your fabric choice on the pattern envelope. Your three pattern choices will be the foundation of your fabric design board.

* The back of the pattern envelope lists suggested fabrics. From the list choose your fabric. Note: if any fabric lining or underlay is needed to add weight to your skirt, choose this fabric also.

* If you decide to choose a type of fabric that is not suggested on the envelope then state your reason why the fabric you chose will work for your skirt.

* Your fabric design board should have three patterns, front and back, with each pattern fabric swatch or swatches choice. The fabric swatch should be a minimum size of six inches by six inches and at least large enough to touch and feel.

* Next to the pattern and fabric choice bullet point your fabric content, texture, design, and care. For example: fabric content—100 percent cotton; texture—smooth with a dull finish; design—blue dye fabric design; and care—machine washable, tumble dry.

* Complete your fabric design board with your fabric choice reasoning. Is the color suitable for your **target market**? Your target market would consist of an age range and other demographic characteristics that your consumer would wear. Who would wear each of these three skirts the best and why?

* What is the occasion for this particular fabric choice and why? Day or evening, dressy or casual?

* Note the fashion personality that would most likely wear your fabric choices. Is it the sporty, dramatic, classic, romantic, or natural fashion personality?

* Conclude with your final thoughts on why your choices were made and why.

This same exercise can be done using any apparel item. The use of a pattern is a good place to start for suggested fabrics but of course it is not always necessary. Applying the principles of design—rhythm, emphasis, proportion, balance, and unity—and your sensory factor of touch, you will be able to make an intelligent decision on your fabric choice.

Fabric Summary

Your personal style goal is to accentuate the positive and de-emphasize the negative. Using your body type and frame as your basis of choice of fabric, you will be able to choose wisely the fabrics that may add or subtract weight depending on its texture. Fabric design is your fashion personality. Choose a design you are drawn to; it can be batik, dyed, embroidered, printed, or painted. Utilize the design principles of rhythm, emphasis, proportion, balance, and unity in your fabric choices, and you will see your own personal style shine through to the world.

Quality

"Buy the best quality you can afford." We've all heard this saying before, but most people do not exactly know what it means. Excellent quality in clothing is defined as: having value and worth; being free of flaws; and generally, although not always, being quite expensive. High quality clothing is made with expensive fabrics such as merino wool, pima cotton, or fine silk. Construction and finishing details are precise; buttons, zippers, linings, pressing, decorative items and the design are exquisite. Not all expensive items are high quality, and not all inexpensive items are poor quality.

Quality Checklist

To determine the quality of an item, use the following **quality checklist**:

* Check the fabric by stretching and balling it up. Does the fabric still hold its shape?

* Check fabric seams. A generous seam allowance will help prevent tearing. Is there any seam allowance in the garment?

* Does the fabric show signs of **pilling**? Pilling looks like fuzz balls on your fabric. It occurs when the fabric fibers are worn or in constant friction. Pilling is an indicator of an old garment, one whose fabric is falling apart, and/or worn to death. When the fabric begins to pill after washing or dry cleaning it is time to get rid of the garment.

* Check buttons and buttonholes. Are they free of threads and not fraying?

* Is the lining laying flat against the garment? The purpose of a lining is to provide a smooth, clean, inside finish. If the garment puckers then it's an indicator of a poorly lined garment. A successfully lined garment will:

  - prevent stretching and wrinkling in a skirt.
  - provide comfort to fabric that has a rough texture.
  - provide a feeling of luxury when the garment is opened. Usually a jacket, coat, or cape is lined because it is taken off and the inside is visible.
  - help preserve the garment's shape by providing extra weight to the garment.

* Check the zipper. Does it lay flat against the garment and work without interruption?

* Check the seams of the garment. Do they run parallel (vertical seams) or horizontal to the floor? No pants will pass a quality test if the vertical seams are crooked. When trying on pants check the side seams to see if they are straight and parallel to the floor. You do not want the seam to veer off to the left or right because visually you will also look crooked. Horizontal seams in waistbands and tops also should lie parallel to the floor. Visually, an unbalanced look will make your entire appearance look unbalanced.

* Are the fabric details staying put on the garment and not falling off when in use?

* Finally, does the garment feel good against your body?

Cost-per-Wearing Formula

Once you have identified if your garment is of excellent, good, or poor quality, you can consider the life of the garment. The **cost-per-wearing formula** is a great way to determine the true value of a clothing item. The formula is:

$$\text{Cost of the garment} / \text{Number of wearings}$$

To demonstrate how to use this formula, let's consider the example of the little black dress that every woman owns or should own. Do you buy the $200 dress or the $100 dress of the same style? The $200 dress will last for four years and the $100 dress will last for one year. If you decide you will wear this dress approximately two times a month or 24 times a year then to compute the cost-per-wearing for each dress the answer is:

$200 / 4 years x 24 wearings per year = $200 / 96 total wearings = $2.08
$100 / 1 year x 24 wearings per year = $100 / 24 total wearings= $4.17

The $200 dress is the better value, lasting four times longer and costing $2.00 less per wearing.

Quality Summary

The basic pieces of your wardrobe, those items that you will wear most often, are the items where quality is vital. Invest in high quality basics; not only will they look good on your body but they will last a lifetime. Trendy items, those that are only important for a season, need not be as costly because the number of wearings will be minimal. A more thorough discussion of basics and trends will be outlined in Chapter 6, the Cluster Concept.

Style

Style is design, and in wardrobe selection the design of the garment that coincides with your body type will make or break an outfit. For example, let's look at various styles of jackets. This is one way we can examine how style can impact your wardrobe.

"The jacket is the mainstay of a woman's wardrobe," according to Linda Allard, a designer for Ellen Tracy. The photographs in Figure 5.14 show a variety of jacket choices available.

Jacket choices include:

* Single-breasted V-neck.

* Three-button closure.

* Double breasted.

* Short-cropped jackets.

* Five button closure.

* Straight cut style reaching below the derriere.

Now, considering each of styles listed above, see how each of the body types listed below match up to its correct style jacket.

Rectangle body types will want to identify a waist. The short-cropped jacket will stop at the waistline and help to define a waist area.

Triangle body types will want to emphasize their upper portion and draw the eye upward. The five-button closure jacket will help to visually bring the eye up.

Inverted triangle body types will want to de-emphasize their top portion and opt for V-neck style jackets to elongate the torso.

Hourglass body types have the ability to wear a variety of styles yet need to define their waists with single-breasted style jackets.

FIGURE 5.14

The jacket. Adding this third piece to your outfit is a basic step in achieving personal style. Choose from the various styles available from manufacturers and make sure the jacket flatters your overall figure. These women would not look complete without the jacket.

Emphasizing style is crucial to achieving your own personal style. Know what works for your body and stick with it. Ultimately, the key point to emphasize is our face, or the personality area of our body. **Design emphasis** means giving special attention to a given area in order to make it stand out. Your goal is to choose a style that emphasizes your assets.

As we all strive to achieve style, flair, and grace, we are also guilty of forming **stereotypes**. This is a label or assumption we place on someone or a group based on how they look. This perception of their image is held in common by a number of people. Complete Exercise 5.3 to see what style of clothing each of these individuals or groups wear.

Exercise 5.3: Common Stereotypes
What would each of these individuals or groups wear? What stereotypes do we form of these individuals or groups? Complete each sentence.

1. A motorcycle rider would wear…
2. A stripper would wear…
3. A computer wiz would wear…
4. A stay-at-home mom would wear…
5. A lawyer would wear…
6. A fashion designer would wear…
7. A doctor would wear…
8. A banker would wear…
9. A teenager with tattoos would wear…
10. A personal trainer would wear…

Compare answers with your classmates to see if there are any similarities in the clothing choices you have chosen for each of the individuals or groups. What factors contribute to your answer? Why is it wrong to stereotype people in categories?

Style Summary

Personal style is what sets us apart from each other and makes us unique and different. Choosing a certain style jacket, pant, dress, skirt, coat or any other clothing item will showcase to the world who you are.

When thinking about style, here are some key points to consider:

* Do invest in classic, quality pieces that will last a lifetime, e.g., trench coat, pencil skirt, blazer, turtleneck.

* Don't stop a jacket at the largest part of the hips if you have large hips.

* Don't divide your body in half with a jacket. Your jacket styles always look more interesting if the jacket is larger or smaller than half.

* Do use color effectively. Monochromatic color will elongate your look, whereas contrasting color will emphasize your bottom half.

* Do check style magazines for the latest fashion trends. Look at the styles of jackets, skirts, and pants that are being worn, and stay current with what is new.

* Do invest in quality accessories to complete your outfit. There are rental accessories companies available if you need the right accessory yet cannot afford it. Chapter 8, Accessories! Accessories! Accessories!, discusses this topic further.

* Do wear what is appropriate for the occasion, time, and place. Style begins with looking your best for all occasions.

* Do invest in proper fitting undergarments to achieve a total look. Further discussion of foundations will be in Chapter 7, Foundation Basics.

Table 5.6
BUSINESS FORMAL AND BUSINESS CASUAL INDICATORS

Business Formal	Business Casual
Matched Suit	Unmatched suit, separates
Tailored jacket	Unstructured jacket
Collar on shirt	Collarless shirt
Natural fabrics—wool, silk, and fine textures that are dry clean only	Cottons, knits, and other washable fabrics
Straight lines and geometrics	Curved, gentle lines
Dark, solid, colors	Bright solid or patterned colors

Style is sometimes in question when deciding what to wear to certain occasions. What is considered business casual and business formal? Table 5.6 examines what clothing items convey formality or casual attire.

Personal style is what we all strive to attain, but do keep in mind the key pointers: invest in classics, your clothing should mirror the current trends; use color wisely, and remember to add the finishing touches of accessories; and wear correct fitting foundations.

Care

Clothing care, the final step in the wardrobe selection process, cannot be overlooked. Achieving personal style is necessary to retain that "just bought look." According to The Soap and Detergent Association, four out of five consumers read care labels before they buy clothing and follow label instructions when washing garments (Soap and Detergent Association, 2006).

Table 5.7

CLOTHING CARE

Refer to the chart on the proper steps to care for your clothing. The fabric care symbols are inserted in your clothing labels.

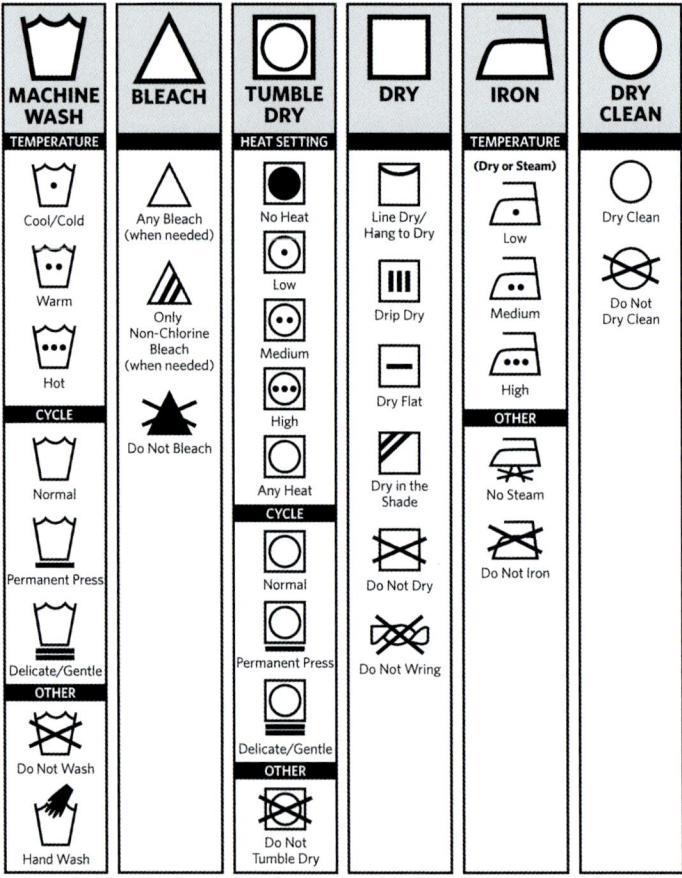

The importance of proper clothing care will be examined in Exercise 5.4. Complete the exercise and add your own list of mistakes in clothing care.

Exercise 5.4: Mistakes in Clothing Care

Preview the list of improper clothing care topics. Categorize the topics in the following broad categories: sewing repair needed, stain removal, pressing, washing, and dry cleaning. Using fashion magazines cut out pictures showcasing proper clothing care in each category. Identify through magazine pictures, the right way to avoid mistakes. What technique would you use to eliminate the improper look?

Mistakes in clothing care include:

- Obvious perspiration stains
- Ring-around-the-collar
- Missing buttons, snaps, or hook-and-eyes
- Ripped clothing and seams
- Makeup stains on clothing
- Not pressed wrinkle clothing
- Broken zippers
- Food stains
- Perfume smells
- Grass stains
- Rust stains
- Ink stains

* Grease and oil stains
* Lining showing below hem
* Belt loops not stitched on properly
* Baggy, ill fitting clothing

Laundry Product Choices

There are so many laundry products in the market that it may be necessary to review the care label for suggestions and advice. The most common categories of laundry products we use are:

DETERGENTS Detergents are used for machine and hand washable garments. The main ingredient used to clean the clothes in detergents is the surfactant or surface-active agent. The surfactant and the movement and agitation of the washing machine or hand washing helps to loosen the soil from the clothing. Some other ingredients used in detergents are builders—used to soften the wash water, brighteners or whitening agents—used to brighten whites and colors, and a variety of other ingredients and fragrances.

LAUNDRY ADDITIVES Laundry additives are optional ingredients used to make clothes look whiter, cleaner, and last longer. They include bleach, pre-treatment products, and fabric softeners. These products do increase your total laundry cost yet the results prove to be long lasting.

FINISHING TOUCH PRODUCTS Fabric finishers, starches, and sizing can all make your clothing look brand new. These products are available in spray or liquid forms with sprays being the most common.

We all have different clothing needs and choose products that we feel are beneficial to and for us. The choice is yours to select the products that are best for your lifestyle and budget.

Care Summary

Following the steps on the care label is a necessary factor in keeping your garments clean and like new. Read the care label carefully to make sure you are able to properly care for the garment.

Making a list of mistakes and mentally checking them off your list is a great way to care for yourself and how you look. Use the magazine pictures you created in Exercise 5.4, Showing Proper Clothing Care, as constant reminders of how your clothing should look.

Spend a day at the store really analyzing what laundry products are best for your clothing needs. Once you choose the right products for your clothing, the care of your clothing will be much easier and your clothing will look their very best. Your garments will last a lifetime if you take care of them properly.

BE AN EXPERT

This chapter covers the basics of wardrobe selection. The six factors crucial to achieving your own personal style are fit, color, fabric, quality, style, and care. Fit, the most important of the style factors, concludes with 10 fit style rules one should adhere to.

Color, a selection factor we are immediately drawn to, emphasizes our skin tone as the foundation for a correct seasonal color wardrobe. Knowing whether you are a cool season, winter or summer, or a warm season, autumn or spring, will help you choose a colorful wardrobe that is perfect for your skin, eyes, and hair.

Fabric wardrobe selection factor utilizes fabric designs and fabric design principles as essential factors. An understanding of the design principles of rhythm, emphasis, proportion, balance, and unity in fabric is placing you on the right track to fabric style.

The quality checklist and style key pointers will point you in the right direction. Don't forget clothing care as the basis for a long lasting wardrobe. Refer to the clothing care label as the beginning of proper clothing care and if necessary, add any optional care items, like starches and other finishers, for further improvement. The fabric care symbols chart is a handy item to keep you abreast of what care symbols mean.

All of the wardrobe selection factors are important and without them, style is just not visible.

KEY WORDS

analogous	emphasis	primary colors
asymmetrical balance	fit	proportion
balance	harmony	quality
batik fabric design	hourglass figures	quality checklist
chroma	hue	rectangle body types
chromotherapy	inverted triangle figures	rhythm
color	laundry additives	sizing
Color Association of the United States	mauveine	stereotype
	manmade fabrics	style
color draping	monochromatic	style mavens
color seasons	natural fiber fabrics	symmetrical balance
complementary	Ott light bulb	target market
contrasting	oval shape	texture
cool hues	painted fabric design	triangle body types
cost-per-wearing formula	Pantone Color Institute	unity
design emphasis	pear shape body type	value
detergent	pilling	wardrobe selection factors
dyed fabric design	printed fabric design	warm hues
embroidered fabric design		

RESOURCES

Color Me Beautiful. (2008). How to determine your season. Retrieved on April 3, 2008 from www.colormebeautiful.com/seasons/index.html.

Dennett, C. (2007). Sewing 101: How to choose fabric, *How to Choose Fabric for Your Sewing Project*. Retrieved on April 21, 2008 from www.associatedcontent.com/article/225146/sewing_101_how_to_choose_fabric.html.

eHow editor. (2008). *How to find the perfect pair of jeans*. Retrieved on April 21, 2008 from www.ehow.com/how_2062439_find-perfect-pair-jeans.html.

Fabrics Manufacturers. (2008). Fabric design. Retrieved on April 21, 2008 from www.fabrics-manufacturers.com/fabric-design.html.

Home Sewing Association. (2008). Learn to sew linings. Retrieved on April 21, 2008 from www.sewing.org/enthusiast/html/el_lining1.html.

Iowa State University Extension Service. (2003). Unraveling the mystery of design elements and principles in clothing. Retrieved on April 21, 2008 from www.extension.iastate.edu/Publications/4H313.pdf.

Jacobs, M. (2008). Bio. Retrieved on April 2, 2008 from www.marcjacobs.com.

Kalisz, K. (2004). Sci-Art™ 12-tone personal color analysis. Retrieved on April 3, 2008 from www.sci-art-global.com/color-analysis/12-tone-personal-color-analysis.htm.

Mississippi State University Extension Service. (2008). Clothing care, information sheet 1248. Retrieved on April 21, 2009 from http://msucares.com/pubs/infosheets/is1248.htm.

Real Simple. (2007, February). Road Test, Jeans, *Real Simple,* pp. 131–136.

Teachinghearts. (2008). Color and psychology, Persecution and the Personality. Retrieved from www.teachinghearts.org/dre00personality.html.

The Soap and Detergent Association. (2007). Your guide to fabric care symbols. Retrieved on April 21, 2008 from www.cleaning101.com/laundry/fabricsymbols2.cfm.

Wikiel, Y. (2005, September). Here's to hue, *Real Simple,* pp. 131–136.

Zafu. (2008). *Here are your jeans, now find the ones you like best*. Retrieved on April 21, 2008 from www.zafu.com/zafu/shape.do?method=CHECK_BROWSER&toolId=1.

CHAPTER SIX

Cluster Concept

"You don't have to be able to afford a whole new wardrobe to indulge in new fashions. Save for a few key items that can be worn multiple ways—jackets, accessories, and a skirt that can be dressed up or down. Thrifty doesn't have to equal boring."

—EMILY STANTON, FASHION ENTHUSIAST AND PERSONAL SHOPPER.

CHAPTER OBJECTIVES
After reading this chapter, you will be able to:

* Define the cluster concept.

* Complete a lifestyle analysis to begin the cluster process.

* Identify one main piece in your wardrobe to begin your first cluster.

* Examine your closet to review additional items that will round out your cluster.

* Complete the cluster worksheet based on clothing items chosen for your first cluster.

* Review additional clothing items for possible additional clusters.

* Compare and contrast fashion personalities with cluster-building concepts.

THE EMERGING STYLE ICON

Forming a **cluster**—a collection, grouping, or assortment of clothing—is the next step in achieving an easy personal style. The word *cluster* can be defined as a mass or pile, an accumulation, or the act of gathering together. Why is forming a cluster an easy progression in achieving personal style? Because it is a natural step that will become a habit and a way of life for you, the emerging style icon.

When you examined the clothing in your closet in Chapter 3, Closet Evaluation, you probably recognized certain items you just can't live without. These **wardrobe staples** are the beginning of what clustering is all about. Examples of staple items are the jacket, the trousers, and the twin set, and each of these pieces can take you from day to night, season to season. Beginning the process of forming your clusters may seem boring and useless, but in the long run it will accentuate your personal style to another level. Knowing your body as you do now; having reviewed the steps in Chapter 4, Body Type Evaluation; and allowing the Wardrobe Selection Factors to guide you as you have learned to do in Chapter 5—you are prepared to learn the cluster lessons.

GETTING STARTED

Where do you begin? Let's analyze your current lifestyle. Do you have a normal weekly routine? Do your clothes match your weekly routine? You began plotting your weekly activities on the lifestyle grid in Chapter One, Fashion Personality Types. Evaluate the grid by analyzing the activities that represent the largest percentage of your life as it is now. It could be school, work, or social activities. Whatever activity it is, analyzing the amount of time spent will help lead you to forming your beginning clothing cluster. Think about the several items of clothing you wear on a continual basis, or at least once a week. Is it the black pants, the little black dress, or your favorite pair of jeans? These items probably fulfill all the wardrobe selection requirements, and each is worthy of being a favorite. As you think about these favorite items, consider where you would wear them. Is it for work, school, play, or a special occasion? Each of these occasions in your life will form a cluster. You can start small, with the cluster that is the biggest percentage of your lifestyle, and add on pieces later.

Cluster Types
The **work cluster** is based on your job, career, and position. If you wear a uniform then this cluster is simplified to include the uniform pieces you are allowed to wear. Preview the work cluster as an example of how to fill in the clothing items suitable for the additional clusters. As you complete the clusters think of the activities associated with each of the clusters. Here are some examples:

Sport cluster—clothing for going to the gym and working out; walking or riding a bike; playing tennis, golf, or any other sport you enjoy.

Casual cluster—clothing for hanging out at home, shopping, visiting friends, going to a movie, and anything else associated with casual activities.

Special occasion cluster—clothing for weddings, funerals, holiday get-togethers, anniversaries, birthdays, retirement parties, baby showers, promotion parties, and any other kind a gathering of people with the purpose of having a good time.

Seasonal cluster—clothing for taking trips to another part of the country to enjoy warm or cold weather.

Complete Table 6.1 with Exercise 6.1 to begin your cluster journey.

Table 6.1
CLUSTER IDENTIFICATION CHART

Clusters	Work Cluster	Sport Cluster	Casual Cluster	Special Occasion Cluster	Seasonal Cluster
Favorite item—base	Black pencil skirt				
Add-on	Two-button black jacket				
Add-on	Blue cardigan twin set				
Add-on	White tailored shirt				
Add-on	Blue/black/white tweed jacket				
Add-on	Accent color trench coat				
Add-on	V-neck pullover sweater–design				

Exercise 6.1 Cluster Model Building

Use Table 6.1 to complete this exercise.

Part I. Cluster Table
Complete the cluster table by identifying the clothing items suitable for sport, casual, special occasion, and seasonal clusters. Keep in mind the clothing items in your closet that you will wear, referring to Chapter 3 Closet Evaluation and to your lifestyle grid. Be specific with your needs and realistic with your budget.

Part II. Cluster Groupings
Take each cluster and make 10 outfits from the seven pieces. For example, the work cluster has the black pencil skirt as its base item (as shown in the outfits on the following pages).

FIGURE 6.1
Black pencil skirt with black jacket buttoned—this is a simple, basic, neutral combination outfit. Add a scarf accessory to be worn over the jacket and the jacket doubles as a top and jacket.

FIGURE 6.2
Black pencil skirt with tweed jacket buttoned—pairing the skirt with a tweed jacket creates interest and a bit of unexpectedness.

FIGURE 6.3

Black pencil skirt with blue cardigan and white shirt—adding a cardigan provides a casual approach to an otherwise business formal look.

FIGURE 6.4
Black pencil skirt with white shirt—the white shirt needs to stand out on its own with this outfit so it will look complete. The cluster-building white shirt is one that is basic yet simple; details on the shirt allow it to be worn by itself. Accessories will help make this simple look complete.

FIGURE 6.5
Black pencil skirt with trench coat and blue shell sweater—adding color close to your face will visually draw the eye upward. The trench coat helps to elongate the upper torso, creating a vertical line.

FIGURE 6.6
Black pencil skirt with V-neck pullover sweater—the sweater providing another casual option but still looking neat and professional.

FIGURE 6.7

Black pencil skirt with white shirt and V-neck pullover sweater—layering the cluster pieces adds interest to your total look. The pullover sweater can also be worn tied over the shoulders as an accessory item.

FIGURE 6.8

Black pencil skirt with blue twin set—the monochromatic look of the twin set is an option that looks good on everyone because of the ability to draw the attention to your face and also the slenderizing appeal of the colors that are exactly the same on the two pieces that make up the twin set.

FIGURE 6.9

Black pencil skirt with blue shell sweater and black jacket—the accent color top adds pizzazz to any neutral color suit.

FIGURE 6.10

Black pencil skirt with cardigan buttoned up—as shown before with the jacket, the cardigan can also double up as a top when fully buttoned.

BUILDING FROM THE BASICS

The clothing items chosen for your cluster consist of quality pieces. As discussed in Chapter 5, Wardrobe Selection Factors, quality clothing items will last long and wear well. Begin your cluster building with the category that will outfit the biggest percentage of your lifestyle at the current time. Refer back to Exercise 2.1, Evaluating Your Lifestyle, in Chapter 2, Personal Style Evaluation, to determine where are you in your life now? If it is school, then the casual cluster will be your first cluster to build on. It doesn't stop with the 7–10 pieces but will continue to build your cluster with additional **basic items** and **accent pieces** that work with each basic item chosen. Because the clothing items chosen are within your color season every item will match and go together. The goal is to continue to build upon each cluster so you have a variety of clothes to choose from each day that is based upon your fashion personality, body type, and lifestyle.

Cluster Planning Chronicle

A **Cluster Planning Chronicle** is a record, a worksheet, a journal, and a spreadsheet outlining the clothing items that will make up each of your clusters. This will make your life easy and simple and keep you on track to becoming a style icon. This sheet can be updated on a seasonal basis to add and/or delete clothing items. Once each of your clusters has a minimum of 3 base items and 7–10 accent pieces, then you can begin to add **trendy clothing items**. The wardrobe selection factors are not necessarily what are needed when choosing trendy items. What is in style at the moment is what is needed to add excitement to a basic cluster. There are various ways to find out what is considered trendy at the time. Current fashion magazines like *Vogue, Glamour*, and *In Style* are examples, as are **trade journals** like *WWD*; entertainment television shows showcase celebrity fashions, and department and specialty stores offer trendy fashions as well. The real fashionista invests in fashion books allowing them to have a library of fashion trends at their fingertips.

The Well-Balanced Wardrobe
There are plenty of theories that explain the concept of clustering or grouping your clothing. One of the best and easiest to understand is "The Well-Balanced Wardrobe," by Karen Zozlowski, fashion editor at *Real Simple* magazine. Zozlowski advises you to compare your wardrobe to a food pyramid using the principles of variety, moderation, and portion control. You can utilize your *staples* (e.g., wool skirt, black suit, pin-striped oxford, black dress, silk blouse, and gray trousers), *basic pieces* (e.g., black tank, crewneck sweater, jeans, long-sleeve white T-shirt, and khakis), *statement pieces* (e.g., printed dress, patterned jacket, bold blouse, graphic sweater, and tweed pants), *evening standards* (e.g., velvet jacket, ruffled shirt, cocktail shirt, sparkly top, and velvet pants), and lastly the *showstoppers* (e.g., the party dress). All of these clothing items put together your balanced wardrobe. To preview more of these suggested items to complete the wardrobe pyramid, visit *Real Simple* magazine's website (www.realsimple.com) and place "well-balanced wardrobe" in the search field.. "How we look to others entirely depends on what we wear and how we wear it," Emily Post wrote in *Etiquette*. Everyone can own a black dress but not everyone wears it the same way. *Your Personal Style* helps you identify and add those touches that are unique to you. This concept will be discussed further in Chapter 12, Tying it all Together... Your Personal Style. (Zozlowski, 2006)

As you work through Exercise 6.2, think of what is current at the present time and follow your instincts incorporating "you" into the wardrobe.

Exercise 6.2: Cutting Trends
Using current fashion magazines, find pictures featuring the current trend of each of the following apparel and accessory categories. As you fill out Table 6.2, describe each trend and show the picture of the trend that will work best for you and why.

A well-organized wardrobe consists of clothing clusters that work well in your current lifestyle. The blank cluster-planning chronicle sheets can be

Table 6.2

TREND-SPOTTING CHART

Trend	Description	Magazine Cutout
Dresses		
Skirts		
Pants		
Tops/blouses		
Blazers		
Outerwear		
Sweaters		
Eveningwear		
Footwear		
Handbags		

copied and used to fulfill your wardrobe goals. Organize your cluster planning worksheets together in a binder under each of the cluster types. Refer to the binder when you need to refresh your memory on the clothing choices that will continue to make your wardrobe your own personal style.

Clustering for Your Fashion Personality

The cluster concept involves using staples, basic clothing items that will allow you to build and expand your wardrobe and suit your current lifestyle. How does the cluster concept work with all the different fashion personalities? Let's take a look at the five basic fashion personalities and see how clustering might work for each of them.

Clustering for the Classic Fashion Personality

For the typical classic fashion personality it's very easy to begin a cluster because clothing choices are mostly tailored and conservative items. The classic personality will begin a cluster with a three-piece suit, consisting of jacket, pants, and skirts in a neutral color and expanding to other items such as sweater twin sets and white shirts. These clothing items are basics for the classic fashion personality and are already part of their existing wardrobe. Items that would expand the cluster for a classic type would be shirts in accent colors, and pants and jackets in plaids and additional colors. Any extremes in fashion styles are not the look for the classic type, yet sticking with the tried and true styles and expanding with color is the way to go for the classic fashion personality. Designer brand investment pieces that are able to be mixed and matched are great choices for the classic type; these include Ellen Tracy, Dana Buchman, and Anne Klein. These brands demonstrate clothing examples that will work for the classic fashion personality.

FIGURE 6.11
The beginning of your cluster can start with one simple jacket. Expand your wardrobe one step at a time by adding additional pieces to your favorite clothing item.

THREAD 6.2

CLUSTER PLANNING CHRONICLE

Name: _____ Date: _____

Worksheet—Cluster Type _____

Your Personal Style _____

	Skirt	Pant	Jacket	Top	Dresses	Sweater	Denim
COLORS							
Neutral							
Accent							
Print							
Shopping List							
FABRIC							
Winter-weight							
Summer-weight							
All seasons							
Shopping List							
ACCESSORIES							
Footwear							
Jewelry							
Belts							
Handbags							
Hosiery							
Shopping List							

FIGURE 6.12

Comfort and relaxed clothing theme is shown in this photograph and is common attire for the sporty fashion personality.

Clustering for the Sporty Fashion Personality

The sporty fashion personality will have in their wardrobe casual, comfortable, and athletic clothing. These pieces might consist of athletic pants and matching jackets made with fabrics such as nylon, spandex, and breathable cotton. Cotton T-shirts, and denim jeans and jackets are also part of the beginning cluster for the sporty personality. Because this personality is always on the go, their clothing should be comfortable, wash-n-wear, with no extra decoration or details. Any additions to the cluster for the sporty personality would consist of items such as brand name jogging suits; Nike, Juicy Couture, or BeBe Sport offer some good examples.

Clustering for the Natural Fashion Personality

The natural fashion personality invests in clothing that is simple, untreated, and in neutral solid, earthy colors. A natural fashion personality would invest in pieces from designer Eileen Fisher, who specializes in minimalist clothing in natural fabrics. The philosophy of this designer is the motto for the natural fashion personality—"styles that last, simple looks, and achieving a sustainable approach to design" (Fisher, 2008). Any additions to the cluster for the natural type would revolve around beautiful fabrics, fabric that is resilient, easy to care for and travels well. As the term *natural* implies, the clothing would be unpretentious yet pure and genuine.

Clustering for the Romantic Fashion Personality

The female who fits into the romantic personality enjoys being a woman and wears clothing that is ultra feminine, delicate, and lacy. The romantic fashion personality would begin her cluster with clothing that would define a woman's shape and body such as fitted bodices in dresses and tops. Clothing that would begin the cluster for the romantic personality would be full skirts, fitted jackets, and lace blouses or tops. Expanding clothing items for the romantic personality would be the same: jackets, dresses, skirts and blouses, yet each item would contain details such as lace and ornate buttons or trims, and fabrics such as chiffon or velvet. Manufacturer's that exhibit these characteristics are Jessica McClintock and Betsey Johnson.

FIGURE 6.13 (OPPOSITE, TOP) The simple style of this Eileen Fisher outfit exhibits the look of a natural fashion personality.

FIGURE 6.14 (OPPOSITE, BOTTOM) The color, pattern, shape, movement, and details in this Betsey Johnson dress are characteristic of a romantic fashion personality.

FIGURE 6.15 (THIS PAGE) The flair and creativity of this look from designer Alexander McQueen is characteristic of the dramatic fashion personality.

Clustering for the Dramatic Fashion Personality

The boldness of a dramatic fashion personality is difficult to cluster because each item of clothing can stand on its own and clothing items are most often very trendy and unique. Extremes in clothing are nothing unusual for this personality; bold colors and high fashion are common. To begin a cluster for this personality you would start with the current trends of the season. Jackets, skirts, pants, and tops all coordinate, but colors and styles may only last one season. Examples of designers who exhibit these types of looks are Dolce&Gabbana and Alexander McQueen. Each piece is unique and sometimes trendy yet showcases the **zeitgeist**, the fashion of the times, and the spirit of the season.

Clustering Summary

Clustering, an important tool in wardrobe planning concludes Part II, What You Should Wear. The tools outlined in this chapter, Cluster Identification Chart, cluster building concept, cutting trends technique, and the Cluster Planning Chronicle are "keepers" in achieving personal style. Form a habit of clustering and make it a way of life by continuing to review your clothing choices, updating your trendy items, and striving to look your very best at all times. Refer back to your fashion personality for suggestions on what clothing items you should choose to form, begin, and expand your cluster. Your personal style is highlighted when the inside of who you are—your personality—matches the outside—your clothing choices.

KEY WORDS

accent pieces	seasonal cluster	work cluster
basic items	special occasion cluster	zeitgeist
casual cluster	sport cluster	
cluster	trade journals	
cluster planning	trendy clothing items	
chronicle	wardrobe staples	

RESOURCES

Dolce&Gabanna. (2008). Retrieved on April 20, 2008 from www.dolcegabanna.com.

Fisher, E. (2008). Retrieved on April 20, 2008 from www.eileenfisher.com.

Johnson, B. (2008). Retrieved on April 20, 2008 from www.betseyjohnson.com.

Post, E. (2006, August). Meet your match, *In Style*, p. 121.

Zozlowski, K. (2006, September). The well-balanced wardrobe, *Real Simple*, pp. 270–281.

PART III

Taking Action: What Should You Add and *Why*?

CHAPTER SEVEN

Foundation Basics

"We have a stronger shoulder. We have a really fitted waist. We have a very accentuated chest . . . the bra is actually the accessory of the season. Every look has got a bra—and those bras, they're not sort of subtle."

—TOM FORD, FASHION AND FRAGRANCE DESIGNER OF TOM FORD INTERNATIONAL, IS ESPECIALLY KNOWN FOR HIS 10 YEARS AS CREATIVE DIRECTOR OF GUCCI AND GUCCI GROUP, WHERE HE INCREASED SALES TO ALMOST 3 BILLION DOLLARS IN 2003.

CHAPTER OBJECTIVES
After reading this chapter, you will be able to:

* Identify the bras that are part of an essential bra wardrobe.

* Compare the variety of underwear available for perfect clothing presence.

* Recognize optional body shapers available to women of all shapes and sizes.

* Identify slips and liner options available to all women.

* Evaluate the variety of hosiery options available.

SHAPE YOUR BODY

Foundation basics consist of the necessary undergarments—bras, panties, body shapers, slips, camisoles, and hosiery—that will shape your body and make or break your image and wardrobe. What's underneath is just as important as what you wear on top. You can ruin an expensive outfit by not wearing the proper undergarments. Having an essential foundation wardrobe is necessary to becoming a true style icon. The complete, essential undergarments that will make an ideal foundation wardrobe will be explained in this chapter. As you assemble your ideal undergarments, start small and continue to build when assembling the rest of your clothing. Previewing the large amount of styles online is a good way to start to narrow down your choices. One website that offers recommendations for lingerie selections is HerRoom Lingerie (www.herroom.com). I will summarize for you the selections in each category.

THE COMPLETE BRA WARDROBE

A **bra** is an undergarment that gives support and contours a woman's breasts. The complete bra wardrobe consists of 17 styles and a variety of specialty bras. These styles can be divided into basics and trends. The basic styles are necessary for every woman to own and the trends are extras—good to have but not necessary.

Basic Bras

Bras that are considered basic are those bras that form the beginning of your foundation cluster. These bras are the necessary foundation pieces that every woman should own as part of their underwear wardrobe. Because we have a variety of clothing in our wardrobe, it is ideal to have a choice of bras that will work under our everyday clothes. The basics can be divided further into the following four styles:

1. **Everyday basic bra**—comfort is key, and you should own at least three to six types of basic bras so as not to have to wear them every day. Similar to

 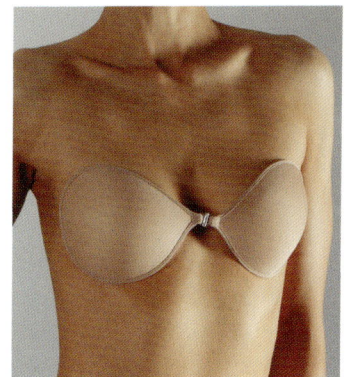 

footwear, we should allow a day for the bra to air out between wearings. This will allow for less washing and the bra will therefore last longer. Your basic bras may all come from one manufacturer and may be of the same style, but owning more than one allows you to rotate your everyday bras and make them last longer.

2. **Backless bra**—important for formal attire where the gowns are backless. Your lifestyle and clothing will let you know if you need to own this type of bra. If there are backless gowns in your current wardrobe or you foresee this in your future then invest in a good backless bra to wear underneath your formal attire.

3. **Black or nude color bra**—a neutral color bra that everyone should own because there are times when you are wearing sheer or see-through tops and do not want your bra to show through your clothing. A bra closest to your skin tone is ideal for sheer tops because the bra blends with your skin tone and doesn't create any breaks in your total look. Nude bras work for lighter complexions and darker complexions work well with a black bra in their wardrobe.

FIGURE 7.1 (LEFT)
An everyday bra should have support and be comfortable. The color of the bra should be as close to your skin tone as possible. Choose a brand that will work for you.

FIGURE 7.2 (MIDDLE)
This bra is essential for formal attire. If you wear low-back clothing.

FIGURE 7.3 (RIGHT)
Invest in a bra that will not show under sheer clothing. This bra should be as close as possible to your skin tone; dark complexions wear black and nude for light complexions.

FOUNDATION BASICS

4. Convertible bra—a bra that has straps that can convert into a variety of configurations such as conventional, halter, one shoulder, off the shoulder, cris-crossed, and strapless.

Trend Bras

Owning just basic bras is the same as owning just basic clothing items. Basic bras will work and provide the comfort and support you will need under your clothing, but trend bras provide that extra added benefit most of us need for special occasions. A trend has been described as a style or look that comes and goes, and in the case of your bra wardrobe it is only needed when certain items are worn. The trends can be divided further into the following 13 styles.

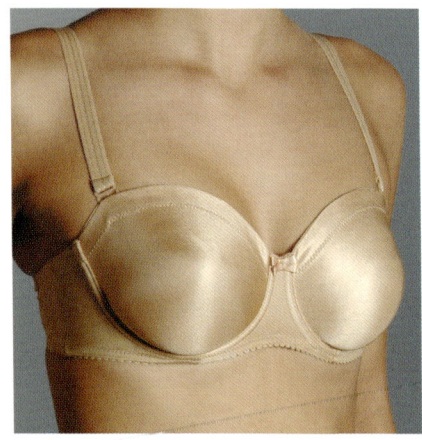

FIGURE 7.4
A convertible bra that can be worn with all the variety of clothing, halters, or racer-backs styles.

1. **Demi-cup bra**—this bra has partial cups or half cups exposing part of the breast but still allowing for support. Perfect for low cut garments where you would like to have some **cleavage** showing.

2. **Lace bra**—in your complete bra wardrobe, a lacy bra is equivalent to a trend. It will lift your spirits and make you feel good.

3. **Long line bra**—this bra reaches the waistline and provides a slimming effect to the midriff area by adding boning and fitting close to the body.

4. **Minimizer bra**—this bra reduces the projection of your breasts by redistributing your breast flesh more under the arms and up towards the chest.

5. **Molded bra**—foam is added to this bra to give it shape and prevent your nipples from showing.

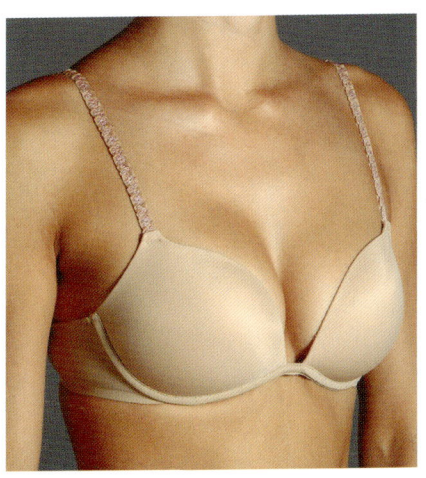

FIGURE 7.5 (TOP LEFT)
A bra to show cleavage is the demi-cup bra. Great bra that has support but also shows the top of your breast.

FIGURE 7.6 (TOP RIGHT)
Every woman should own a pretty lace bra. What's underneath your clothing is just as important as what you show to the public. It makes you feel good inside and out.

FIGURE 7.7 (BOTTOM LEFT)
Do you want to hide the extra roll around your tummy? Wearing a long line bra can hide a multitude of sins; it pulls you in and slenderizes your total body frame.

FIGURE 7.8 (BOTTOM RIGHT)
Full-busted woman can redistribute their breast in bra cups that spread horizontally creating an illusion of smaller breasts. Great to wear with button front tops.

FIGURE 7.9 (TOP LEFT)
If you want to add shape without showing any nipples, add a molded bra to your lingerie wardrobe. The thin foam the molded bra is made out of totally eliminates anything showing through your clothing.

FIGURE 7.10 (TOP RIGHT)
When shopping for a certain style in clothing, don't forget to buy the undergarments to showcase the style chosen. The plunge style bra is essential for those plunging necklines.

FIGURE 7.11 (BOTTOM LEFT)
Small-breasted women can add a push-up bra to create an illusion of fuller, larger breasts.

FIGURE 7.12 (BOTTOM RIGHT)
Workout clothing and swimwear are two examples of clothing that could use a racerback bra. No need to show those bra straps when you have this bra in your wardrobe.

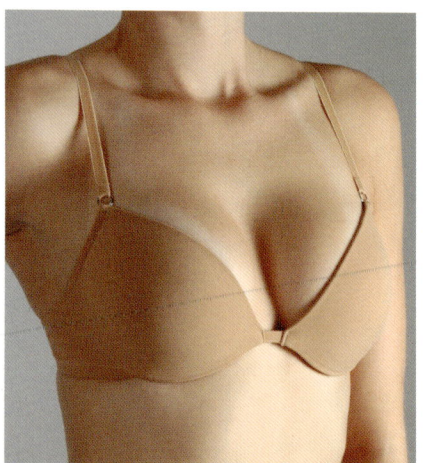

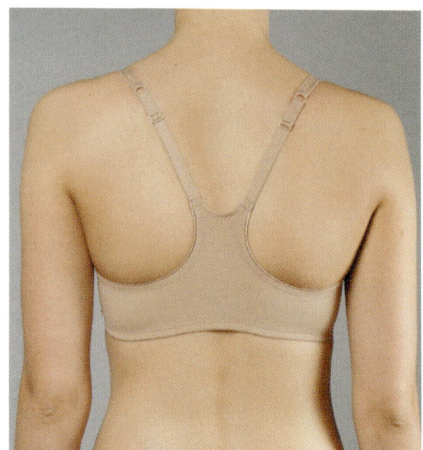

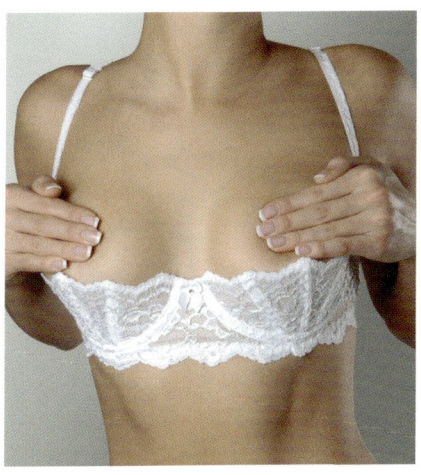 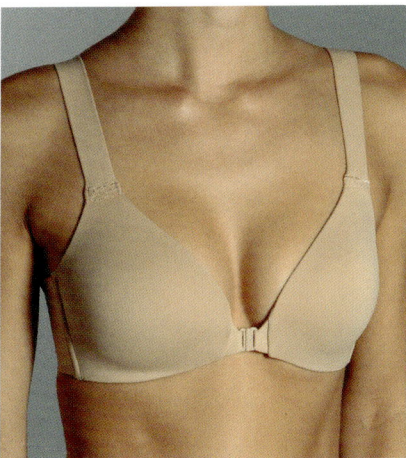

FIGURE 7.13 (LEFT)
A shelf bra equals support. This bra provides some support without making your breasts sag.

FIGURE 7.14 (RIGHT)
For that smooth look under clingy fabrics, wear a seamless bra to achieve that invisible look

6. **Plunge bra**—a low center front accommodates low cut styles.

7. **Push-up bra**—additional padding in the bra lifts the breasts and gives the illusion of a full bust line.

8. **Racer back bra**—the straps of the bra form a racer back, curving between the shoulder blades, as shown in the photograph.

9. **Shelf bra**—constructed for small-breasted women, cups sit on your breast. Allows you support without going braless.

10. **Seamless bra**—molded cups and no seams. Perfect for clothing that clings.

 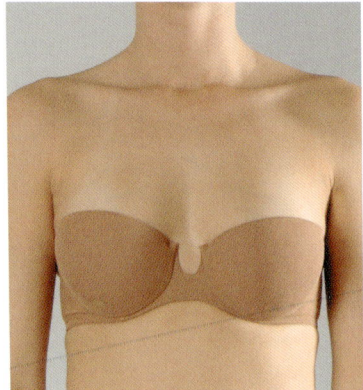 

FIGURE 7.15 (LEFT)
A sports bra is designed especially for active sports and helps to prevent damage to your breasts.

FIGURE 7.16 (MIDDLE)
Evening wear and strapless tops require a strapless bra to showcase your shoulders and not your bra straps. For that clean look with support, add this bra to your wardrobe.

FIGURE 7.17 (RIGHT)
Some manufacturers make bras that have wide-set straps to allow for boat neck and wide necklines in clothing.

11. Sports bra—a bra that provides support and helps to prevent breast sagging.

12. Strapless bra—a bra with no straps and can be worn with strapless tops and gowns.

13. Wide-set straps—the straps are set wide apart for boat and wide necklines.

Specialty Bras

There are also a variety of specialty bras that may be necessary depending on where you are in your current lifestyle. These bras include *nursing bras, mastectomy bras, arthritis bras,* and plenty more. At certain times in your life you may need to wear a special bra that will allow ease of movement yet look and feel comfortable. Fit is crucial even with lingerie. It is important to remember that no matter what challenges or expectations you are going through in your life—mastectomy, pregnancy, or illness—there is a bra wardrobe that will satisfy this point in your life.

No matter what you do or where your life may take you, a good bra is essential to making your outfit look its very best. Bra fitting is a science, and major department and specialty stores have bra fitters that will help you get the perfect fitting bra. Thread 7.1 offers tips for finding the right fit for you.

Bra Checklist

Now that you have the correct size bra and are beginning to try on the variety of brands that are available, there are certain indicators to look for to achieve that just right fit. The following bra checklist will make sure you are reaching your goal of attaining the perfect fitting bra. Your perfect fitting bra should have:

1. smooth fitting cups.
2. a center panel that lays flat against your breast bone.
3. a bottom in the front and back that is parallel to the floor or slightly lower in the back.
4. straps that stay put and don't dig into your shoulders.
5. an underwire that encircles your breast.
6. good breast uplift.
7. your breasts face front and not sag or fall to the sides.
8. the ability to have a finger placed under the front band without strain or resistance.
9. comfort when sitting.

Source: www.herroom.com.

Bra Manufacturers

Just as in apparel, bra manufacturers vary in their sizing. The aim in finding the perfect fit is to first try on a variety of manufacturers to find the right fit and brand for *you*.

Lingerie and underwear expert Tomima Edmark started the website HerRoom after realizing there was a gap in the retail places and style choices women had for buying lingerie. From HerRoom's beginnings in 1999 until today,

Tomima continues to "pick the brains of designers, manufacturer's and consumers" to offer women the best styles, sizes, and products. HerRoom consumers rate the following brands with high accolades:

- **Wacoal**—best overall fitting bra.
- **Chantelle**—best plus-size bra.
- **Vanity Fair**—full figure test bra and best comfort bra.
- **Fantasie**—full coverage bra.
- **Goddess**—bra with stretch shoulder straps.
- **Natori**—great bra for determining bra size.

Exercise 7.1: The Perfect Bra for Me
Visit your local department store and go to the lingerie department. Locate a bra fitter and get measured the proper way. Find a minimum of three bras from three different manufacturers to try on. Spend up to an hour trying on bras to find the perfect fit. Review the bra checklist to make sure that it's the right bra

STEPS TO FINDING THE CORRECT BRA SIZE

Step 1. Measure the band size—measure around the bra directly under your bust line.

Step 2. Measure the cup size—measure at the fullest part of your bust.

Step 3. Subtract the larger number; the full bust measurement called the **overmeasure**, from the smaller one; the measurement under the bust called the **undermeasure**, and this number will help to determine your bra size.

Some bra fitters use this number difference as a guide to cup size. A 1-inch difference equals an A cup, a 2-inch difference equals a B cup, a 3-inch difference a C cup, and a four-inch difference a D cup. For example, your overmeasure equals 36 inches and your undermeasure equals 33 inches. The fitter in this example would begin with a 34 C cup bra. The band size is based on the undermeasure number and in this case its 33 inches, therefore 34 inches is the closest measurement to this number. The difference between 36 and 33 is 3 inches, which corresponds to a C cup bra. The following table illustrates the cup size based on the difference in measurement between the overmeasure and undermeasure numbers.

Table 7.1

CUP SIZE BASED ON OVER- AND UNDERMEASURE CALCULATION

Difference	Standard Cup Size
0"–½"	AA
½"–1"	A
2"	B
3"	C
4"	D
5"	DD or E
6"	DDD or F
7"	G
8"	H
9"	I
10"	J

Source: Herroom, www.herroom.com/measure-bra-cup-and-band-size,903,30.htm

These steps are a guide to finding your correct bra size but it's only that—a guide. This measurement process narrows down the many choices that are available. In the previous example it is much easier to begin with a specific bra size, 34C, then to begin with a B cup size that may be too small.

THREAD 7.2

TIPS WHEN TRYING ON A BRA

* Bend at the waist, slip the straps onto your shoulders, and allow your breasts to fall into the bra. The cup of the bra will adjust to your shape and hug your breast.

* Move around in the bra, bend over, swing your arms around, hug yourself, and reach up high.

* Put on a tight T-shirt to reveal any unfitted areas.

* Fasten the bra on the loosest hook and see how it feels. After several washings and wear and tear the bra can be worn on the tightest hook and still fit comfortably.

Following these four simple steps when putting on a bra will make you look and feel your absolute best.

Source: www.thebudgetfashionista.com, 2008.

---

for you and for your needs. Once you find the bra manufacturer that is right for you, grab it and wear it!

Are you able to complete this exercise on someone else? Can you complete the measurements, fittings, and find the right bra manufacturer for the individual? If so, you are well on your way to looking your bra best! You know what it takes to look right underneath your clothing.

THE COMPLETE PANTY WARDROBE

"VPL," or visible panty line, is a definite wardrobe liability and consistently appears on every stylist, magazine and television DON'T list. Investing in the right panties will help eliminate panty lines and provide a smooth finish to your entire outfit. Nine styles of panties are recommended for a complete panty

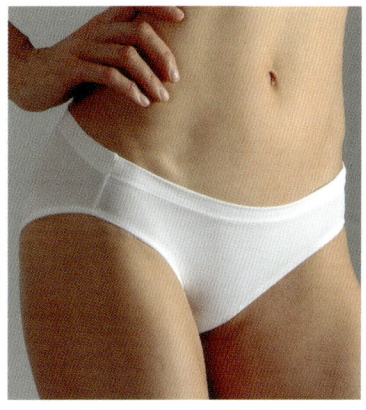  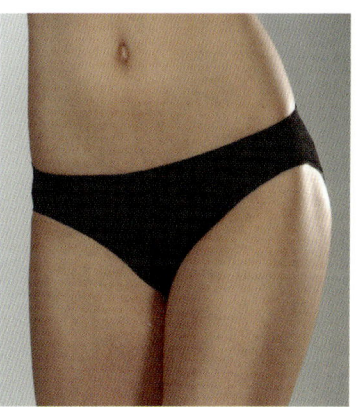

wardrobe. As with bras, panty styles fall into the two categories—the basics and the trends.

Basic Panties

Panties that are considered basic are not to be worn just for special occasions or for a specific activity yet are useful, essential styles that can be included in any woman's panty wardrobe. Basic panty styles can be further divided into five types:

1. Everyday basic panties—your choice of style, but panties that provide comfort and are non-binding. You should have at least 7–14 of these.
2. Bikini panties—waistband sits below the belly button, has high-cut legs, and provides back coverage.
3. Black panties—the color does not show stains and are great to wear during that time of the month.
4. Boy short—the cut is similar to hot pants.
5. Briefs—waistband sits at the natural waistline.

FIGURE 7.18 (LEFT)
Everyday basic panties consist of styles that are comfortable to you.

FIGURE 7.19 (MIDDLE)
Bikini panties are suitable for swimwear and rests just below your belly button.

FIGURE 7.20 (RIGHT)
Black is a slimming color, and black panties look good with your black bra.

FIGURE 7.21 (LEFT)
A style panty that can double as loungewear because of its look—the female version of the boxer.

FIGURE 7.22 (RIGHT)
Briefs reach to the waistline and give total coverage.

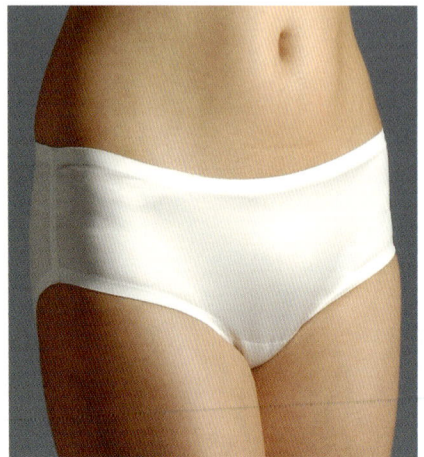
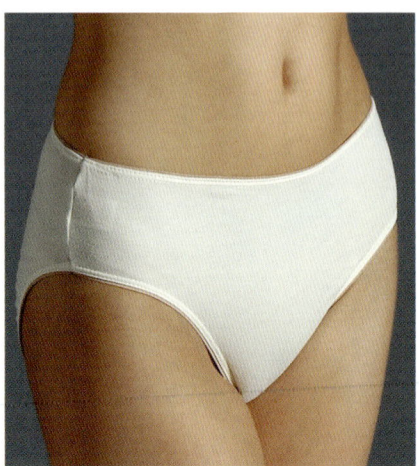

Trend Panties

There are many reasons why fashion trends have crossed over to underwear and other lingerie items. One reason trend panties are becoming more popular is the popularity of retailer Victoria's Secret and its annual televised lingerie fashion show. In addition, certain clothing has dictated the use of unique styles of underwear, e.g., seamless underwear for tight-fitting pants and athletic panties that allow for comfort and ease of movement. The trends in underwear may come and go just as in clothing, but knowing these styles are available is a positive statement for the fashionable woman. Trend panty styles can be divided into four types:

1. Athletic panties—made to be worn during your workouts.
2. Crotchless—not literally crotchless but has a slim fabric seam down the center.
3. G-string—backless; just a string.
4. Thong—bikini panty with a high-cut leg and a strip of material up the back.

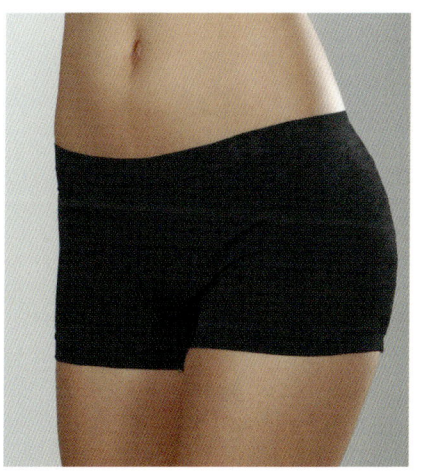

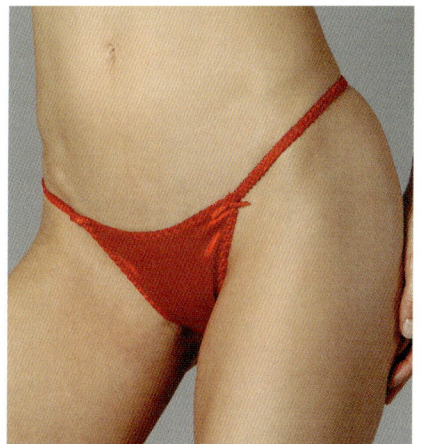
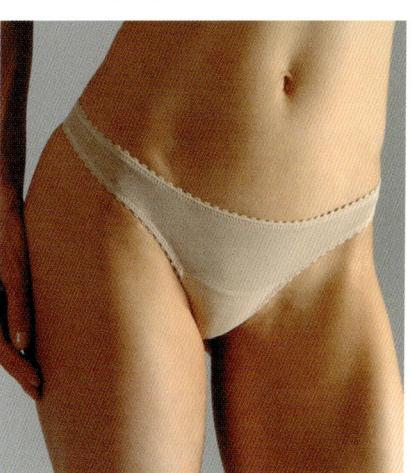

FIGURE 7.23 (TOP LEFT) Panties worn during workouts should be provide comfort and sweat protection.

FIGURE 7.24 (TOP RIGHT) These are not necessary for everyone's panty wardrobe but can add excitement to your collection.

FIGURE 7.25 (BOTTOM LEFT) No VPL! G-string style provides no visible panty line.

FIGURE 7.26 (BOTTOM RIGHT) Thongs are similar in style to the G-string; some people find them more comfortable.

FIGURE 7.27 (TOP LEFT)
The biker short is an excellent shapewear item that can slim your bottom and thighs.

FIGURE 7.28 (TOP RIGHT)
The body briefer is a popular shapewear item that slims your waist and provides a smooth silhouette.

FIGURE 7.29 (BOTTOM LEFT)
The camisole can be worn as a top under a suit jacket showing a hint of lace. Here is another shapewear item providing a smooth overall look to your total look.

FIGURE 7.30 (BOTTOM RIGHT)
Just as its name implies, the control brief pulls your tummy in and provides a slimming overall look.

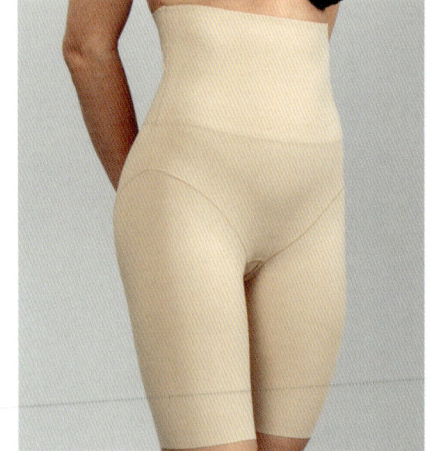

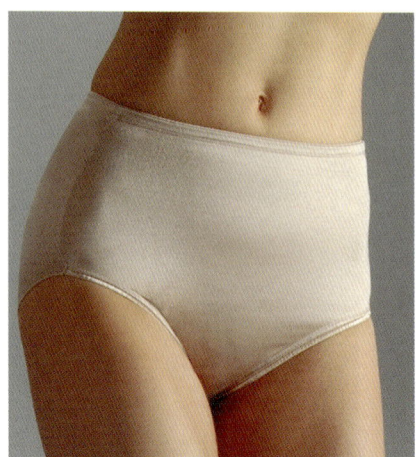

BODY SHAPERS—DO YOU NEED THEM?

Shapewear helps all figure types by tucking your body in at just the right spots. If you're looking for smooth lines, invest in the right shapewear for the bumps, lumps, and curves you are trying to hide. There are seven items needed to complete your shapewear wardrobe, which, again, can be categorized into the basics or the trends.

Basic Body Shapers

Who has the perfect body? I bet no one has answered that they are perfect. In Chapter 4, Body Type Evaluation, you visually and physically measured your body. You know by this time which parts of your body you would like to emphasize and which parts to de-emphasize. Becoming a style maven means being realistic on what body parts need help. **Body shapers** are available to help complete the process. Basic body shaper styles can be further divided into four types:

1. Biker shorts – full panty with legs that hit right above the knee. Great for firming up the buttocks and tightening the waist.
2. Body briefer – looks like a one-piece bathing suit that helps control the tummy.
3. Camisole top – full top undergarment perfect for knit tops.
4. Control brief – provides a flat tummy.

Trend Body Shapers

The basic body shapers discussed previously covers the body parts most women have difficulty concealing—rear, waist, and tummy. Lingerie designers have created looks that will accommodate any style of clothing and allow for smoothness and comfort. These trend styles are needed with certain types of clothing and add extra support in parts of the body that are sometimes neglected like the sides, thighs, and legs. Trend body shaper styles can be further divided into three types:

1. High-waisted brief—extended waistband that gives support to the waistline and smoothes the sides.
2. Long leg—control brief also shapes the thighs and legs.
3. Waist cincher—similar to a corset.

Exercise 7.2: The Perfect Shapewear for Me
Visit your local department store and go to the lingerie department. Locate three different types of shapewear from three different manufacturers to try on based on your body type. Spend up to an hour trying on shapewear to find the perfect fit. Put your clothes on over the shapewear to see the difference in your look. Once you find the shapewear that is right for you, wear it all the time to enhance your overall appearance.

THE COMPLETE SLIP WARDROBE

A **slip** is the one lingerie category that is sometimes forgotten and rarely worn. Just as the male wears a T-shirt under his shirt, a female can, and most of the time should, wear a slip under her best clothing. A slip can provide comfort under rough fabric, allow garments to lie flat, and create an opaque look under sheer garments. Slip fabric is usually made of nylon, silk, rayon, satin, or taffeta. These fabrics, because of their smoothness, lies comfortably against your body and adds that touch of femininity for any woman. The slip wardrobe is not basic or essential, but it can definitely add excitement to your wardrobe.

The six items needed for a slip wardrobe are:

1. **Camisole**—great as a cover-up for the top part of your body to prevent itching from fabrics and to provide warmth during the cold months. It can also be worn as a top under a jacket for a very feminine look.
2. **Culotte**—a pant-style slip; great to be worn under skirts and full slacks. A culotte is a trouser that is cut full in the leg and resembles a skirt. The

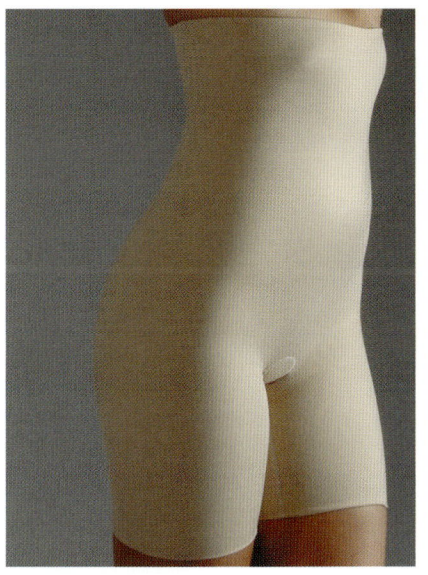

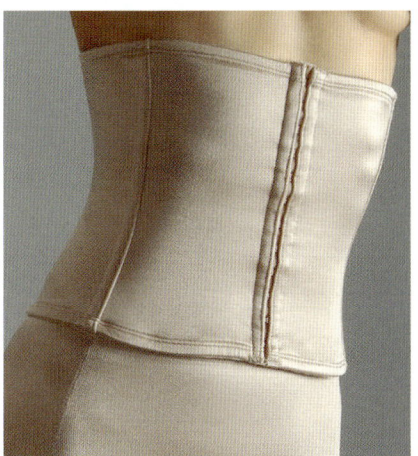
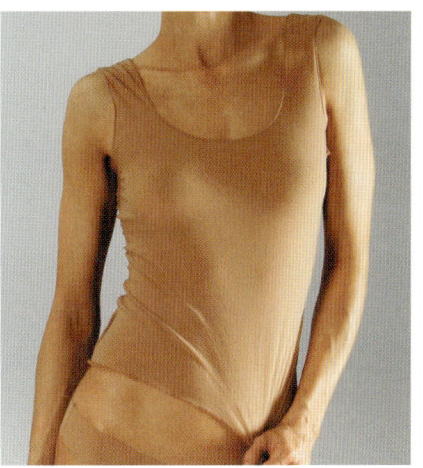

FIGURE 7.31 (TOP LEFT) Achieving a smooth look is necessary for great style. A high-waisted brief does just that—adds style, support, and smoothness.

FIGURE 7.32 (TOP RIGHT) No panty lines with the long leg shapewear. It's also useful under white pants.

FIGURE 7.33 (BOTTOM LEFT) A waist cincher helps to provide an hourglass figure, similar to a corset that was worn in the early nineteenth century.

FIGURE 7.34 (BOTTOM RIGHT) The multi-functional camisole.

FIGURE 7.35 (TOP LEFT)
A culotte provides additional shape and prevents your legs from rubbing together.

FIGURE 7.36 (TOP RIGHT)
As an underpinning for suits and/or dresses, a full slip provides shape and form to your overall look.

FIGURE 7.37 (BOTTOM LEFT)
Similar to a full slip, a half slip provides the same shape and smoothness as skirts and suits.

FIGURE 7.38 (BOTTOM RIGHT)
Some manufacturers recommend pantyliners for their unlined pants. The pants lay better without the added weight and lining fabric.

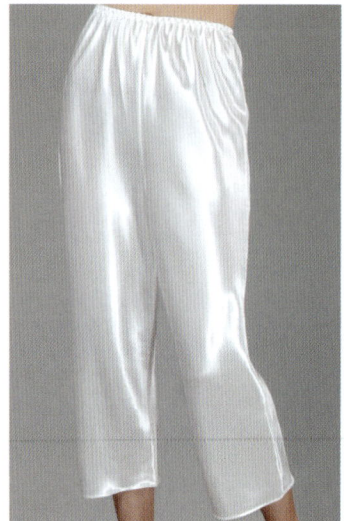

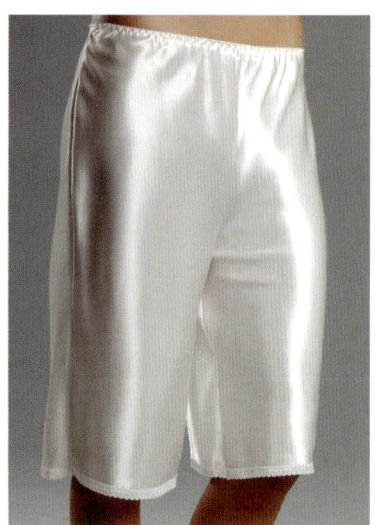

culotte acts as an **underpinning** and provides comfort to the body when garments are made of rough fabrics.

3. **Full slip**—a silk slip is a luxury that every well-dressed woman should have as part of her lingerie wardrobe. As an undergarment to be worn under your best clothing, a slip acts as an extra layer of protection against your skin, which helps keep your garment in superlative shape.
4. **Half slip**—helps to provide a totally smooth look under skirts.
5. **Pantyliner**—sometimes called an underliner. Worn under pants to provide a smooth finish.
6. **Tap pant**—short-shorts with a small flare. Great item to be worn under short skirts because it provides a little more coverage than a regular panty.

FIGURE 7.39

If you are wearing a short skirt and want that extra coverage, a tap pant is the way to go.

PRIORITIZE TO PERFECTION

It may take time to build an essential foundation wardrobe. But, start small, and begin with the category that you wear the most. Build that category first and then expand the other categories. Compare your foundation wardrobe to apparel essentials; those items you really need, such as bra and panties should be the basics, while those that are nice to have, such as camisoles and tap pants, should be considered the trends.

HOSIERY

The word **hosiery** is defined as leg coverings that include stockings, pantyhose, tights, and socks. A woman's need to wear stockings consistently to work has changed throughout the years. Stockings have been largely relegated to formal attire. It is not uncommon to see women wearing a suit without hosiery and they still can be considered dressed for business. The casual workforce has changed the hosiery business to add much more than just stockings. Women are looking for support, comfort, and good looks in their hosiery. Hosiery has become a hot accessory item to jazz up your wardrobe. Hosiery completes an outfit and adds the finishing touch.

Types of Hosiery

The types of hosiery are many and vary by brand. The terminology associated with hosiery refers to the sheerness, support, and type.

Pantyhose

Pantyhose are usually made of nylon, spandex, and lycra blends and extend from the waist to the toes. It is a combination of the panty and hosiery. Many women wear pantyhose to cover their legs for warmth during the cold season, to cover bruises and scars, hide hair stubble, and for overall attractiveness.

Common styles of pantyhose are:

* **Ultra sheer control top**—very sheer hosiery with a panty top that is composed of a heavier lycra content and weight. This panty top acts as a body shaper adding extra support to the tummy area. Standard denier, thickness and weight of hosiery fiber are 15, and ultra sheer falls below this number. Ultra sheer hosiery is worn for dressy occasions.

* **Shimmer sheer control top**—dressy hosiery with metallic threads for shine and glitter and also with a support panty.

- **Ultra sheer non-control top**—very sheer hosiery with no added support in the panty.
- **Ultra sheer shaper top**—very sheer hosiery with a foundation panty top.
- **Toeless and footless**—to be worn under garments adding support and warmth when sandals or other footwear is worn that shows the toes.
- **Day sheer shaper top**—not as sheer as ultra sheerness yet slightly sheerer than the norm of 15 denier. Pantyhose meant to be worn during the day, work or other day occasion. Panty top is of a body shaper style providing support.
- **Day sheer control top**—not as sheer as ultra sheer but panty top provides some support and control.
- **Day sheer non-control top**—same as above but without a control top.
- **Opaque**—hosiery that cannot be seen through, heavy denier than the standard thickness of 15. Opaque hosiery is usually colored and is worn mostly for casual looks.
- **Fishnets**—an open mesh weave hosiery usually worn for dressy or special occasions.
- **Maternity**—hosiery that pregnant women wear that allow for the pregnant belly to breathe and feel comfortable. The hosiery does not confine the belly and are made either with a sheer no control front panel or no panel at all.

Stockings

Stockings are a type of hosiery that has been worn for a long time and may appear to have a "sexy" image because of the attachment of a garter at the top for support to hold them up. Stockings are referred to by the sheerness and also by the look of the top of the stocking. Stockings can be:

- **Plain top**—the top of the stocking band has no decoration or adornment.
- **Satin top**—the top of the stocking band is made of satin material.
- **Lace top**—the top of the stocking band is made of lace fabric.

Tights

Tights are the casual, durable, sporty type of hosiery. Tights are very durable because of the use of a heavier **denier.** A denier is used as a measure of density of weave; it is defined as a mass in gram per 9,000 meters. The denier system of measurement is used on two and single filament fibers. The heavier the denier the more durable the hosiery, and hosiery is considered to be tights when the denier measurement is 40 and higher. Tights come in a variety of colors and prints and are usually worn during the fall and winter months. Footless tights, called **leggings**, are popular items and are worn to be seen under tops, skirts, and even dresses.

Socks

Lastly, **socks** are a basic item worn not just for sports but also with trousers to create a vertical line. Socks are defined as a short stocking reaching the point between the ankle and the knee. There are a variety of socks available that fall into the two categories of basics and trends.

Basic Socks

Under the category of hosiery we also have socks, a knitted garment that is worn covering the foot. Socks can be made of cotton, wool, or even cashmere or mohair. Sock sizes are based on shoe sizes; women's shoe sizes 4-10 wear a sock size 9-11. Basic socks styles can be further divided into four types:

1. **Athletic**—to be worn for athletic events and made of heavy weight fabric.
2. **Outdoor**—socks that are worn for outdoor events like hiking and are made of heavy weight fabrication for added support and comfort.
3. **Trouser**—socks that are to be worn under trousers and are knee high in length. Fabrication ranges from wool to silk.
4. **Casual knee-high**—socks that are knee length high and are made of casual fabrics such as cotton or wool blends.

Trend Socks

The trends in socks are extras and are only needed for a special occasion or incident. These socks are considered trends because you would not miss them as part of your hosiery wardrobe if you did not own them. Trend socks styles can be further divided into three types:

1. **Slipper**—a sock that covers the foot snugly and made of warm, comfortable fabrics like chenille.
1. **Liner**—socks that are meant to keep the feet warm and dry and acts as a friction buffer to prevent blisters. Fabrication is usually made with high performance wicking properties such as Dri-weave™ or Coolmax™.
1. **Medical**—those with diabetes, arthritis, or sensitive feet would wear medical socks. These socks are made with high performance wicking properties to keep the feet dry, healthy, and comfortable.

Devil in Detail

It never hurts to have several pairs of socks in neutral colors and prints. Socks can provide comfort and style and be the one item people remember if you have a hole in them or they don't match! Don't let your hosiery become an image breaker.

All of the categories of hosiery—stockings, pantyhose, tights or socks—should own space in your closet or in your dresser drawers. The basic items described in each category are essential items to add to your personal style wardrobe. This is also one area you can show your individuality by wearing the unexpected, such as fishnet stockings or brightly colored socks.

Two-Out-of-Three Hosiery Rule

Hosiery or leg coverings, no matter what type you are wearing should also follow the **hosiery rule**—two out of three should match: consider 1) skirt or trouser bottom, 2) your legs, and 3) your footwear as the three parts of the hosiery rule. To create a lean vertical line you would want to have the apparel bottom complement your leg covering. If your bottom is not a solid but a print, use the base color of the print as the color to match.

WHAT EVERY GREAT WARDROBE RELIES UPON

"One of my ex-husbands thought I had a breast job. They looked bigger. I just got the proper lingerie." This quote from actor Cybill Shepherd conveys the importance of a good foundation garment. Good foundation garments, as mentioned before, can make or break an outfit. Don't stop with the perfect suit, but remember to begin with what's underneath the suit. The exercises in this chapter are all crucial in making the decisions needed to guarantee a proper-fitting foundation garment. Take the time to invest in good foundations; it will improve your image and your attitude.

KEY WORDS

body shapers	leggings	shelf bra
bra	long line bra	slip
camisole	minimizer bra	socks
cleavage	molded bra	sports bra
convertible bra	overmeasure	stockings
culotte	panty	strapless bra
demi-cup	pantyhose	tap pant
denier	pantyliner	tights
foundation basics	plunge bra	undermeasure
half slip	push-up bra	underpinning
hosiery	racerback bra	
hosiery rule	seamless bra	

RESOURCES

The Budget Fashionista. (2008). Best Bras on a Budget: Quick tips for finding the Perfect Fit. Retrieved on April 21, 2008 from www.thebudgetfashionista.com/archive/best_bra_finding_the_perfect_fit/.

Cabela's. (2008). Cabela's liner socks. Retrieved on April 21, 2008 from www.cabelas.com/spodw-1/0005495.shtml.

Ford, T. (2008). Retrieved on April 21, 2008 from www.tomford.com.

Fox River Mills. (2005). Comfort/Medical Socks. Retrieved on April 21, 2008 from www.foxsox.com/Categories/Commed.aspx.

HerRoom. (2008). Consumers rate the brands. Retrieved on April 21, 2008 from www.herroom.com/bra-styles-help-determine-bra-size,908,30.html.

Tomima Endika. (2008). Retrieved on April 21, 2008 from www.tomima.com.

CHAPTER EIGHT

Accessories! Accessories! Accessories!

"The accessory is always a delicate balance between good and bad taste. In other words, a handbag may either make or break an outfit."

—VALENTINO GARAVANI, KNOWN AS VALENTINO, THE POPULAR ITALIAN FASHION DESIGNER.
IN JULY 2007, HE CELEBRATED HIS ANNIVERSARY OF 45 YEARS IN THE FASHION INDUSTRY.
VALENTINO'S FINAL HAUTE COUTURE SHOW IN PARIS WAS HELD ON JANUARY 23, 2008.

CHAPTER OBJECTIVES
After reading this chapter, you will be able to:

* Define the word *accessory* and its usage with style and wardrobe planning.
* List the current trends in all categories of accessories.
* Categorize accessory styles into essential and trend items.

CHARACTERIZING YOUR PERSONALITY

Phrases that come to mind when we think of accessories include "the finishing touch," "icing on the cake," "the last drop," "the bold and the beautiful," and "that extra-added attraction." **Accessories** are articles worn that complete an outfit such as a purse, a pair of gloves, etc. Most women want to accessorize and show who they are to the world. The accessories we will discuss in this chapter are handbags, footwear, and jewelry. Accessories such as scarves, belts, glasses, and hats will also be included as part of an exercise.

In Part I of this book, we discussed who we are, in Part II what we should wear, and now in Part III adding the extras. The extras express who you are on the outside, in a physical manner. Like a painting on a wall, the accessory items you choose characterize you and your personality. You are the one carrying the handbag and wearing the jewelry. Make it a standout that expresses who you are.

I love handbags, jewelry, and footwear. I may only buy accessories and not buy any clothing items in a season. Accessories totally change an outfit and can make them look new. In this chapter, we will review the accessory categories mentioned above and place them in two groupings—basic, or essential, and trendy, or nonessential.

HANDBAGS

We need to look at accessories just like we do apparel and apply the wardrobe selection factors—fit, color, fabric, style, quality, and care. These same principles apply to accessories, and we will call them **accessory selection factors**. The fit of your accessories relate to your body frame. Your body frame can be measured by the size of your wrist. To determine your body frame measure your wrist just below the bone on the arm that is used the least. The measurement of your wrist in relation to your height determines your frame. (See Table 8.1.)

Table 8.1
BODY FRAME SIZES

	Height less than 5ft 2inches	Height 5ft 2inches– 5ft 5inches	Height more than 5ft 5inches
Small frame	Less than 5.5 inches	Less than 6 inches	Less than 6.25 inches
Medium frame	5.5 inches–5.75 inches	6 inches–6.25 inches	6.25 inches–6.50 inches
Large frame	More than 5.75 inches	More than 6.25 inches	More than 6.50 inches

Source: www.am-i-fat.com/body_frame_size.html

Relate your body frame to the size of your handbag. Someone who is very large would look very inappropriate carrying a tiny bag. Consider how the trend of oversize bags looks on a small frame person. If you are small framed, the bag will weigh you down and you will look totally out of proportion. Adjust the bag to your body frame.

Kinds of Handbags

There are at least as many different kinds of handbags as types of occasions to carry them. The possibilities may seem infinite. But most every kind can be placed into the following categories: the essential—including the everyday, tote, and evening bags; the trends—including the print, colored, sporty, and humorous bags; and the icons.

Essential Handbags

Essential handbags are bags that are necessary to carry your essential items; items that you can't do without. An essential handbag will carry you through every season, withstand wear and tear and add the finishing touch to any day outfit. Let's begin by looking at the essential handbag wardrobe.

FIGURE 8.1

Everyday handbags should be distinctive, stylish, and able to withstand everyday use. These examples show styles that will work for any classic individual.

1. **The everyday handbag**—should be in a neutral color, and its shape should be the opposite of your body. If you are round, you should not carry a round handbag because it will only accentuate your roundness. Comfort and versatility is also important for your everyday bag. You do not want to be called a "bag lady" because you carry more than one bag to accommodate your necessary items. Having two to three everyday bags in your wardrobe will help prolong the life of your bags.

EXERCISE 8.1: THE ESSENTIAL HANDBAG Work with a classmate and pull out all the items you are carrying in your handbag. Categorize each item as **essential,** (this category could include car keys, money and credit cards, cell phone, drivers license, glasses, etc.) and the items you feel you can't live without. Also look for **nonessential** items (gum, entire makeup bag, candy, etc.), or those items that you wouldn't miss if you did not carry them in your bag.

Table 8.2
ESSENTIAL HANDBAG CHART

	Your Handbag	**Your classmate's handbag**
Essential items		
Nonessential items		
Keep or change? Reasons why		
New ideal essential bag would look like…		

Complete the chart above and state whether or not the size of your bag is suitable to carry just your essential items. Be honest in what is truly considered essential for you. Consider adjustments to your current bag, (change of shape, color, or quality), that may make an ideal everyday essential bag for you.

At this point you can describe the ideal essential bag for you based on your lifestyle and the number of essential items you need to carry (see Table 8.2). Remember your body frame size, your personal coloring, and comfort.

FIGURE 8.2 (THIS PAGE, TOP)
The classic "noel mark" style Kate Spade handbag is noted for it's graphic icon, whose shapes when viewed alone form the letters "k" and "s".

FIGURE 8.3 (THIS PAGE, BOTTOM)
The Bhar bag shape is long, rectangular, and covered with quartz and other stones retailing for thousands of dollars depending on the amount of stones embellished on the bag. Designed by Sonal Gandhi.

FIGURE 8.4 (OPPOSITE, TOP)
This popular bag is in an animal print and will add pizzazz to any wardrobe.

FIGURE 8.5 (OPPOSITE, BOTTOM)
The brightly colored handbag is a perfect accent piece to any outfit.

2. **Tote bag**—a handbag that can work as an everyday bag and a carry all. Usually made out of a durable fabric such as canvas or nylon. This bag is suitable for the busy, active, commuting woman who needs to carry more than just her essential items. The shape of the tote bag would be able to carry your work papers, shoes, and other large items.

3. **The evening bag**—the **clutch** is considered the universal evening handbag. It's small enough to not take away from your evening attire and can be carried in your hand. The dressy, glossy, glittery fabric and jewels that an evening bag is usually made out of can make the price range from $20 to more than $1,000.

Trend Handbags

Consider those handbags that aren't really necessary but you would like as part of your wardrobe. These bags can be added at any time to round out your handbag assortment. For these items, cost may be the major factor for purchase.

1. **Print handbag**—a bag that wouldn't necessarily go with all of your clothing but adds spark to certain outfits.

2. **Colored handbag**—colors are all the rage and definitely are a standout with classic attire or casual attire. The wide range of colors available can put your mind in a

FIGURE 8.6 (LEFT)
Sport bags, such as this soccer bag, are perfect to carry not just for your soccer ball and cleats but also as a fun bag to carry.

FIGURE 8.7 (RIGHT)
This Stella McCartney bunny-shaped bag is something that will make you smile.

flurry but remember your personal color tones (cool or warm). If you stick with colors that fall within your category, you can't go wrong.

3. **Sporty handbag**—a sporty bag is one that has vivid colors, bold and unusual shapes, and may have a logo or another decorative symbol or picture.

4. **Humorous handbag**—the name says it all; these bags make you smile and laugh. They may be in the shape of a piece of fruit, or taking on another item such as a clock purse. These bags are usually given as gag gifts and are not meant to be an everyday bag.

CHANGING TRENDS Trends change depending on the season and what's hot for that moment in time. Examples of trends that have occurred throughout the years in handbags are:

* **Fabrication**—tartans and tweeds, patent leather, animal print.
* **Chains**—a chain shoulder strap adds a bit of glamour to a handbag.
* **Quilted bags**—popular style where the leather or fabric is of a quilted pattern.
* **Gold hardware**—the hardware on the handbag (closures and fasteners) is gold.
* **Jewel tones and any current color of the season**—handbags coincide with apparel colors popular for a particular season.
* **Glitter**—handbags that are to be worn for eveningwear are adorned with sparkle, shine, and glimmer.

The cost of a trend bag can be just as expensive as a status bag. Celebrity Beyoncé Knowles was spotted carrying a Louis Vuitton Tribute bag that costs $52,500! This bag is a patchwork of fourteen of Louis Vuitton's latest designs. A total of five bags were made for North America and Beyoncé was lucky enough to get one.

FIGURE 8.8
Celebrities in the public eye like Beyoncé Knowles carry the "best of the best." Beyoncé is one of 5 North American customers to carry this unique, expensive handbag.

ACCESSORIES! ACCESSORIES! ACCESSORIES! 217

The Icons
An elegant bag that announces status, substance, and prestige becomes an **icon**. It represents importance and everything you want to be in society. The establishment of iconic bags began during the nineteenth century but became perfection during the twentieth century. These bags are classic and the envy of every woman, young and old. Let's begin with Emile-Maurice Hermès who transformed feedbags and saddlebags into four classic handbag shapes.

THE FOUR CLASSICS Most classic bags today are based on these **four classic Hermès handbag forms:**

1. **Haut a Courroies** (1892)—an elongated triangle; tall shape and long straps meant to hold a saddle.

2. **Bolide bag** (1923)—an elliptical square and the first bag in history to feature a zipper.

3. **The Plume** (1930)—a soft little box shaped liked a camel. This handbag was based on a horse blanket bag but is much more modern.

4. **The Trim** (1958)—shaped like a hobo; bucket-like feed bag with a scooped gusset and skinny strap.

OTHER ICONS In addition to the four bags mentioned above the following bags are also classified as part of this iconic category:

* **Hermès Birkin bag**—featured as the "it" bag on the television show *Sex and the City*. Originally designed for actress Jane Birkin who was known to carry her reading material in a straw basket when traveling.

FIGURE 8.9 (LEFT)
The iconic handbags featured are classic and will remain in the mind of women young and old. This photograph features Princess Grace Kelly holding a Hermès Kelly bag, a style that was named after her.

FIGURE 8.10 (BOTTOM)
The Trim, year 1958, shaped like a hobo handbag.

FIGURE 8.11

Hermès Birkin bag.

FIGURE 8.12
Hermès Kelly bag.

FIGURE 8.13
Louis Vuitton, 1932, the Noe bag, bucket–shaped shoulder bag.

- **Hermès Kelly bag**—it takes 18 hours for a single craftsman to make this bag from first to last stitch. Distinctive characteristics of the bag are the locking belt hardware, arc shape handle, and goat skin lining.

- Louis Vuitton **Noe bag** (1932)—bucket-shaped shoulder bag originally designed to carry five bottles of champagne.

- **Chanel 2 (1955)**—square quilted bag with a chain strap. Introduced in February 1955, this bag went well with Chanel's signature jersey suits.

FIGURE 8.14 (LEFT)
Chanel, 2/1955, square quilted bag with a chain strap.

FIGURE 8.15 (RIGHT)
Gucci Cane Handle bags, 1969–1975.

* **Gucci Cane Handle bag** (1969–'75)—after World War II there was a leather shortage. Gucci made his handles out of cane to compensate for the shortage.

EXERCISE 8.2: THE ICONIC HANDBAG Wouldn't we all like to have an authentic iconic handbag as part of our accessory wardrobe? Iconic handbags are a status item, and owning one could cost a fortune. This exercise will take you through the process of acquiring the best look-alike iconic handbag.

There is no shortage of websites available to find the handbag of your dreams. Examples are: www.handbag.com, www.mypurseworld.com, www.zhefiry.com, www.bagborroworsteal.com, and (one of the best examples) www.like.com. Like.com sorts through celebrity accessories and gives you a shopping list of similar styles at a variety of prices. The search categories are by fabrics, function, pattern, size, sale, and merchant.

Using the iconic list of bags mentioned previously, search through any of the handbag websites to find the best three look-alike bags. Complete Table 8.3 and exchange your paper with a classmate. Compare notes and bags. The entire class votes on the best look-alike at the best price.

What should you look for to find a great iconic bag? Experts give the following pointers to spot an "it bag" (*Glamour*, 2007):

- Soft squarish shape
- Flap Closure
- Textured leather
- Chain strap
- Oversize grommets
- Contrast color piped seams
- Metal-Y hardware closures
- Oversize buckles
- Patent leather touches

Table 8.3

LOOK-A-LIKE ICONIC HANDBAGS

Iconic Handbag	Look-alike bag 1 Website Price	Look-alike bag 2 Website Price	Look-alike bag 3 Website Price

FOOTWEAR

"I did not have three thousand pairs of shoes; I had one thousand and sixty," said Imelda Marcos, wife and confidante of Philippine dictator Ferdinand Marcos, who reined over the Philippines from 1965 to 1986.

Footwear is the accent piece to a woman's wardrobe. We wonder about the size of Imelda Marcos' closet to hold all of her shoes. Wouldn't we all love to have a different pair of shoes for every single outfit? What an ideal situation.

The parts of the shoe are the **sole,** or the bottom of the shoe; **insole**, or the interior bottom of the shoe that sits directly under the foot; **heel**, or the bottom rear part of the shoe; and **vamp** (also called the "throat"), or the front or upper part of the shoe. The vamp helps hold the shoe on your foot and is the part that is considered most flattering.

The most flattering shoes on any woman have slim heels—about two inches, considered to be a medium height; a V-shaped vamp; and thin soles when looked at from the side. These shoe styles have the most leg-lengthening characteristics.

Categories of Footwear

Footwear categories are many and each group has a certain look with specific wardrobes. The categories are:

- **High heels**—heel height three inches or higher.
- **Wedges**—wedge shape piece under the heel that forms a solid sole.
- **Low heels**—heel height less than two and a half inches.
- **Platforms**—a thick sole of cork, leather, etc.
- **Flats**—having little or no heel or elevation.
- **Sandals**—the sole is fastened in various ways to the foot by straps over the instep or toes, or around the ankles.

- **Boots**—protective covering of leather, rubber, cloth, etc. for the foot and part or all of the leg.
- **Loafers**—moccasin-like sport shoe for informal wear.

Applying Selection Factors to Footwear

For most women a two-inch heel is ideal to feel the most comfort and still look your very best. This heel height also flatters almost everyone. Apply the selection factors to footwear, and the shape of you heel should closely match the shape of your body. For example, if you are heavy then a thin heel will make you look even heavier. Opt for a thicker heel to make you look in proportion and the best you can look.

Podiatrist Jaleh Hoorfar has eight rules for shoe comfort and sensibility (Hoorfar, 2007):

1. Shoe sizes are not standardized and vary from one designer to another.
2. Heavy shoes are just too heavy to walk in.
3. Choose flexible materials that will allow your shoe to stretch.
4. Cushioning is key; invest in gel inserts.
5. Three inch heels are the limit for comfort.
6. Select soles that have substance; no thin soles.
7. Covered toe casings means less pain and bunions.
8. Styles that allow for adjustability feature laces, straps, or ties.

Pairing in Proportion

Pairing your clothes and footwear in the right proportions is what makes a woman have a great sense of style. Some general rules of thumb:

- **Kitten heels** (very low heels) are universal and work well for the office and evening attire.

FIGURE 8.16 (OPPOSITE)
What woman doesn't love a great pair of shoes—heels, sandals, and pumps, in all colors and styles.

FIGURE 8.17 (ABOVE)
Crocs, a boat shoe, are being worn by the masses as a casual shoe. To prevent any accidents, shoes like Crocs should only be worn for their intended purpose. Crocs are a popular style with women, men, and children alike.

THOSE RUBBER AND PLASTIC SHOES!

The popularity of rubber, flat-soled shoes has expanded beyond their intended use. **Flip-flops**, or thongs, are rubber sandals held loosely on the foot by a U-shape strap that passes between the big and second toes and around either side of the foot. It is believed that the flip-flop sandals were developed based on traditional Japanese woven or wooden-soled sandals. There are now a variety of styles, some with heels, of these popular thong type sandals. Because these sandals can be easily removed and their rubber sole can withstand water, these shoes are meant to be worn at places such as the beach, spas, and in the shower. They are also known as "beach shoes."

The biggest fashion image breaker occurred in July 2005 when some members of the Northwestern University national champion women's lacrosse team were criticized for wearing flip-flops to the White House to meet with President George W. Bush. The women felt their footwear was dressier than flip-flops, yet others, including myself, felt it was inappropriate for the occasion.

The lightweight plastic shoes called **Crocs** were developed to be worn as boat shoes because of their light weight, slip resistance, and comfort. They come in a variety of colors. These shoes were not meant to be worn as an everyday shoe with all your casual clothing. Crocs became popular in the United States mainly by word-of-mouth beginning in 2002.

Flip-flops and Crocs have both had health and safety concerns. There are reports of children suffering injuries when their shoe gets stuck in the escalator mechanism and the child's leg is injured. When worn for their intended use, neither of these styles of footwear would have these health and safety concerns.

Footwear Selection Factors

The same selection factors that apply to other accessories also apply to footwear. Consider the occasion and the type of shoe. *Each type of footwear is made with a specific purpose in mind.* Keep this thought in your mind when choosing appropriate footwear and you will never be in doubt or questioned on your choice of shoe.

- **Stiletto heels** (very high heels) are best worn with slim skirts and dressy wide leg pants.
- **Stacked heels** are thick and therefore more comfortable and appear business-like in appearance.
- **Loafers** are casual shoes and look best with pants, but someone who is very tall can get away with pairing loafers and skirts.
- **Boots** create a slimming look when paired with the same color pants. The knee-high boot looks best with skirts.

Maintaining and Building Your Shoe Wardrobe

A great pair of black pumps is a smart investment. Choose your heel height and wear your pumps casually with jeans or to work with a suit. Just as you should find a good tailor for your clothing, you should also find a good shoe repair person or store. Replace the heels on your favorite black pumps so as not break the image of your total look. Heels can be lowered, raised, or changed depending on the shoe.

Begin to establish your footwear collection. Start with the *basics*—black heels, brown heels, and a colored or other trendy pair; black boots, brown boots, and black flats. This is the minimum assortment for your footwear wardrobe as you continue to add basics and trendy items.

JEWELRY

In the 1953 movie *Gentlemen Prefer Blondes*, Marilyn Monroe sang the song "Diamonds are a Girl's Best Friend." In every stylish woman's essential jewelry list are diamond studs. They go with everything and provide the perfect complement to a variety of necklaces. The jewelry category is the icing on the cake to your wardrobe. Jewelry can show your personality in many ways by portraying conservativeness, boldness, uniqueness, or elegance.

The essential jewelry assortment consists of (*In Style*, 2007):

* **Diamond studs**—timeless beauty with diamond stud earrings can be worn day and night.

* **Pearls**—gems are noted to be a symbolism for purity and perfection. Pearls come in a variety of sizes, shapes, and colors.

* **Classic watch**—leather or metal band is meant to complement your wardrobe, simple in style.

* **Evening watch**—metal band, gold or silver, with diamonds or glitter can be worn for special occasions.

* **Oversize cocktail ring**—top trend adds instant bling to any wardrobe.

* **Charm bracelet or necklace**—personal charms, pendants, or trinkets adorn a bracelet or necklace.

* **Long linear earrings**—day or evening earrings that dangle and are vertical in style.

* **Long chains**—necklace that that is long in length creates a vertical line calling attention to your face.

* **Bangles or cuff**—bangles and cuffs are usually made out of metal. Bangles are usually worn in pairs and the cuff style bracelet hugs the wrist.

Earrings Size, Shape Comparison

A simple, quick way to add a finishing touch to your wardrobe is with a pair of earrings. The same selection factors that apply to your wardrobe apply to your earrings. Style of earrings and the shape of your face determine which style of

Jewelry Web Search

Jewelry sold over the Internet has become very popular, and jewelry making has become a fast moneymaking business. What jewelry websites entice you to buy, and why? Search the web to find three unknown jewelry designers and state their strengths and weaknesses compared to each other.

Table 8.4

JEWELRY WEB SEARCH CHART

Website	Strengths	Weaknesses
1.		
2.		
3.		

Conclusion—which site would you purchase jewelry from and why?

earrings is best for you. Examining the different facial shapes the best styles for each facial shape are:

* **Round face**—best to wear oblong, rectangles, and vertical style dangle earrings. These shapes are the opposite of your round face and help to elongate a round face.

* **Square face**—best to wear hoops, or small shapes, oval, oblong earrings. The opposite earring shape of your face is best.

* **Rectangular face**—because the face is long, the best styles are hoops or other round styles.

* **Heart-shaped face**—styles that are most flattering are those that are wide at the bottom.

* **Oval shape face**—this facial shape can wear any style earring. Hoops, round, or dangle styles are all flattering.

FIGURE 8.18
Jewelry can freshen up an outfit and update the look. Invest in classic jewelry pieces that will last a lifetime.

PUNCTUATE YOUR STYLE

Begin your accessories wardrobe with the essential items and then add the trends slowly as you build the basics. Remember to consider the selection factors— fit, color, fabric, style, quality, and care—when choosing accessories. Choose a smart style handbag for everyday use and a great evening clutch that suits your lifestyle. Invest in quality footwear that highlights your best assets and acquire essential jewelry such as diamond earrings, a classic watch, and long chains or pearls. Consider shape and size when choosing accessories. For example a small body frame should carry a small handbag. The shape of your face should dictate the shape of your earrings. Opposite is best; round shape face should wear dangle or rectangular shape earrings.

Jewelry selection is very personal yet still requires a look at who you are, your lifestyle, and your overall body shape and size. You can't go wrong with completing your outfit with jewelry as an accent.

Without accessories, your style would be incomplete, plain, and boring; no stylish person is any of these things, so go ahead and accessorize, accessorize, accessorize!

KEY WORDS

accessories	four classic Hermès handbags	loafers
accessory selection factors	Gucci cane handle handbags	low heels
boots	heel	Noe handbag
Chanel 2/1955 handbag	Hermès Birkin bag	nonessential
clutch	Hermès Kelly bag	platforms
crocs	high heels	sandals
essential	icon	sole
flats	insole	stiletto heels
flip flops	kitten heels	vamp
footwear	learning partner	wedges

RESOURCES

Glamour (editors). (2007, June). "Nine details for an it bag." *Glamour*, p. 104.

Fifield, K. (2007, September) "Style 101." *In Style*, p. 111.

Hoorfar, J. (2007, February). "The shoe doctor is in." *Oprah*, p. 210.

PART IV

Focus on the Future: *Where* Do You Go?

CHAPTER NINE

Shopping Basics

"Shopping is a woman thing. It's a contact sport like football. Women enjoy the scrimmage, the noisy crowds, the danger of being trampled to death, and the ecstasy of the purchase."

—ERMA BOMBECK, WRITER AND HUMORIST KNOWN FOR HER WITTY COLUMNS ON SUBURBAN FAMILY LIFE.

CHAPTER OBJECTIVES

By the end of this chapter, you will be able to:

* Discuss various types of retail store formats.
* List clothing items needed to complete wardrobe clusters.
* Identify wardrobe journal components listing each of your personal wardrobe selection factors.
* Recite the best places to shop online for unique categories of clothing.

YOUR SHOPPING STRATEGY

I've been in the retailing industry for many years and know a little bit about shopping. There are certain days that are best for shopping and other days you would rather wait it out and not go shopping at all. Shopping can be therapy for some, providing that extra feel of satisfaction and glee; for others, shopping can be a nightmare, providing information (e.g., sizing!) that one would rather not know. Knowing when and where to shop can save you time and money. Upon completion of your closet in Chapter 3, Closet Evaluation, you now have discarded the old, tired, and ill-fitting clothing from your wardrobe. Shopping is necessary to fill in the blanks, purchasing basic and trend clothing items, and sprucing up your wardrobe. In this chapter, we will review the various retail formats for shopping, "big shopping," and sale days, and provide the necessary steps to begin a style journal.

WHAT'S MY CLOTHING ALLOWANCE?

Financial advisor and author Suze Orman says there is no such thing as a "one size fits all" budget for clothing. There are various factors included in figuring out how much you have to spend on clothing. How much money do you have going out, or your total expenses, compared to what is coming in, or your total income? Orman also advises looking at your savings, four to six months of living expenses, and retirement savings. If your expenses outweigh your income, then your clothing allowance might be one place to cut back spending. (Orman, 2006)

Typically, experts recommend spending no more than eight percent of your monthly income on clothing. Wardrobe costs should also include upkeep, dry cleaning, tailoring, and other maintenance issues that may be associated with a garment. For example, buying leather and suede requires special cleaning techniques that are more expensive than washable fabrics.

PLAN TO SHOP

Filling in the gaps in your wardrobe requires careful planning. Refer to the Cluster Planning Chronicle completed in Chapter 6, The Cluster Concept. Consider the following as you shop for clothes and build your wardrobe:

* Have a plan when you shop and know what you want and need *before* you enter a store. This will help you avoid impulse buying. Shopping without a plan is a lot like going to the grocery store when you're hungry.

* Shop when you are feeling and looking good. This makes it easier to determine if something looks good on you.

* Gain the support of a knowledgeable salesperson. Gain her assistance when shopping and expect her to keep you informed of new pieces that come in and future sales.

* Buy *quality,* not quantity.

* If you aren't sure you will wear an item of clothing, you probably won't, so don't buy it.

* Pay attention to details. Does it hang nicely, do the seams match, is there any pulling, and can you move freely?

* Employ a tailor for a proper and flattering fit.

* If you don't like shopping by yourself, find a shopping companion you can trust.

* Be patient. A stylish wardrobe takes time to compile. Build your wardrobe slowly so the items that you accumulate you will wear year after year.

What Kind of Shopper Are You?

The coupon industry identified five types of shoppers:

* **The Traditionalist**—a disciplined purchase planner who makes lists, has coupons, and shops like a pro. About 32 percent of shoppers are considered to be this type.

* **The Striver**—someone who strives to be a better shopper. About 23 percent of shoppers are strivers.

* **The Stresser**—you want to save but are not organized enough to know where to begin. About 16 percent of shoppers. The striver and stresser are both impulse shoppers with hectic schedules and limited time. For these types, shopping is very stressful and disorganized. Shopping trips are generally unplanned.

* **The Anti-Shopper**—does not like to shop and considers shopping a chore. About 21 percent of shoppers are anti-shoppers.

* **The Casual Shopper**—doesn't mind paying more if there is little effort involved. About seven percent of shoppers are casual shoppers. The anti-shopper and casual shopper are not interested in how much they save and in changing their shopping habits. (ABC News, 2007)

Do you recognize yourself in any of the above examples? The coupon industry identified the shoppers mentioned above. How often do you use coupons? Do you really want to save money when you shop? If so, Exercise 9.1, Savvy Savings Shopper, will guide you on a shopping journey that is just right for your lifestyle and your budget.

Table 9.1
COUPON SHOPPERS

Garment Category	Regular Price	Sale Price	Savings	Coupon Source
1.				
2.				
3.				
Accessories				
Total Costs & Savings				

Exercise 9.1: Savvy Savings Shopper

Your goal in this exercise is to buy a complete outfit, three pieces plus accessories, all on sale. The more savings you get the better. In addition, try to use at least one coupon. Coupons are not just available from the retailer but also from a variety of websites. Examples of coupon savings websites are www.savingsmom.com, www.couponwinner.com, and www.greatcoupons-online.com.

   Choose from any of these websites or from a website or retailer of your choice. Begin your shopping excursion by completing Table 9.1, Coupon Shoppers.

   How much did you save? Was this exercise easy or hard for you? After completing this exercise, what type of shopper do you think you are—traditionalist, striver, stresser, anti-shopper, or casual shopper?

RETAIL FORMATS

There's not a big city that doesn't have a multitude of places to shop for apparel. There are also a variety of retail formats to choose from for your shopping destination. According to the National Retail Federation (NRF), in 2006 consumers favored traditional department stores as their favorite shopping destination followed by specialty stores and online retailers. The NRF specified the type of department store on the rise in consuming spending in recent years is the discount or mass merchandising department stores. In addition, productivity gains during the years 1987–1999 increased in **variety stores**. A variety store sells an assortment of merchandise at inexpensive price points. (Vargas, 2006)

THREAD 9.1

THE RETAIL COLLECTIVE

Many new artists and designers don't have the time or the space to showcase their wares. Teaming up collectively with other individuals can cut costs while providing that needed visibility. For this purpose, the **retail collective** format was born as an ideal solution for many retailers.

Retail collective format provides retail space and advertising at reduced costs. Staffing is also provided for the entire collective, usually consisting of a manager and two sales clerks. Andersonville Galleria in Chicago, Illinois, is an example of this format. This galleria features the works of more than 50 artists and designers who share booth space and all costs associated with space. Typically, the designers who share the space rotate their shifts selling their own and each others works. One example at this galleria is six designers who rent two four-by-eight feet booths at $650 per month plus a 20 percent advertising fee that comes to about $130 a month per designer. This rental and advertising fee is a lot less expensive than what the designers could get by themselves. In addition, the designers save time by dividing up the work hours between all individuals. (Meyer, 2007)

Retail Shopping Breakdown
Retail formats have expanded throughout the years with Internet shopping becoming a popular choice for most shoppers. A **department store** merchandises both **hard and soft goods** under one roof. A **specialty store** limits its merchandise selection and creates an image for a particular lifestyle. **Mass merchants**, or **discount stores**, sell large volumes of merchandise at low prices with very little customer service. **Outlet stores** sell excess inventory from name brand designers. Outlet stores are typically located in an outlet mall that houses outlet stores from a variety of well-known designers. **Off-price stores** sell designer apparel anywhere from 20 to 60 percent lower than department stores. Typical off-price stores are Marshalls, T. J. Maxx, Loehmans, and Ross. Some retailers have increased their selection of merchandise by offering catalog shopping. According to the Direct Marketing Association, 2005 holiday shopping report, catalog sales were slightly ahead of 2004 sales by 0.2 percent. (Emerson, 2005)

Internet Shopping
The many advantages of Internet shopping include convenience and the ability to shop anywhere, anytime, day or night. Every year online sales continues to grow. According to the National Retail Federation, the year 2007 showed the slowest rate of growth for holiday sales up only four percent for the November/December time period. This was the slowest growth since a 1.3 percent rise in 2002. (Money, 2007)

      Internet sales have become so popular that huge online shopper Hilary Mendelsohn developed **Thepurplebook**, an encyclopedic guide to more than 1,600 Internet stores. Mendelsohn, owner of a marketing consulting firm, wife, and parent, was frustrated from not finding what she wanted online. It took her three years to compile the information but she is satisfied with the result. Thepurplebook has been in existence since 2000 and has proven to be a valuable resource for online shopping. Mendolsohn has taken the exhaustive search of sources that are available online and has chosen the most relevant sites in each category. In

Table 9.2
INTERNATIONAL WEBSITES

Price point	Website	Country of origin
Inexpensive	Laredoute.com	France
	Bodenusa.com	England
	Goodorient.com	China
European-designer sites	mulberry.com	England
	eileenshields.com	Ireland
	net-a-porter.com	England
Boutique sites	havaianasus.com	Brazil
	canfora.com	Italy
	figleaves.com	England
	hunterboots.com	Scotland
	espadrillesetc.com	Spain
	saltwater.net	England

Source: Wikiel, Y. (2006, November). "Shop the world," *Real Simple*, pp. 155–162.

Chapter 10, A Global Perspective: International Shopping, we'll explore how shopping online across the world is a valuable way to achieve personal style. Thepurplebook will come in handy when searching the Web for unique and different clothing items. Browse the list of international websites in Table 9.2 for all kinds of unique apparel, accessories, footwear and other merchandise.

BIG SHOPPING DAYS AND SALES

The holiday season is the busiest time of year for shopping. Individuals shop not only for themselves but also for friends and family. According to reports from Shopper Track, the biggest shopping days are typically:

- **"Black Friday"**—the Friday after Thanksgiving
- The Saturday after Thanksgiving
- "Cyber Monday"—the Monday after Thanksgiving, Internet sales are huge on this day.
- The Thursday before Christmas
- The Friday before Christmas
- "Super Saturday"—the Saturday before Christmas
- The Sunday before Christmas
- The day after Christmas
- The first weekend in December

These days and weekends vary depending on the actual day Christmas falls, but are increasingly high in sales volume. (Shopper Track, 2006)

FIGURE 9.1
You can travel the world and find a clothing style that is totally new to you and the place you call home. Bring back that look and see how many compliments you may get for being unique.

SHOPPING BASICS **245**

Monthly Specialties

Every year, the big holiday shopping days for most all goods are clustered around Christmas Day. Thanksgiving weekend begins the big rush of sales. But for specific categories of goods, yearly markdown bets occur during the following months:

> January—outerwear and winter accessories.
> February—fine jewelry, boots, and cashmere sweaters.
> March—linen suits and separates, handbags, and spring raincoats.
> April—silk separates, spring raincoats, and dresses.
> May—spring shoes, dresses, and suits.
> June—swimwear, casual shorts, T-shirts, and summer dresses.
> July—summer shoes; drastic reductions on swimwear.
> August—summer clearance and fall season sales.
> September—lined raincoats, wool blend blazers, handbags, and backpacks.
> October—leather jackets, fall suits, career, and casual sweaters.
> November—eveningwear, fall shoes, and boots.
> December—clearance coats, cashmere sweaters, and fine jewelry.

PLAN, PLAN, PLAN!

Planning is the best advice concerning when and where to shop. Make a list and stick to it. You'll know what to buy, how much you're going to spend, and how to add the right garments to your wardrobe. You'll be a much happier person when you get home. If you discover a store and sales person you like, then shop at that location more often depending on the items they have in stock. As always, remember the wardrobe selection factors fit, color, fabric, quality, style, and care. Keep these six points in mind when choosing a garment or accessory item. And of course, have fun!

KEY WORDS

anti-shopper	hard and soft goods	stresser
Black Friday	mass merchants	striver
casual shopper	off-price stores	thepurplebook
catalog shopping	outlet stores	traditionalist
department stores	retail collective	variety stores
discount department stores	specialty stores	

RESOURCES

ABC News Internet Ventures. (July 20, 2005). *What Kind of Shopper are You?* Retrieved November 26, 2007 from abcnews.go.com/print?id=950906.

CNN. (2007). Retrieved from http://money.cnn.com/2007/11/24/news/economy/bc.holidayshopping.ap/index.htm?section=money_topstories.

Emerson, J. (2005). Catalogs and the web: A beautiful friendship. Retrieved on April 23, 2008 from http://directmag.com/exclusive/specialreports/2005_05_20_especial_report/#top.

Meyer, A. (2007, December 3) "Artist mall keeping dreams alive," *Chicago Tribune*, Business, Section 3, p. 4.

Orman, S. (2006, September). "What's your number?" *Oprah*, p. 324.

ShopperTrak. (October 4, 2006). Shoppertrak predicts top 10 shopping days of holiday 2006 (Press release).

Retail Perspectives. (2004). Three questions with Hilary Mendolhosn. Retrieved n April 23, 2008 from www.newgistics.com/downloads/nl/0409/ThreeQuestoins.html#Guest.

Smart Girl. (1996–2000). Report on Shop Till you Drop. Retrieved on April 23, 2008 from www.smartgirl.org/reports/2833263.html.

Vargas, M. (2006). Black Friday weekend. Retrieved on April 23, 2008 from http://retailindustry.about.com/od/sales_holiday/a/holidayspend06_3.htm.

Wikiel, Y. (2006, November). "Shop the world," *Real Simple*, pp. 155–162.

CHAPTER TEN

A Global Perspective: International Shopping

"We are proud to bring the excitement and talent at our shows to people all over the world who love fashion. We are continuing to connect the global fashion community."

—FERN MALLIS, SENIOR VICE PRESIDENT OF IMG FASHION. MALLIS WAS INSTRUMENTAL IN LAUNCHING NEW YORK FASHION WEEK, WHICH IS HELD TWICE A YEAR IN NEW YORK CITY. AT ITS SPRING 2008 EVENT, IT GENERATED MORE THAN $235 MILLION FOR THE CITY.

CHAPTER OBJECTIVES
After reading this chapter, you will be able to:

* Identify what makes each of the top fashion markets around the world distinct.
* Define *transumerism* and its effect on the shopping industry.
* Explain leasing options for luxury items.
* Prepare and pack a simple and complete travel wardrobe.
* Shop globally like a celebrity.
* Research fashion from a global perspective.

A GLOBAL PERSPECTIVE

As a reader of *Your Personal Style*, you most likely love fashion. Every month there is a fashion show taking place somewhere in the world. Financially, if I could afford it, I would attend all the women's apparel and accessories shows around the world. What a fabulous way to see a variety of looks from across the world. It would be a chance to accumulate a knockout wardrobe none could emulate.

A **fashion week** is a trade event that lasts about one week where members of the press and buyers can view fashion design collections for the following season. They usually take place twice a year; once for the spring/summer season and once for the autumn/winter seasons. Fashion weeks are trade events not open to the general public. Registered buyers, press, and members of the fashion industry are the only attendees.

So what are considered the top cities around the world for fashion? The **Global Language Monitor** (GLM) documents, analyzes, and tracks trends in language the world over, with a particular emphasis upon Global English, and posts its results on its website (www.languagemonitor.com). The list is based upon GLM's Predictive Quantities Index, "a proprietary algorithm that tracks words and phrases in the print and electronic media, on the Internet, and throughout the blogosphere. The words and phrases are tracked in relation to their frequency, contextual usage and appearance in global media outlets," according to Millie Lorenzo Payack, fashion correspondent and director of the Global Language Monitor. In 2007 the annual global survey ranks the top 25 global fashion cities in the following order:

1. **New York**—number one on everyone's list.
2. **Rome**—beat out Paris and London for the second spot.
3. **Paris**—considered to be the "heartbeat" of the fashion world.
4. **London**—creativity abounds in this city.
5. **Milan**—persistent contender for number one.
6. **Tokyo**—global influence is gaining.

Table 10.1
INTERNATIONAL FASHION WEEKS BY CITY/COUNTRY

Fashion Week	City/Country
EUROPE	
A Fashion Week—Benelux Fashion Week	Antwerp, Belgium
Albania Fashion Week	Tirana, Albania
AltaRomaAltaModa	Rome, Italy
Amsterdam International Fashion Week	Amsterdam, Netherlands
Andalusian Fashion Week	Andalucía, Spain
Athens Exclusive Designers Week	Athens, Greece
Austrain Fashion Week	Vienna, Austria
Baltic Fashion Week	Riga, Latvia
Barcelona Bridal Week—Noviaespaña	Barcelona, Spain
Belgrade Fashion Week	Belgrade, Serbia Montenegro
Budapest Fashion Week	Budapest, Hungary
Copenhagen Fashion Week	Copenhagen, Denmark
Dublin Fashion Week	Dublin, Ireland
Fashion Week Zagreb	Zagreb, Croatia
Glasgow Fashion Week	Glasgow, Scotland
Iceland Fashion Week	Iceland
London Fashion Week	London, United Kingdom
Madrid International Fashion Week	Madrid, Spain
Mercedes-Benz Fashion Week Berlin	Berlin, Germany
Milan Fashion Week	Milan, Italy
ModaLisboa / Lisbon Fashion Week	Lisbon, Portugal
Oslo Fashion Week	Oslo, Norway
Prague Fashion Week	Prague, Czech Republic
Paris Fashion Week	Paris, France
Romanian Fashion Week	Romania
Sarajevo Fashion Week	Sarajevo, Bosnia Herzegovina
Stockholm Fashion Week	Stockholm, Sweden
Ukrainian Fashion Week	Ukraine

Fashion Week	City/Country
RUSSIA	
Fashion Week in Moscow	Moscow, Russia
Russian Fashion Week	Russia
Ural Fashion Week	Yekaterinburg, Russia
NORTH AMERICA	
Atlanta Fashion Week	United States
Chicago Fashion Week	United States
Fashion Week Cleveland	United States
Funkshion: Fashion Week Miami Beach	United States
Haute.Lanta Fashion Week (Atlanta)	United States
Los Angeles Fashion Week	United States
Mercedes-Benz Fashion Week Los Angeles	United States
Mercedes-Benz Fashion Week Miami Swim	United States
Mercedes-Benz Fashion Week New York	United States
Miami Fashion Week	United States
Nolcha Fashion Week	United States
Portland Fashion Week	United States
San Francisco Fashion Week	United States
Seattle International Fashion Week	United States
CANADA	
British Columbia Fashion Week	British Columbia, Canada
L'Oréal Fashion Week Toronto	Toronto, Canada
Montreal Fashion Week	Montreal, Canada
LATIN/SOUTH AMERICA	
Buenos Aires Fashion Week	Buenos Aires, Argentina
Caribbean Fashionweek	Jamaica
Fashion Week Mexico	Mexico
Fashion Santiago	Santiago, Chile

Fashion Week	City/Country
Fashion Rio / Rio De Janeiro Fashion Week	Rio De Janeiro, Brasil
São Paulo Fashion Week	São Paulo, Brasil

AUSTRALIA

Air New Zealand Fashion Week	New Zealand
L'Oréal Melbourne Fashion Festival	Melbourne, Australia
Rosemount Australian Fashion Week	Australia
Southern Trust id Dunedlin Fashion Week	New Zealand

AFRICA

Addis Ababa Fashion Week	Ethiopia
Audi Joburg Fashion Week	South Africa
Coca-Cola Light Zambia Fashion Week	Zambia
Kenya Fashion Week	Kenya
Liberia Fashion Week	Liberia
MTN Durban Fashion Week	South Africa
Nigeria Fashion Week	Nigeria
Nokia Cape Town Fashion Week	South Africa
Sanlam SA Fashion Week	South Africa
Tunisia Fashion Week	Tunisia

ASIA

Bali Fashion Week	Indonesia
Bangkok Fashion Week	Thailand
China Fashion Week	China
Ho Chi Minh City Fashion Week	Vietnam
Hong Kong Fashion Week S/S	China
Hong Kong Fashion Week F/W	China
International Fashion Week Qingdao China	China
Japan Fashion Week in Tokyo	Japan
Kazakhstan Fashion Week	Kazakhstan

Fashion Week	City/Country
Lakme Fashion Week	India
Malaysia International Fashion Week	Malaysia
Shanghai International Fashion Week	China
Singapore Fashion Week	Singapore
Sunsilk Nepal Fashion Week	Nepal
Wills Lifestyle India Fashion Week	India
MIDDLE EAST	
Beirut Fashion Week	Lebanon
Dubai International Fashion Week	UAE

Source: Cosmoworlds (www.cosmoworlds.com/fashion_weeks.htm)

7. **Los Angeles**—celebrity packed city may impact rating.
8. **Hong Kong**—in South Asia considered to be number one.
9. **Las Vegas**—continues to emerge as a fashion center.
10. **Singapore**—regional hub with a strong presence.
11. **Berlin**—pushing to put fashion on the map in their city.
12. **Sydney**—one of two Australian cities in the top 25.
13. **Barcelona**—continues to grow, regional center.
14. **Shanghai**—China is making a fashion presence.
15. **Melbourne**—highly regarded for fashion.
16. **Moscow**—slowly making a presence.
17. **Bangkok**—gaining momentum.
18. **Mumbai**—Indian global influence.
19. **Santiago**—continues to push fashion.
20. **Rio de Janeiro**—beginning to make a fashion statement.
21. **São Paolo**—rich, fashion-filled city.

22. Buenos Aires—known for its classic beauty.
23. Johannesburg—Africa on the list for the first time.
24. Dubai—new city making a strong push in fashion.
25. Krakow—unique, neo-bohemian fashion vibe.

Source: Global Language Monitor, 2007

Cities that have emerged as newcomers on the list are Berlin, Moscow, Shanghai, and Dubai. As the fashion industry continues to change and expand into new territories, cities like Dubai may come as a surprise. For many years before 2007, the top four cities considered to be the fashion capitals were New York, Paris, London, and Milan. As of 2007, Rome has come forward as a contender in the top four and Milan has dropped to number five. Also in 2007, Johannesburg, an African city, appears on the list for the first time. Australia and Asia continue to have cities that make the list and push fashion forward in their cities.

As we continue to strive to have a signature style that is uniquely our own we can begin by shopping the world to help us achieve our goals. Remember to keep in mind the wardrobe selection factors studied in Chapter 5, Wardrobe Selection Factors—fit, color, fabric, quality, style and care, when shopping the world. Those individuals that achieve an authentic style find uniqueness within the global assortment of merchandise that is available.

FASHION MARKET CHARACTERISTICS

When shopping globally you may become aware of the fashion personality of each of the top fashion cities. What do the locals wear and how do they look? What makes each fashion city distinctive? Continually appearing at the top of the list for fashion is New York City. Let's begin with the "Big Apple" as the city is sometimes called.

FIGURE 10.1
In New York City, the fashion capital of the United States, the garment district is the area of the city where fashion rules around the clock.

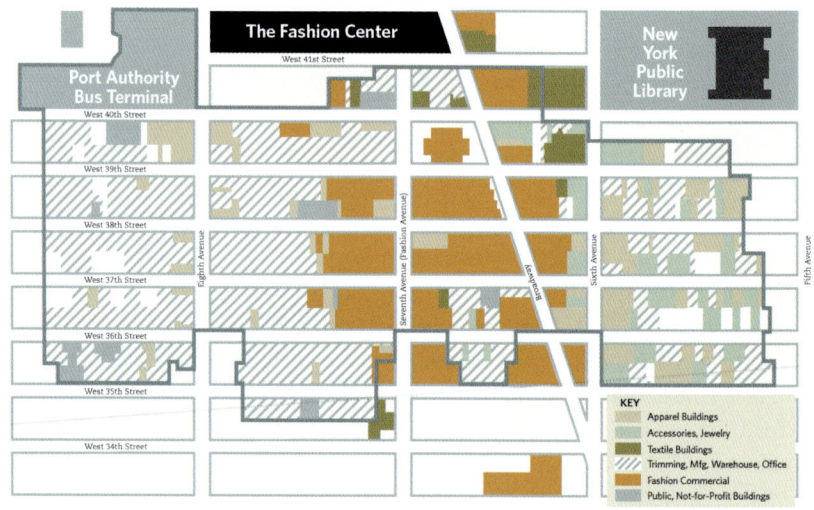

New York City

New York City's garment district neighborhood is located between Fifth and Ninth Avenues from 34th to 42nd streets. In this area you will find the warehouses and workshops of the fashion industry. Fabric stores, ribbon stores, trimmings, buttons, beads, and **notions**—needles, threads, zippers and the like—are in abundance in the Garment District. The vibrant fashion industry in New York City continues to expand and seek assistance and notoriety with the non-for-profit organization The **Fashion Center Business Improvement District (FCBID)**. Established in 1993 the organization markets and promotes the New York fashion business, and provides economic development, security and sanitation services, street improvements, and community service.

The New York Lifestyle

New Yorkers are known to have **Type-A personalities**. Characteristics that describe these individuals are impatience and time consciousness; they are often considered high-achieving, workaholic, multi-taskers who are incapable of relaxation. A busy, vibrant city that is filled with clothing designers, fashion buyers, attractive models, make-up artists, actors, and hair stylists—together, hundreds of thousands of this personality type all live and work in one city, helping to bring in billions of dollars in revenue from their work and from the tourists who come to see such a place in action. As the FCBID continues to work hard to promote its largest employer, the fashion industry, rents continuously rise even as manufacturing has declined in size due to global market and labor forces. Non-fashion tenants have moved into the area and the FCBID has broadened its programs to appeal to a mass community. As the neighborhood continues to change, the fashion industry in New York City still brings in more than $14 billion in annual sales revenue.

It is believed that New Yorkers are characterized by wearing only one color and that color is black. Approximately 18 million people live in New York City and not everyone wears black every day. The typical New Yorker wears the color and styles of the season. Most New Yorkers are very accepting of an individual's taste and lifestyle and really don't analyze a person's choice in clothing. A typical answer from a New Yorker may be "I wear black because it's slimming, chic, and can be accessorized in a million different ways!"

Notable New York fashion designers are Michael Kors (who regularly appears as a judge on the top fashion designer show *Project Runway*), Donna Karan, Ralph Lauren, Tommy Hilfiger, Marc Jacobs, and Vera Wang.

Paris

Paris, France is widely known as the fashion capital of the world. So much so that when you mention the city you automatically think fashion. It is widely said that the French regard fashion as a business, not a frivolity. The French textiles and clothing industry is the second leading industrial employer in the country and the second largest market in Europe. The fashion industry in Paris in the year 2000 was valued at approximately $18.3 billion. Fashion in Paris is constantly being heralded as one of the pillars of the French economy.

Paris has the support of the **Fédération française de la couture, du prêt-à-porter des couturiers et des créateurs de mode.** The members consist of Couture Houses and Fashion Designers of women's ready-to-wear. This organization, established in 1973, is derived from the **Chambre syndicale de la haute couture** created in 1868. The members of the Chambre syndicale are from the couture houses benefiting from the "haute couture" label. Lastly, the **Chambre syndicale de la mode masculine** created in 1973 is composed of the Couture Houses and Fashion Designers of men's ready-to-wear.

The, Fédération along with the three chambers, has about 100 members. The Fédération members assist the Paris fashion industry in many ways striving to achieve the following:

* To provide Paris with locations to house the fashion shows so as still to be known as the world capital of creation.

* To increase the visibility of new brands.

* To establish synergies between the major players in the fashion industry (buyers, subcontractors, weavers) mainly by using new technology.

* Defend intellectual property rights. The Federation works closely with the government to fight against any type of forgery.

* To develop training to keep up with global competition.

* To solve problems; a place for discussion on social, tax, or economic issues facing its members.

Source: Mode à Paris, 2008

All of the help and exposure the Fédération brings to the city has helped to keep Paris on everyone's mind as being the fashion capital of the world.

The Paris Lifestyle

Stylish Parisians tend to be feminine yet functional, often seen in subdued color clothing and elegant accessories. Stylist Lisa Jouvin from the French magazine *Muteen* cites Parisian style as a "blend of luxury brands with high street, creating a look from clothes that appears effortless yet is reasonable and has recognizable detail." (*Muteen*, 2007)

Couture

Couture, the business of designing, making, and selling highly fashionable, usually custom-made clothing for women, originated in Paris, France. The term **Haute Couture** is the leading establishments or designers for the creation of these exclusive fashions. To earn the right to call itself a couture house and to use the term haute couture in its advertising and any other way, members of the Chambre syndicale de la haute couture must follow these rules:

* Design made-to-order for private clients, with one or more fittings.
* Have a workshop (atelier) in Paris that employs at least 15 people full-time.
* Each season (i.e. twice a year) present a collection to the Paris press, comprising at least 35 separate outfits for both day and eveningwear.

In 2007, there were 10 official haute couture member houses:

* Adeline André
* Chanel
* Christian Dior
* Christian Lacroix

* Dominique Sirop
* Emanuel Ungaro
* Franck Sorbier
* Givenchy
* Jean Paul Gaultier
* Jean-Louis Scherrer

In 2007, there were three correspondent (foreign) member houses. These member houses have shown their haute couture collection in Paris but they are not based in Paris. These members are:

* Elie Saab—Lebanon
* Giorgio Armani—Italy
* Valentino—Italy

Milan

Milan, just like its other fashion capital counterparts, is known as a great place to shop, notably for its original design. The core of the fashion district in Milan is **Via Montenapoleone**. Luxurious boutiques of top Italian and international designers, antique shops, and tearooms are the physical proof of Milan's status as the capital of European fashion. Via Montenapoleone is the most important street of the Milan's Fashion District. All major Italian fashion designers have their main **ateliers** and shops here: Giorgio Armani, Dolce&Gabbana, Dior, Fendi, Gucci, Kenzo, Krizia, Prada, Valentino, Versace, Vuitton, and Zegna. Shoes, clothing, and textiles are Italy's biggest exports.

The Milan Lifestyle
It is often said the Italians dress more formally than Americans. Men always wear collared shirts and both genders wear mainly dark or subdued colors. Designer labels are a plus in this fashionable city. Some Italians think dressing well is an act of courtesy towards others.

London
The height of London fashion begins with the exquisite tailoring of **Savile Row**, a street in Mayfair central London sometimes known as the "golden mile of tailoring." Tailors have been hand-sewing suits for royals, statesmen, film stars, and men of distinction and style for almost two centuries on this street. **Bespoke** tailoring originated on Savile Row. Bespoke is an English term meaning made at a customer's behest and exactly to the customer specifications. Bespoke tailoring originally started in the nineteenth century when the British occupied the sea port cities of Shanghai and Ningbow in China; to these places, the British brought made to measure and other handmade skills with them. It is said that after the customer chose a bolt of cloth from which they wanted a suit made the fabric was said to "be spoken for." No pattern is used in the process and the tailors may take up to 35 measurements and require up to four fittings to achieve that perfect fit. Therefore, the cost is expensive yet worth it. The suit may take up to 12 weeks to make and cost upward of $6,000.

The London Lifestyle
Even with this eminent sophistication from Savile Row, the fashion in London is very edgy and individualistic. The Internet generation, or those individuals born in 1986, is coming of age now and seeking the fashion that London has to offer. They do not follow the mainstream and crave individualism. (*Business Week,* 2006)

    Notable London fashion designers are Stella McCartney, Paul Smith, Alexander McQueen, Matthew Williamson, and Neil Barrett.

Lost in Translation?

A comparison list of American and British terms that can somehow be lost in translation is as follows:

Table 10.2
LOST IN TRANSLATION CHART

AMERICAN	BRITISH
Barrette	Hairclip
Button-down shirt	Shirt
Gaucho	Culottes
Hose	Stockings
Jean jacket	Denim jacket
Jumper	Pinafore
Panties	Knickers or undies
Pin	Brooch
Plaid	Check
Pumps	Winkle pickers
Sweater	1. Jumper, jersey, or pullover
	2. Cardigan
Sweater vest	Sleeveless pullover
Sweats	Tracksuit
Sweatshirt	Sweater
Swimsuit	Bathing costume or cozzie
Tall boots	Long boots
Tennis shoes	Trainers, plimsols, or fashion sneakers
Thong	G-string
Turtleneck	Polo neck
Vest	1. Waistcoat (part of a formal suit)
	2. Bodywarmer (casual sleeveless jacket)

Source: Lost in translation blog, Friday, September 14, 2007

Other Remarkable Fashion Cities

The growing fashion industry is evident in all of the top 25 cities and it's becoming very difficult to pinpoint who is the favorite. The world of fashion is a revolving door as is the ranking of the top fashion cities. Thus, it is worthwhile to mention five other fashionable cities—Rome, Dubai, Berlin, Shanghai, and Moscow.

Rome

The Italian city, **Rome**, has recently surpassed Milan as the place to watch for fashion. The top fashion houses Valentino and Fendi acquired their start in Rome. While Milan has ready-to-wear, Rome has haute couture and hosts couture houses Sorelle Fontana, Gattinoni, and Renato Balestra. The **AltaRoma Organization** helped propel Rome to the top of the fashion industry. Each year the organization hosts AltaRomAltaModa, a fashion show showcasing haute couture selections from existing and new designers.

Dubai

Dubai, a city in the United Arab Emirates, is built around the principles of free trade, foreign investment, and sound business practices. Tourism is expected to triple from 6 million visitors to 15 million by 2010. Once you visit Dubai you are immediately attracted to two things the city has to offer: the sea and the desert. Shopping is also a tourist paradise with Dubai's low import duties and no taxation. Like all top fashion weeks, Dubai's international event brings together designers, buyers, and others associated in the fashion industry.

Berlin

Fashion in **Berlin** is a mix of looks. In the last 10 years there has been a surge of young designers along with the burgeoning music and club scene. Berlin's main shopping center is the **Ku'damm.** International labels such as Prada, Versace and Cartier populate this fashion area.

Shanghai
Shanghai, known as "the Paris of the Orient," is one of the world's busiest ports and is regarded as the center of finance and trade in mainland China. Shanghai is undergoing in-depth urban planning and its population is expected to grow to more than 20 million. Shanghai hosts four fashion weeks per year with support of its government and continues to promote young fashion designers and the latest creations from the international fashion houses.

Moscow
Fashion week in **Moscow** occurs twice a year, at the end of March and October, and features the presentation of ready-to-wear clothing. Moscow is still searching for its fashion identity and has not yet gained international recognition in the fashion industry. Within the past year the number of designers and people attending the fashion events has almost doubled thanks to the help of the founder of Russia fashion week **Alexander Shumsky.** Shumsky, known as the "Producer General" of Russian Fashion week, is often the very positive spokesman to the media for the increasing growth of Russian fashion in the global arena.

As fashion becomes more global and expands into unknown territories the competition between who will end up on top is anyone's guess.

TRANSUMERISM AND THE LEASING OPTION

In today's culture, we move fast; we are consumers in a state of transition—boarding a plane, catching a bus, train, or ship, always on the go. Global design and business consultancy firm Fitch coined the term **transumerism** to describe this phenomenon. The website trendwatching.com defines **Transumers** as "consumers driven by experiences instead of the 'fixed', by entertainment, by discovery, by fighting boredom, who increasingly live a transient lifestyle, freeing themselves from the hassles of permanent ownership and possessions. The fixed is replaced by an obsession with the here and now, an ever-shorter satisfaction span, and a lust to collect as many experiences and stories as possible. Hey, the past is, well, over, and the future is uncertain, so all that remains is the present, living for the 'now'." (trendwatching.com, November 2006) These individuals involved in this mass escape connect back to their home country through the Internet, cell phone, and a variety of other electronic means. Traveling provides a consumer an opportunity to see and buy that which is different and unique to them. This is a quality someone with personal style would want to acquire.

As we continue to see and travel, we begin to want more and more. As a result, the status items we see around the world are things we want to seek, have, and flaunt. These status luxury items can be ours through the multitude of **leasing** options. Not only is leasing considered an option for automobiles, but in the fashion industry it's become an avenue to access evening gowns, jewelry, and handbags. We want to look our best, so why not seek to have the goods any way possible?

FIGURE 10.2
H&M retail store is noted for its trendy styles and up-to-the-minute fashions.

Retailers and Transumerism

Retailers have responded to transumerism by providing the latest apparel trends in a matter of weeks. Consider retailers H&M, Zara, and Forever 21.

H&M

H&M was established in Sweden in 1947. The company's philosophy is to provide fashion and quality at the best price. Located in 28 countries with more than 1,500 stores, H&M continues to provide the latest in fashion at breakneck speeds. New, trendy, fashionable merchandise for both men and women are delivered daily. The store is packed with a wide selection of garments in the

FIGURE 10.3
Spain-based Zara stocks trendy items that are swept up by the fashion-conscious consumer in its more than 60-plus retail locations.

FIGURE 10.4
Trendy, inexpensive, fast, and fashionable clothes are part of retailer's Forever 21 philosophy. This Los-Angeles-based store makes it a point to keep up with the latest trends.

casual and dressy categories. There is usually a waiting line for the fitting rooms at peak shopping times. In March 2000, H&M opened its first store in New York City and since then has been expanding worldwide.

Zara

In 60-plus countries, Spain-based **Zara** clothing store stocks new items regularly to keep the store fresh with the latest trends. The normal length of time for new products to reach stores are usually nine months, but Zara beats all records with a claim of just two weeks for new product development and a three to four week timeframe for arrival to all of their stores. Zara products include men's and women's clothing and also cosmetics. Zara's catalog also carries a children's line of clothing in addition to men's and women's. Shortening the timeframe for product development has helped Zara become a retailer to watch. **Vertically integrated retailers** such as Zara are able to meet consumer demands for fashionable merchandise. They design, produce, and distribute the products themselves.

Forever 21

In 1984, the Los Angeles clothing store **Forever 21** opened with the philosophy to offer the latest fashion at great prices to its consumers. Men's and women's clothing offerings are accessible to all ages and demographics. The range of merchandise is endless, from lingerie, sportswear, and eveningwear to designer collections. Always changing and always carrying the latest styles, Forever 21 operates more than 355 locations nationwide.

  These three retail operations, H&M, Zara, and Forever 21, exemplify the best retail options for the transient style-conscious individual. As a consumer you are able to look current at affordable prices. You are never at a loss for finding what you need when fashion, quantity, plentiful locations, and affordability are right at your fingertips. You can achieve your personal style by looking your best at an affordable price and enjoying the experience as you wear these luxury items.

INTERNET RETAILERS

Internet shopping is the wave of the future. In Chapter 9, Shopping Basics, we discussed thepurplebook and exploring the best sites to shop. To review, the advantages of shopping online include the following:

* Shop anytime, day or night.

* No salesperson to deal with when shopping, freedom is yours.

* No traffic problems, easy delivery of merchandise.

* Convenience of location, home or office, and a variety of options are available.

* Secure servers allow for the Internet to be a safe place to shop.

Retailer's websites provide the consumer the opportunity to see their merchandise without leaving their homes. It's now common practice for a retailer to have a website as part of their marketing strategy.

Leasing Fashion via the Internet

Internet retailers offer products to transient style-conscious consumers through their websites by offering leasing as an option. Consumers pay a monthly fee to borrow the handbags for an agreeable length of time. High-price status handbags are popular rental items. Shopping globally on the Internet provides you the opportunity to search the world and lease items you normally wouldn't or couldn't afford to buy. Being able to possess something temporarily is a fantastic option for a style maven.

Leasing high-priced clothing and accessory items may seem like an easy option for most, but for those of you who don't return the items in tip-top shape it is best to acquire insurance. This inexpensive option gives you peace of mind if the merchandise is returned with excessive wear and tear.

Leasing Handbags
Consider the following rental handbag sites:

- Bag Borrow or Steal—www.bagborroworsteal.com/
- Be A Fashionista—www.be-a-fashionista.co.uk/
- From Bags to Riches—www.frombagstoriches.com/rentbag/pc/index.asp
- Shoulder Candy—www.shouldercandy.com/

These sites are based all over the world; your handbag could come from Canada, the United Kingdom, or any other country.

Leasing Jewelry
Jewelry is another popular leasing category and Bag Borrow or Steal has expanded their merchandise selection to include jewelry. Examples of popular jewelry leasing sites include:

- Borrowed Bling—www.borrowedbling.com/
- RK Jewellery Hire—www.rkjewelleryhire.com/

Leasing Clothing
Clothing items, especially evening gowns, are becoming an ideal category for leasing. If you are a person who occasionally attends a formal event, leasing an outstanding evening gown offers the possibility to wear the latest and best styles. Popular sites for this category include:

- One Night Stand—www.onenightstand.co.uk/
- Estella's Wardrobe—www.estellaswardrobe.co.nz/
- Salon Maure—http://salonmaure.com/

Auction and Trade Sites

In addition to leasing consumers may choose to trade, barter, or auction goods with other individuals. **eBay,** an online marketplace for all kinds of goods, has become the champion of the auctioning firms. For a reduced fee you are able to purchase from an assortment of items including jewelry, handbags, and clothing. This method of using an online marketplace is not desirable for some because of the time it may take to search the web for just the right item. But like the rental option, eBay offers the opportunity to own or rent luxury items.

In Chapter 9, Shopping Basics the advantages of Internet shopping are explored. Table 9.2 lists a selection of places to shop internationally to find the look you want. To explore your unique style even further, the Internet can not only help you find the right style but also the right fit. Answering a set of questions before you select your items may help you find not only a unique clothing item but also the right fit. Two popular sites where you can do this is are www.zafu.com and www.myshape.com. Zafu.com helps you find the right pair of jeans by allowing you to custom make the pair to your size and shape. A short questionnaire asks you to answer questions based on your perfect fit. The choices are narrowed down for your choosing. Myshape.com is described by Helena Paulin, Vice President of Marketing, as the "Internet matchmaker for your wardrobe and truly changing the way women shop." After entering your style preferences and measurements, My Shape chooses styles suitable for your figure and taste.

The website www.like.com allows you to choose accessories just like the celebrities wear by typing in the search engine, their name, and item.

Celebrity Copy Cat (www.celebritycopycat.com) is another website to shop and help you look like a celebrity for 50 percent or less.

TRAVEL—PACK LIKE A PRO

If the option you choose to find your personal style is flying across the world, then you need to travel like a pro carrying just the right items. Tips from travel stylists are many, but all tips lead to one word—*comfort*—as the main objective for your clothing. Tips for what to pack in clothing and accessories:

* Bathing suit
* Bras
* Panties and/or thongs
* Lingerie—including robes, night gowns and other sleeping items.
* Costume jewelry—earrings, necklace, bracelets
* Fake diamond engagement ring—leave the real one in a safety-deposit box till you return.
* Dress
* Heels
* Pareo/sarong/big scarf
* Robe
* Sandals
* Shorts/Capris
* Skirt
* Slacks
* Slip/Bodyslimmer/Spanx (compare prices)
* Sneakers or walking shoes

* Socks
* Stylish shirt
* Sweater
* Straw/wide-brimmed hat
* Tank/halter/sleeveless tops
* Workout clothes

Source: honeymoons.about.com, 2008

Layering your tops will help with changing climate or adapting to air-conditioned environments. This packing list is just the beginning and definitely includes just the basics. Inquire about the assistance of a personal shopper that specializes in packing if you need help. Your goal is to minimize wrinkles and reduce the size and amount of luggage you have to carry. Learn the steps to pack like a pro so as you shop internationally you not only look like a style maven but pack like one too.

WHAT MAKES YOU UNIQUE?

Technology has provided a means to access a variety of goods and services. As we discover who we are—our fashion personality, our body type, and our overall look—we can expand our search to update and include that which makes us special—our **signature style,** what helps us distinguish our look from others'.

Shopping internationally, either physically or via the Internet, is an excellent way to achieve uniqueness. The top fashion cities, Paris, London, Milan, and New York are each explored in this chapter, and each of their distinctive characteristics are explored. As fashion continues to expand to other countries we can also look to cities like Rome, Dubai, Moscow, and Shanghai to expand our

Table 10.3
HOW TO PACK LIKE A PRO

Things you'll need:

- Plastic Storage Bags
- Toiletries
- Toiletry Bags
- Garment Bags
- Carry-on Bags
- Luggage Sets

Pack Clothing
Step 1: Remember this order of operations: shirts on the bottom, then dresses (if applicable), then pants.
Step 2: Stack tops, unfolded, by placing wrinkle-prone tops toward the bottom of a pile and less easily wrinkled ones toward the top.
Step 3: Fold the sleeves in toward the shirts' torsos.
Step 4: Fold the shirts in half from the bottom. You now have a rectangular bundle of shirts; place it in your suitcase.
Step 5: Drape long dresses in the suitcase so that the ends hang over the sides.
Step 6: Place pants and skirts on a flat surface; fold each in half lengthwise.
Step 7: Stack pants and skirts on top of one another, with easily wrinkled ones on the bottom and sturdier ones, such as jeans, on top. Fold the stack over, so that its length is halved.
Step 8: Place your stack of pants and skirts on top of the dresses, then fold the ends of the dresses over the pants and skirts.

Pack Accessories
Step 1: Roll ties loosely.
Step 2: Stuff socks in shoes. Pack underwear in mesh laundry bags or side pockets to save space.
Step 3: Arrange each pair of shoes so that the heel of one aligns with the toe of the other.
Step 4: Wrap pairs of shoes in separate plastic bags, and place them along the border of your suitcase.
Step 5: Protect clothes from leaks by placing toiletries in a plastic bag.
Step 6: Pack essential toiletries in a carry-on bag. Include your toothbrush, toothpaste, makeup, medication and other important items.

Reference: eHow, How To Do Just About Everything, www.ehow.com/how_3403_pack-suitcase.html

fashion outreach. We can begin to match our needs and wants by city, exploring the Internet, traveling and reaching out to those experts who will be there to assist.

As you travel and explore other countries, make it a point to take photographs, obtain fabric swatches, and identify key retailers and designers. This information will all be included in your personal style journal, which will be discussed in Chapter 12, Tying it all Together…Your Personal Style. This final project will make a great reference point to look back at when previewing your fashion options and a keepsake to look back on in years to come.

KEY WORDS

Alexander Shumsky	fashion week	Savile Row
AltaRoma Organization	Fédération française de la couture, du prêt-à-porter des couturiers et des créateurs de mode	Shanghai
atelier		signature style
Berlin		transumerism
bespoke tailor		transumers
Chambre syndicale de la haute couture	Forever 21	type-A personality
	Global Language Monitor	Via Montenapoleone
Chambre syndicale de la mode masculine	H&M	vertically integrated retailer
	haute couture	Zara
couture	Ku'damm	
Dubai	leasing	
eBay	Moscow	
Fashion Center Business Improvement District	notions	
	Rome	

RESOURCES

Breslow Sardone, S. (2008). Vacation packing list, the ultimate packing list for travelers heading for vacation. Retrieved on April 24, 2008 from honeymoons.about.com/cs /travelplanner/a/Packing_List.htm.

Business Week. (2006). Retrieved on April 24, 2008 from www.businessweek.com /globalbiz/content/oct2006/gb20061030_512497.htm

Forever 21. (2008). *About Us*. Retrieved on April 24, 2008 from www.forever21.com/forever/about.asp.

Global Language Monitor. Retrieved from www.cosmoworlds.com/fashion_features /global_language_monitor-fashion_cities-07192007.htm.

H&M. (2008). New locations. Retrieved on April 24, 2008 from www.hm.com/us/workingathm/newlocations__worknewlocations.nhtml.

Hurley, L. (2007). Fashion passion. Fern Mallis, retrieved on April 24, 2008 from specialevents.com/corporate/events_fashion_passion_20070604/.

Mode à Paris. (2008). Retrieved from www.modeaparis.com/va/toutsavoir/index.html.

Montrose, N. (2007). Young Parisians accentuate the practical with vintage accessories. Retrieved on April 24, 2008 from www.iht.com/articles/2007/03/05/news/rfash.php?page=1.

Norton, K. (2006). Savile Row never goes out of style. Retrieved on April 24, 2008 from www.iht.com/articles/2007/03/05/news/rfash.php?page=1.

Sameth, C. & Kelly, N. (2007). Online women's fashion retailer MYSHAPE names Linda Freedman chief marketing officer, Helena Paulin is named vice president of marketing; Both marketing veterans specialize in building e-commerce businesses. Retrieved on April 24, 2008 from www.myshape.com/images/main/static/pdf/press_releases/MS_MRKT_ releaseFINAL.pdf.

Tiplady, R. (2006). Zara: Taking the lead in fast fashion, *Business Week*. Retrieved on April 24, 2008 from www.businessweek.com/globalbiz/content/apr2006/gb20060404_167078. htm?chan=innovation_branding_brand+profiles.

Trendwatching.com. (November, 2006). *Transumerism*. Retrieved on April 24, 2008 from www.trendwatching.com/trends/transumers.htm.

CHAPTER ELEVEN

Going Green with Your Personal Style

"There's no denying that green and eco-based issues are currently very hot. They mirror our global angst about climate change and resource depletion."

—LUCY SIEGLE, IN HER BOOK *RECYCLE THE ESSENTIAL GUIDE*

CHAPTER OBJECTIVES

After reading this chapter, you will be able to:

* Define the term *green* and its relationship to the fashion industry.

* Categorize types of green fashions.

* Identify key brands and designers in the green fashion movement.

* Prepare, select, and analyze an action plan for current or future green clusters.

* Identify sources of all natural, green fabrics.

* Explain the difference between recycled, sustainable, and organic clothing.

* Describe the relationship of eco-fashions and the millennial generation.

BALANCING THE EARTH AND THE INDIVIDUAL

I don't know about you, but when I think of anything that is related to the environment or the "greening of America" I think of former Vice President of the United States, Al Gore. He wants all of us to take bold action steps to "right the balance of our earth" and take the necessary steps to improve the world we live in. This chapter focuses your attention on what you can do with your wardrobe to become a green, environmentally focused fashion individual.

What is Green?

The word *green,* as it is used in this book, refers to a broad definition—that which is sustainable, organic, recyclable, recycled, alternative, or repurposed. Each of these terms will be defined, explained, and discussed in relationship to its role within the fashion industry.

As of the writing of this book, green fashion manufacturing is still in its infancy but slowly gaining momentum. The environmental movement's main focus is on global warming due to many occurrences not limited to but including the 2005 Hurricane Katrina and Al Gore's Academy Award-winning 2006 documentary *An Inconvenient Truth*. In 2007, the United States began to experience many grassroots rallies and demonstrations in green activism. Now, green has expanded to include clothing as a major player in helping the environment. The cost of acquiring the materials to produce green clothing is currently very high and the manufacturers are few. As individuals become more familiar with the type of clothing available to them, designers will find the need to make more garments that are considered green and more consumers will be asking for these garments. Eventually, green fashion will become second nature to all of us. Individuals looking to start families that are conscious about the environment and what they put on their body are going to become very vocal and begin the green clothing movement on their own.

WHAT DO WE MEAN BY GREEN?

The use of the term *green* in fashion refers to nature, cleanliness, environmentally friendly, ecologically aware, conservational, and recyclable—in other words, that which does not disturb or disrupt the environment. Green, as it relates to fashion, includes garments that are considered organic, pure, whole, and natural. Nature and textiles are intertwined to form green fashions.

Natural Fibers

The natural fibers that we are familiar with but are not necessarily considered "green" are cotton, linen, wool, and silk. These fibers fall in three distinct groups: 1) vegetable fibers that come from plants, 2) protein fibers that come from the wool and hair of animals, and 3) silkworm larvae used to create silk.

Familiar Naturals

Fabrics reviewed in Chapter 5, Wardrobe Selection Factors, all play an important part in the greening of fashions:

COTTON It's known as the fabric that "breathes" because the cotton fiber absorbs and releases perspiration easily. Cotton also stands up to abrasion well and can be washed and ironed easily and often wrinkles. Cotton is often blended with other fabrications like linen or polyester to create a strong, smooth fabric.

LINEN A very strong fabric, linen is cool to wear yet wrinkles easily. Linen comes from flax, which is a fiber taken from the stalk of the plant. Linen has poor elasticity and therefore does not spring back easily. Linen does wrinkle easily, but is also very easy to iron.

WOOL Cozy and warm, wool has crimps and curls in its fibers that create pockets and provide insulation to the wearer. Wool is dirt resistance, flame resistant, and does not wear and tear easily. The following specialty wool fibers are named from the animal the fibers come from:

- **Alpaca** fleece from the alpaca.
- **Mohair** from the angora goat.
- **Angora** wool is from the angora rabbit.
- **Camel hair** is from the undercoat of the camel.
- **Cashmere** is from the Kasmir goat down.
- **Vicuna** is from the lama family.

SILK   A strong natural fiber noted for its elegance, silk is used especially in the summer and winter months because of its strong filaments. Silk, a natural protein fiber comes from the cocoon of the silkworm. Silk garments can shrink if the fabric is not washed before the garment is made. It is best to use shampoo to wash silk; do not wring the fabric, but roll it in a towel to dry. Because of the delicacy of the fibers, silk should avoid perspiration and sunlight which can weaken the fabric.

New Green Naturals

Natural fibers that are new to the green category of fabrics are bamboo, corn, coconut, crab shells, eucalyptus, metal, milk, seaweed, and soybeans.

BAMBOO   Because of its all natural qualities and Asian origins, **bamboo** has become the most popular natural fiber amongst green designers. China is the country that produces the majority of bamboo whose properties include the softness of silk and the strength of an oak tree. Bamboo is a grass, not a tree, and similar to linen, another plant-like fiber. Bamboo was first introduced in the sheet category because of its properties but has now expanded to items of clothing, most notably t-shirts.

COCONUT The **coconut fiber** fruit husk is packed with tight fibers called coir, which is also considered part of the plant family in textiles. This fiber is obtained from the outer layer of the coconut husk and is currently being used in bedding, automobile upholstery, and doormats. The company, Shikibo Ltd. in 2006, has succeeded in developing a fiber from coconuts that is suitable for making clothing. The firm extracts a thin fiber by heating and softening the coconut, then processing the material in a proprietary machine that separates the thin, pliable strands. The fiber becomes extremely porous and lighter than cotton, making it an ideal candidate for polo shirts, jeans, and jackets. This company, an innovator in making fibers from unconventional plant sources, is also using sugarcane and bamboo as fiber sources to become clothing.

     All of these new fibers are either intertwined with synthetics or used alone to form fabrics that are significant for our well-being and provide comfort. In other words we are using what nature has placed before us, and experts refer to this as the **3 Rs**—reduce, reuse, and recycle.

Recycling

Recycling, as part of the definition of green, is "adapting or processing used or waste material so that it can be converted for a new use or used again for the same purpose" (Hanaor, McCorquodale, and Siegle, L. 2006). When we recycle we reuse or use again that which once was rubbish. Some of us are of the mindset that recycled garments are not good and they lack value and have no taste. That is not the case anymore. There are recyclable fashions that could rival that which is considered couture.

     Recycling can be used in all categories of clothing; from sportswear to couture. When you recycle you're reusing materials that you already own. It becomes a savings to the environment and also for you as the owner. In addi-

THREAD 11.1

RECYCLABLE CLOTHING

Designers are jumping on the bandwagon turning old clothing into stylish new looks. One designer, Nick Graham of Joe Boxer fame, uses clothing from a Goodwill store to make his stylish outfits. Selecting items that have been sitting in the store for 30 days or longer, Graham reconstructs the outfit making it into something that will sell. The Goodwill store in San Francisco is the first to have these garment remakes done, but Graham plans on expanding to other Goodwill stores across the country.

Graham's Goodwill store garments are a very good example of recycled garments because used clothing is the basis for the fabric construction. The William Good line, as the new clothes are called, is taking off with the millennial generation. This new generation considers these items "chic" and wearable. As discussed in Chapter 2, Personal Style Evaluation, the millennial generation (1982–2002) considers individuality their right, and this is very much reflected in their clothing choices. What a perfect way to express yourself to have something truly unique and special. If the millennial generation has their way, this is just the beginning of recycled clothing.

Source: www.Iconoculture.com, 2007

tion to William Goode's clothing line, a web search for recycled manufacturers' lists a variety of companies that sell used clothing. Turning vintage clothing into clothing that is hip, cool, and totally wearable has been popular in Japan for years, but it's just now becoming commonplace here in the States. In 1984, Tony Mahagamage and Leeba Marks, designers at the company Trash Clothing, blended old and new styles to form their company. Trash Clothing operates under Denim King Vintage Wholesaler, whose primary products are used and vintage clothing and denim jeans. Primary owner Mahagamage has been tracking down any type of clothing for customers since the company's founding in 1984. In the United States, Trash Clothing is just one example of the recycled movement in existence for quite some time.

FIGURE 11.1
Repurposed clothing can be just as stylish as manufactured ready-to-wear. Designer Nick Graham proves that fashion can look just as good when made from recycled Goodwill clothes.

A company like Tropical Mixed Used Clothes recycles and sells clothing to more than 20 countries worldwide. Based in Atlanta, Georgia, this company recycles up to 40,000 pounds of clothing a day. The clothing that makes up the "mix" is mainly from store returns that aren't suitable to re-sell in the store. The mix of clothing could contain 180 to 190 pieces from a variety of categories that include women's pants, women's skirts, blue jeans, dresses, and shorts.

Recycling can take many forms as you can see from the previous examples. You can take clothes and change them from their original look to something new, or you can take used clothing and sell them to a new owner, recycle them so as not to just throw them away. Find new ways to use and re-use and re-use again.

FIGURE 11.2
Recyclable clothing is also used clothing. Only the wearer needs to know how many times the garment has been made to look like it is now.

FIGURE 11.3
Developing countries appreciate the used clothing that is sent to them from companies. Instead of throwing these items away, send them to the needy.

As the experts say, we must begin the recycling process as space becomes an issue and landfill is getting more expensive. Recycling is a means of extending our resources and evokes creativity in all of us. Recycling is an investment in our future and we must continue to look at nature for clues. For example, compare the structure of a leaf to the ultimate solar appliance. In nature itself, is there such a thing as waste? (Siegle, 2006)

Sustainability

The word ***sustain*** can be defined as to maintain and nourish. To become a green fashion-focused individual means we are continuing to use what we already have and we will support, aid, help, and assist in any way possible to keep what we already have and own. **Sustainable design** attempts to assist in increasing the value and survival of the earth's resources and its existence for future generations.

Institute for Market Transformation to Sustainability
The environmental movement has expanded the need for sustainable clothing. The **Institute for Market Transformation to Sustainability (MTS)** has developed the Unified Sustainable Textile Standard. The MTS attempts to establish standards that address what MTS calls the "triple bottom line of economic, environmental, and social performance for all aspects of the supply chain—from the acquisition of raw materials and natural resources through manufacturing to shipping and transportation of the finished garments and textiles." (Organic Clothing, 2006)

The MTS Unified Sustainable Textile Standard examines garment sustainability in five areas of sustainability:

1. Safe for Public Health and Environment
2. Renewable Energy and Energy Efficiency
3. Material, Biobased, or Recycled
4. Facility or Company Based
5. Reclamation, Sustainable Reuse, and End of Life Management

Within each of these five areas of sustainability there are twelve categories a garment is measured for sustainability. These twelve areas are:

1. Global Warming
2. Acidification
3. Ozone Depletion
4. Eutrophication
5. Photochemical Smog

NORM THOMPSON OUTFITTERS

"Escape from the ordinary" is the tag line used by casual clothing company Norm Thompson. This company developed a sustainability toolkit and scorecard for consumers and manufacturers to use to help them understand the differences in the growing production, manufacturing, shipping, and transportation issues that will affect the decisions of the company. The overall effect on its sustainability ranking and environmental impact is also evaluated. To remain a role model, Norm Thompson Outfitters incorporates several practices. The company:

* searches for products that have an environmental conscience such as sustainable salmon and organic cotton through the efforts of its buyers.
* gets involved in local community activities and donates profits to social service and environmental causes.
* believes in protecting the world's forests and resources by reviewing the need to minimize the overall impact of paper and other forest products. The goal is to consume paper wisely and efficiently.
* uses recycled content in its catalogs.
* ensures that virgin fiber comes from well-managed forests.
* makes decisions through a life cycle filter taking into consideration suppliers and their production capabilities.
* pursues alternative fibers so as not to make a burden to the forest and the trees.
* utilizes a third party to verify and communicate sourcing and other practices of their suppliers.

The company's guiding philosophy is "Limit nothing. Examine everything. Search without boundaries." As a role model in the eco-fashion movement, Norm Thompson Outfitters continues to lead the way.

FIGURE 11.4
Norm Thompson Outfitters is one of many new manufacturers with a philosophy based on producing clothing that is "environmentally responsible."

6. Human Health
7. Ecological Toxicity
8. Fossil Fuel Depletion
9. Habitat Alteration
10. Criteria Air Pollutants
11. Water Intake
12. Solid and Hazardous Waste

The Sustainable Company

To achieve a favorable rating in the five areas of sustainability, a garment most often has to achieve positive ratings in only seven out of the twelve categories. In order to help companies incorporate sustainability in the design and manufacturing of their products, the McDonough Braungart Design Chemistry (MBDC) organization introduces sustainable practices to all companies and awards certificates to companies wishing to be certified against the sustainability standards set by the organization. Sustainability is achieved through hard work and setting goals.

As mentioned before the environmental movement is the catalyst for sustainable designs. Designers continue to look for fabrics and notions that will help to make their looks part of this movement. To be considered a sustainable company would involve a myriad of responsibilities including but not limited to "reusing environmentally friendly packaging, reducing manufacturing, and operational waste and pollution, improving building energy efficiency and reducing energy consumption, moving towards the use of renewable energy, improving shipping and transportation efficiencies, and designing sustainability into the products and services that are sold to the public." (Organic Clothing, 2006)

This is truly just the beginning of an environmental movement that will continue to surge on into the future. As people begin to understand what it means to have sustainable fashions, then wearing sustainable clothing may soon become a common value for those environmentally conscious people.

FIGURE 11.5 (OPPOSITE) Designer Vivienne Westwood's look is making a resurgence with younger new designers as they copy the punk rock fashions of the Seventies.

Organic

The Organic Trade Association (OTA) is a membership-based business organization that focuses on promoting and protecting the growth of the organic trade industry. According to the OTA, the definition of *organic* refers to the way agricultural products are grown and processed. An organic product ensures consumers the product is maintaining the organic integrity that began on the farm. The standards include a national list of approved substances for organic production. This detailed list may be found on the following website www.ota.com. (Organic Trade Association, 2008)

The terms *organic* and *natural* are often used interchangeably, yet they are different. Natural fibers, coming from nature, are not necessarily organic. Organic fabric manufacturing is free of toxic chemicals and thus healthy for the consumer and the environment. To be considered organic the garment must be made with earth-friendly natural fibers such as organic cotton**, hemp**, wool, alpaca, and **tencel**. Hemp is fabric similar to linen, and tencel is from cellulose from managed tree farms. Organic garments are also manufactured under ecologically and ethical conditions.

In a survey conducted by the OTA to its members, the following question was posed: What percentage of all clothing worn by the average U.S. consumer will be made with some or all organic fiber? The OTA group felt that anywhere from 1 to 10 percent of all clothing would be organic by the year 2025. The average number was 6.25 percent. (Organic Trade Association, 2005).

Buying organic clothing is one way you can help safeguard the environment.

Alternative or Repurposed

Repurposed designs, or "vintage store cut-ups," have become big business. To become a repurpose designer means to take what you already own or can find in thrift stores, vintage stores, or even the Salvation Army and re-design or re-use the garments again. (See Thread 11.1.)

Fashion company Preloved's designer Julie Grieve recycles thousand of garments to complete her collections. The Toronto-based company in 2006 used 20,000 sweaters and 8,000 pairs of jeans to complete its fall collection.

Another company, based in Washington DC, Unsung Designers stocks its online store with looks that are repurposed. The website features a wide selection of merchandise from cutting-edge designers from around the world. Co-founder Grace Wang believes that people are trying to get back to basics and get rid of the over-processed, over-done, mass-produced garments we have been used to seeing in the stores.

The millennial generation has used terms such as *punk rock* or **alternative clothing** to describe repurposed clothes. The uniqueness and one-of-a-kind garments that are fashioned from used clothing are reminiscent of the mid-Seventies style punk fashions that began with designer Vivienne Westwood and the Sex Pistols. Zippers, rips, torn clothing, and bright colors are all examples from the punk movement.

Whether or not these used garment designs are called repurposed, recycled, or alternative, the result is the same from all of these designers—to save the planet earth.

GREEN—THE DESIGNERS AND RETAIL STORES

Five years ago we never heard about the current trends in green, eco-friendly fashions. Today, fashion designers are getting on the bandwagon to do their part in saving the planet. Retailers are assisting these designers in providing space to highlight these special garments. The following list will not contain all the names of designers who are involved in this movement, but these are the ones with the loudest voices and saleable designs at this time.

Stella McCartney

Stella McCartney, fashion designer and daughter of Paul McCartney of the Beatles and strict vegetarian mother Linda McCartney (who died in 2000), translates her own vegetarian beliefs to her clothing line. As creative director for Chloe, in 1997 McCartney had included in her contract that she will not work with either fur or leather. She branched out on her own in 2001 creating her own fashion line, and her clothes ring true with her beliefs: saving animals, sustaining the planet, and practicing an overall respect for nature.

High fashion retailer Barneys New York has teamed up with McCartney to present her eco-collection. Her fabrics either remain natural in color or if a dye is used it is one that does not contaminate the water supply. Bamboo and organic cotton are included in her new spring collection garments, and accessories such as synthetic flats and recycled nylon bags, are also part of her collection.

John Patrick

John Patrick, the designer of clothing line Organic, founded in 2004, has created garments made from raw materials such as bamboo, hemp, soybean,

FIGURE 11.6
Designer Stella McCartney is in the forefront of organic fashions and does not use fur or leather in any of her designs.

FIGURE 11.7
Designer John Patrick's Organic clothing line is reaching new heights with environmentally conscious individuals. He uses raw materials such as bamboo, hemp, soybean, and seaweed to make his clothing.

FIGURE 11.8 (LEFT)
Designer Linda Loudermilk uses hemp, soy, and bamboo in her eco-friendly clothing line. Linda strives to create clothing that celebrates the beauty of nature.

FIGURE 11.9 (RIGHT)
Retailers such as Barney's New York have tapped young, new designers like Phillip Lim to produce organic, environmentally friendly clothing.

recycled plastic, and even seaweed. Patrick's suppliers and manufacturers are based mainly in Peru, a country where Patrick is a frequent visitor. He has used organic bed sheets as his staple fabric to make simple white shirts. He is passionate about not having chemicals and pesticides in his fabric. Patrick has said he can't wait for the day when we can say not "is it organic, but of course its organic."

John Patrick's Organic clothing line is carried at a variety of department stores, including JC Penney and Nordstrom, and online with Mick Margo.

Linda Loudermilk

In 2003, Linda Loudermilk launched her "luxury eco" collection consisting of sustainable fabrics that bears her creativity. These fabrics are **seacell—**woven from seaweed, **sasawashi**—a blend of Japanese paper and herbs with antibacterial properties, and **milk silk**—a combination of silk, cashmere and milk fiber. In addition Loudermilk uses the raw materials hemp, soy, and bamboo to create her designs. Loudermilk believes that nature is beautiful and we should celebrate it through our clothing.

From the beginning, Loudermilk's background in costume design from Oxford University in England and her training as a sculptor has helped her to lay the foundations for her organic fashion design line.

Phillip Lim

Young designer Phillip Lim has teamed up with retailer Barneys New York to create high quality organic designs. This new organic collection is called Go Green Go. His organic clothing consists of high quality, undyed organic fabrics. His pale, natural tones remain a standout on the runway.

FIGURE 11.10 (LEFT) Designer Behnaz Sarfpour focuses on innovative fabrics and interesting designs.

FIGURE 11.11 (RIGHT) Rogan Gregory is best known for his partnership with U2's Bono and his wife to create eco-friendly clothing for his company Loomstate.

Behnaz Sarafpour

Behnaz Sarafpour's limited spring 2008 collection of green looks uses organic fabrics and employs natural dying techniques. Sarafpour has not completely expanded into the green world because as she has said in her own words "it is quite labor intensive and expensive." She admits going green is used successfully as a marketing strategy with all of the hype about the environment.

Sarafpour's ready-to-wear business began in 2001 after working with designer Isaac Mizrahi, with whom she found her niche in appreciating innovative fabrics and a love for precise design.

Rogan Gregory

Rogan Gregory has three labels: he is cofounder of the ethical t-shirt line Edun, designer and co-founder of Loomstate, an all organic line of t-shirts and jeans, and he designs his own line Rogan. His eco-friendly lines are featured at Barneys New York and also set to debut at Target. As a champion of environmentally responsible practices he uses organic fabrics and makes sure all stages of manufacturing maintains the highest environmental standards.

Designer's reference: *O, The Oprah Magazine, March 2008, pages 115–120.*

GREEN CLUSTER

In Chapter 6, Cluster Concept, we identified several clusters you may have as part of your wardrobe. The green movement in clothing has only just begun and consequently the prices of most organic, sustainable clothing are expensive. If clothing and saving the environment are passions of yours, begin to collect pieces of organic clothing. You will be able to see a wide variety of clothing at a range of price points from Target to Barneys New York.

Consider your fashion personality when choosing organic clothing. Most of the clothing, because of the nature of the fabrication, falls within the sporty, natural classifications. It's best to begin with classic categories of organic clothing to get the most out of the garment and also to expand your current clothing options. Jackets, simple tops and skirts, dresses, and trench-type coats are all great starter organic options.

Fashion is beginning to transition into the green movement. Preview your personality, your closet, and finally analyze your clusters to begin to get involved in the green movement.

ACHIEVING GREEN

Who would have thought simple, organic, eco-friendly clothing would be all the rage for designers and retailers? The food industry began the trend with organic grocers leading the pack with healthy, pesticide-free fruits and vegetables. In the clothing category, green clothing includes a variety of industries, ranging from the OTA to MTS, striving to help set standards for the industry.

Understanding "green talk" is important in making your way through the industry. The following words are unique and special to the industry yet different in their meanings; organic, sustainable, recycle, green, and raw materials such as bamboo, hemp, soybean, organic cotton, seaweed, and soybean. As the green industry blossoms, it becomes necessary for us to read, study, and listen to all discussions on the topic. Your goal is to explore the designers and expand your clothing options to include this wonderful category as an option for your wardrobe. It will only prove to be beneficial and unique for you and your personal style.

KEY WORDS

- 3 Rs
- alpaca
- alternative clothing
- angora
- bamboo fiber
- Behnaz Sarafpour
- camel hair
- cashmere
- coconut fiber
- green
- hemp
- Institute for Market Transformation to Sustainability (MTS)
- John Patrick
- Linda Loudermilk
- milk silk
- mohair
- organic
- Organic Trade Association (OTA)
- Phillip Lim
- recycling
- repurposed clothing
- Rogan Gregory
- sasawashi
- seacell
- Stella McCartney
- sustain
- sustainable design
- Tencel
- vicuna

RESOURCES

Denim King Vintage Clothing Wholesaler. (2008). Retrieved on April 25, 2008 from www.alibaba.com/member/denimking/aboutus.html.

Gore, A. (2006). *An Inconvenient Truth.* New York: Rodale Books.

Hanaor, C., McCorquodale, D., and Siegle, L. (2006). *Recycle, the Essential Guide.* London: Black Dog Publishing, p. 16, 33, and 246.

Iconoculture. (2007). William Good makes stylish duds out of throwaway clothes. Retrieved on April 25, 2008 from iconoculture.com, p. 1.

Natural Fibers. (2008). Retrieved on April 25, 2008 from www.fabrics.net/natural.asp.

Oprah (editors). (2008, March). Green is the new chic, *O, the Oprah Magazine*, p. 115–120.

Organic Clothing Weblog. (2006). Retrieved on April 25, 2008 from http://organicclothing.blogs.com/my_weblog/2006/05/sustainable_clo.html.

Organic Trade Association. (2005). Retrieved on April 25, 2008 from www.ota.com/pics/documents/Forecasting2005.pdf.

Organic Trade Association. (2008). Retrieved on April 25, 2008 from www.ota.com/listbackground05.html.

PART V

Discovery: Uniquely Your Style

CHAPTER 12

Tying It All Together... Your Personal Style

"I dress for the image. Not for myself, not for the public, not for fashion, not for men."
—MARLENE DIETRICH, (1901–1992), GERMAN BORN ACTRESS,
SINGER, AND ENTERTAINER WHO BECAME A HOLLYWOOD MOVIE STAR IN THE 1930S.

CHAPTER OBJECTIVES
After reading this chapter, you will be able to:

* Compare and contrast total looks for each of the body types—hourglass, rectangle, triangle, inverted triangle, pear, and apple.
* Compare and contrast total looks for each of the fashion personalities.
* Establish personal style techniques and criteria for each of the fashion personalities.
* Complete your own personal style journal.

THREAD 12.1

TURNING A POSITIVE INTO A NEGATIVE
Growing up, supermodel Cindy Crawford was always very self-conscious about the mole above her upper lip. The first modeling agency she went to told her to remove her mole. Instead, this beauty mark has catapulted her to the top of the modeling world since 1983. She is beautiful and unique. She stood apart from the rest of the models during the late 1980s early 1990s. Since then she has turned her modeling success into a career as a successful entrepreneur, establishing Cindy Inc. What you may see as a negative may be a positive to others. Don't be afraid to highlight your total self. In Cindy's words, "for every thing you don't like about yourself come up with something you do like. It could be as simple as long eyelashes. A great shaped mouth. Lips with natural color. Once you start thinking in positive terms slowly you'll begin to appreciate other things." (Cindy.com, 2004).

YOUR PERSONAL IMAGE

Image is a vivid representation, mental impression, and concept of a person held by the general public. More than your wardrobe alone constitutes your image. In Chapter 1, Fashion Personality Types, we discussed the fact that effective communication makes up 55 percent the way we look, 38 percent comes from how we sound, and 7 percent from the words we use. Our body language, tone of voice, etiquette, grooming, hair and skin color, attitude, and self-concept all contribute to how others see us. With this definition in mind, what image would you like to portray? In Part I we examined *who* we are, in Part II *what* we should wear, and in Part III *why* we should add the extras. This chapter binds together all of these factors—the *who*, *what*, and *why*.

Individuality is an important factor in attaining personal style. As you think back to all the exercises you have completed so far, it's time to find the common denominator—your individuality—in all of your answers. In Exercise 1.1, for example...What is it that sets you apart from everyone else? What if that appears to be something negative? Think about making a negative trait a positive one. (See Thread 12.1.) Our goal throughout this book has been to accentuate the positive and work with the negative. In pulling together a complete image, you'll do the same.

Your Signature Style
What is it that everyone compliments you on continuously? Your **signature style** can be based upon just about anything—a piece of jewelry, any accessory

HAIR AND MAKEUP TIPS FOR THE IMAGE-MINDED

- Rule of thumb for both hair and makeup—keep it simple!

- Play up one feature when applying makeup. Eyes, lips, or cheeks. Too much of one thing is too extreme and unprofessional.

- The shape of your face is the foundation to a good haircut and style. Your hair should be the opposite of the shape of your head.

1. The **oval facial shape** can wear any hairstyle.
2. The **round facial shape** should draw the attention down by covering your cheeks and/or adding diagonal bangs. Hair style should be cut at the cheek bone or collar bone to de-emphasize the roundness of the face.
3. The **square facial shape** should add height to cover the temples to lengthen the square shape and add diagonal bangs to draw the attention down..
4. The **rectangle facial shape** should add fullness to the sides of the face.
5. The **oblong facial shape** should fill out the cheek area of the face and partially cover the forehead.
6. The **diamond facial shape** should cover the ears and fill out the jaw.
7. The **triangle facial shape** should fill out the jaw area and the temple area of the head.
8. The **inverted triangle facial shape** should add height leading the attention outward and cover the temple area while also filling out the jaw line.

THREAD 12.2

Carrie Underwood

round

Tyra Banks

oval

FIGURE 12.1

The shape of your face provides clues to your perfect hairstyle. Once you analyze your facial shape you can then play around with the hairstyle that will work for you.

Nicole Kidman

reverse triangle/pear-shaped

Nicole Richie

square-shaped

Reese Witherspoon

heart-shaped

Mandy Moore

oblong/rectangle

item you wear all the time, a favorite color, a category of clothing that is your favorite, your hair or eye makeup could even be considered your signature style.

Personal Style Techniques for Your Fashion Personality

Have you thought about why you wear the things you do? As discussed in Chapter 1, Fashion Personality Types, your style and personality coincide. Who you are is expressed outwardly in your clothing. Each of the unique personalities has its own personal style. The following are style tips for each fashion personality.

Sporty Fashion Personality and Style

Key word for this personality is *comfort*. The sporty fashion personality should look for styles that are simple and casual. Solid, bright colors exemplify this personality. Athletic shoes or flats are perfect for this personality that is always on the go. Wash and wear fabrics that are comfortable against the skin is a must. The total package for the sporty type is exhibiting enthusiasm, and portraying an energetic, wholesome look.

Romantic Fashion Personality and Style

The key word for this personality is *femininity*. Romantic fashion personalities should look for styles that are dainty yet graceful and elegant. Soft, feminine colors are best and nothing too extreme or bold for this type. Low or high heels and dresses showcase the womanly side of this personality. Fabrics would include floral and lace patterns. The total package would include a personality full of charm, grace, and somewhat flirty.

Classic Fashion Personality and Style

The key word for this personality is *conservative*. The classic is very traditional in style and looks should be timeless. The key basic pieces in your cluster are classic items. Classics should look for fabrics for every season, and can stand the test of time. Colors are neutrals and each clothing item can be worn to mix and match with other classic wardrobe items. Basic pumps in a low heel or sling backs would work for the classic personality. The total package would include a sense of professionalism, balance, well mannered, and under control.

Dramatic Fashion Personality and Style

The key word for this personality is *bold*. The styles for the dramatic personality would be extreme, high fashion, and striking. Stilettos and high heels in a variety of styles and colors would suit this personality type. Fabrics are deeply textured; prints in bold colors and unique fabric types such as leather and suede are suitable for the dramatic. The total package would always stand out in a crowd, remain trendy yet fashionable, and confident.

Natural Fashion Personality and Style

The key word for the natural personality is *casual*. The styles that are appropriate for this type are simple and free of decoration. Fabrics are natural or organic with rough textures and natural finishes such as raw silks and tweeds. Flats, loafers, and simple comfortable shoes would complete the look. Colors mirror the earth—browns, greens, stone, and sky blue. The total package consists of being free, friendly, open and honest.

Your Image Inventory

Now it's time to describe your image in words and on paper. Complete the image inventory to use as a guide when dressing. Begin your discovery by completing Exercise 12.1 to describe the image you would like to present to the world.

Table 12.1

MY IMAGE INVENTORY

Classic	Enduring	Romantic	Lively
Prim and proper	Natural	Colorful	Flamboyant
Traditional	Modern	Simple	Energetic
Stern and austere	Eclectic	Flirty	Bohemian
Stylish	Dramatic	Feminine	Masculine
Sloppy	Polished	Boring	Risk taker
Elegant	Sensational	Sophisticated	Unique
Neat	Chic	Plain	Young
Timeless	Exciting	Sporty	Perky
Sexy	Contemporary	Professional	Icon

Exercise 12.1: My Image Inventory

PART I: TAKING COUNT Circle the words in Table 12.1 that best describe the image you would like to portray.

PART II: IMAGE COLLAGE Cut out pictures from magazines that represent the words chosen. This collage is the image viewpoint you are striving to achieve. This collage can be updated seasonally. There is no magic number of pictures to choose, but the goal is to be able to visualize and express in words your ideal image.

THE TOTAL LOOK

You now have your clusters formed and the basics in place, but are they the right pieces for you? Women's clothing designers that sell basic items routinely partner with the retail buyers to have their basic items on an **automatic replenishment system**. The retail store computer system recognizes what has been

FIGURE 12.2
Your signature style is what makes you stand out from the pack. Your clothing, jewelry, hairstyle, and the way you walk and talk is all part of style. Let it shine!

sold in the store and automatically orders replacements to be delivered from their central warehouse to their stores. When the agreed upon replenishment number of each item goes below the standard then the system is triggered to re-order the item. For example, if the **model stock** for black pants is 200 units, the number of units ideally on hand, and the replenishment number is 120, if the inventory reaches 119 then the system will automatically reorder. With the re-order system manufactures will consistently make their money on the staples (e.g., black pants, white blouse, the jacket, and the little black dress). Several vendors have established key looks for certain body types. Price points vary so choose the right price for you. When considering your choice of vendor make sure to review the following points from Chapter 2, Personal Style Evaluation:

* What is your current lifestyle?
* How much disposable income do you have to spend on clothing?
* What is the cost-per-wearing for the article of clothing, and is it worth it?
* Does the item meet all or most of the wardrobe selection factors?

Let's take a look at a sampling of "the total look" for each body type. (See Table 12.2.)

Denim
Denim is a unique category because it crosses both the sportswear and evening categories. It's a definite staple to include in your cluster; in fact three denim jeans are ideal: one hemmed for your flats, one for your heels, and one for mid-heel height. There are more than 30 denim manufacturers with different fits and looks, so schedule enough time to shop for the perfect fit. Just like

Table 12.2

THE PERFECT STAPLE ITEM

Inexpensive = $
Moderate = $$
Expensive = $$$
Very Expensive = $$$$

Body type	Manufacturer/Price Point	Description
PANTS		
Belly, a little tummy	Alvin Valley/$$$	Leather waistband, low rise
Small waist but bottom heavy	Michael Kors/$$$$	Lightweight stretch wool, full legs
Any body type	Premise's Grace pants/$$$	Straight and narrow but not skinny
Pear shape	Raven Tailored/$$$	Classic boot cut, wide hemline
Rectangle shape, boyish figure	Tevrow + Chase/$$$	Wide, dropped waistband, belt loops, easy fit
WHITE BLOUSE		
Small bust	Anne Fontaine/$$$	Three rows of ruffles
To frame the face...	Club Monaco's Kara shirt/$$	Built-in scarf to frame the face and vertical placket
Curves	Lafayette 148 New York/$$$	French cuff, vertical seams, added stretch, 100% cotton
Nipped in waist	Ann Taylor/$$	Ruching down the center
Rectangle, boyish figure	Tevrow + Chase/$$$	Balloon sleeve creates femininity and adds volume to the rectangle shape
DRESS		
Wide hips	Diane Von Furstenberg/$$$	V-neck top, loose fit skirt bottom
Long torso	Julie Haus/$$$	High empire waist
Boy shape	J. Crew/$$ to $$$	Diagonal patterns to create curves
Petite frame	Isaac Mizrahi for Target/$	Narrow pleats

Body type	Manufacturer/Price Point	Description
DRESS		
Plus size	Lane Bryant/$$	Solid colors, fitted cut
Thick waists	Behnaz Sarafpour for Target/$	Dark lace detailing around the waistline
Small bust	Anthropologie/$$$	Stripes—vertical and diagonal
All body types	Banana Republic/$$$	U-shape neckline, dark color belted waist, full bottom skirt

JACKETS	**Guidelines**
Neckline	Fit snugly around neckline, no gaps or wrinkling
Shoulder seams	Lie flat on top of the shoulder and end at the joint unless design indicates otherwise
Armholes	No gaps, binding or restriction; lowest point 1–2 inches below the armpit for ease of movement
Sleeves	One and a half inch ease around the arm. One finger should fit easily under short sleeves. Long sleeves should end at wrist bone. No puckers in set-in sleeves.
Waists	Fit comfortably when standing, all buttons can button, two fingers can slip easily inside the waistband.
Darts	If any they should point toward and end 1-1 ? inch from the fullest part of the curve. Dart should taper and end smoothly.
Pockets	Lie flat without pulling or gaps.
Linings	Cut on the grain, lie smooth and allow for ease of movement.

Table 12.3

THE PERFECT FIT JEANS

Body type, flaw	Denim guideline
Flat bottom	Stretch jeans that hug the butt, slim legs, avoid stiff denim, loose fits, and boy cuts.
Curvy	Straight cut that fits hips and butt (may have to have waist taken in).
Petite	Classic style, natural waistline to add length to the legs.
Tummy	Styles that sit below the natural waistline.
Short waist	Lower rise to elongate torso—rise that is 7.5 inches or less.
Long waist	Straight legs. Waistline is near your natural waist, 8 inches of rise to make legs look longer; avoid flares and wide legs.
Bottom-heavy	Lower rise, dark denim, stretch denim with a fitted waist. Avoid tight legs.
Tall	Low rise with long inseams at least 36 inches.

jackets category in Table 12.2, Table 12.3, The Perfect Fit Jeans, lists the guidelines to look for when trying on jeans. There are many websites with denim manufacturer suggestions. One to try is Couture Candy (www.couturecandy.com). Its denim fit guide includes manufacturer recommendations for every body type www.couturecandy.com.

FASHION PERSONALITY TOTAL LOOK

Tying it all together means you are expressing your total package to the world the way you want to be presented and not by trying to squeeze yourself into the trends or what someone else is telling you; the discovery of *who* you are,

FIGURE 12.3

Celebrities have the opportunity to look their best at all times. Each of these celebrities has a style they can call their own. Note how through poise and style, each of these celebrities expresses her style: Grace Kelly (this page), Jackie Kennedy (opposite), Jessica Alba, Halle Berry, and Gwyneth Paltrow (following, clockwise from top).

FIGURE 12.4
Journal page example

Source: BCBG Le Journal, spring 2007.

how you want to be presented to the world, and *why* this image is important to you in your life right now. If you are preparing to enter a professional work arena for the first time the total package you present to your colleagues will be an important career move. Is it one of professionalism, or does it scream, "I don't care?" Your fashion personality, as discussed in Chapter 1, is who you are. Taking bits and pieces of this discovery will help you to narrow down your signature style. Refer to Table 1.8, Fashion Personality Vendor Table, to see where you can begin to hone in on your style.

YOUR PERSONAL STYLE JOURNAL

Now it's time to tie everything together. By now you have assembled a multitude of ideas, photographs, images, swatches, and style muses. Your personal style journal will encompass these items. The *intro* to your personal style journal will consist of the information obtained in Part I, Who Are You? The *body* of the journal will include Chapter 5, Wardrobe Selection Factors, focusing on fit, color, style, fabric, quality, and care. The *conclusion* of your journal will be the extras, or your accessories, and here you will refer to Chapter 8, Accessories! Accessories! Accessories! Because this is a journal, a record of your thoughts and inspirations that might include pictures from magazines, books, or from your travels, will be part of the personal style journal.

Complete Exercise 12.1 to begin your journal discovery. This is your opportunity to brainstorm and make choices. Once complete, you can incorporate your ideas from the exercise in your final journal.

Exercise 12.2: My Personal Style

Part I. Who Are You?
Complete the following sentences:

1. My fashion personality is...
2. Fashionable adjectives that describe me are...
3. My style icon is...
4. My three best colors are...
5. My three favorite fabrics are...
6. My three top clothing items (and why) are...
7. My favorite place to shop if money is no problem is...

Describe your ideal life. Be specific and make it ideal! How do you want to look and feel? List activities you plan on participating in now and in five years.

THE TOTAL PACKAGE

Are you ready to show the world the style maven you have become? The exercises and tables studied in this chapter summarize the steps to becoming a style maven who has it all tied together. The image collage visually outlines your look. Your physical features are meant to be highlighted. The manufacturer tables in this chapter will assist in leading you to choose a proper fit by making it easy for you to narrow down your choices of the variety of goods that are available for us to choose.

If you feel that you need additional help and assistance in choosing the look that's right for you, employ the services of an **image consultant,** an individual who specializes in visual appearance, confidence building, and behavior and communications. The Association of Image Consultants International (AICI) is dedicated to educating image professionals and membership is worldwide. Visit the website at www.aici.org for more information or to find an image consultant near you.

Begin to list your favorite clothing items, fabrics, colors, and patterns. Memorize a positive descriptive phrase to use that encompasses and stands for your total look. You are now well on your way to achieving your own personal style and having a signature style that no one will forget.

KEY WORDS

automatic replenishment system	individuality	rectangle facial
	inverted triangle facial shape	round facial shape
diamond facial shape	model stock	signature style
image	oblong facial shape	square facial shape
image consultant	oval facial shape	triangle facial shape

RESOURCES

Bessic, J. (2008). Hair tips. Retrieved on April 25, 2008 from www.salonblonde.com

Cindy.com. (2004). Keeping it all together: Beauty. Retrieved on April 25, 2008 from www.cindy.com/keeping/beauty.php

Dicks, S. (2007). *What is your Fashion Personality?* Retrieved on April 25, 2008 from www.sheilasfashionsense.com/personality.htm

Fever, E. (2007, September). *O, The Oprah Magazine.*

Glossary

3 Rs Reduce, reuse, and recycle.

Accent pieces Clothing items that provide details and artistic expression to an outfit; usually worn with basic items of clothing.

Accessory An object or device not essential in itself but adding to the beauty, convenience, or effectiveness of the outfit.

Accessory selection factors Fit, color, fabric, style, quality, and care.

Age group A way to categorize people who may often share common experiences, values, and beliefs: preteen (12-14 years old), teenager (15-17), young adult (18-24), adult (25-34), middle age (35-44), mature (45-54), older (55-64), and senior citizen (65 plus).

Alexander Shumsky Known as the "Producer General" of Russian Fashion week; a very positive spokesman for the increasing growth of Russian fashion in the global arena.

Alpaca Wool of the alpaca, a domesticated mammal (Lama pacos), especially of Peru, that is probably descended from the guanaco. A thin cloth made of or containing this wool.

AltaRoma Organization Provides opportunities and fosters relationships between the traditional couture of famous Italian designers and the creativity of new, creative up-and-coming designers. The organization also encourages the growth of the fashion sector through the promotion of training by striving to become the driving force of innovation, creativity, and technology.

Alter To make different without changing them into something else. One phase of closet evaluation (choosing to wear, discard, or alter clothing).

Alternative clothing Another name for repurposed clothing; clothing that has been re-designed and re-used.

Analogous Colors that appear next to each other on the color wheel.

Analyze To dissect and break down your clothing for individual scrutiny; to discover the true nature of why you have the clothing you do.

Angora The hair of the Angora rabbit or Angora goat—also called angora wool.

Anorexia Nervosa Eating disorder where people starve themselves. Symptoms include extreme weight loss (usually 15 percent below one's normal body weight) and nevertheless believing that one is overweight.

Antique Clothing older than 1920 is considered antique.

Anti-shopper About 21 percent of shoppers, whose motto is "Shopping is a chore I could live without."

Apple body type A body shape with a full bust and midsection. Assets are great lower legs and bust.

Assumptions A fact or statement that is taken for granted.

Asymmetrical balance Not symmetrical, out of balance; for example, two sides of a garment of different appearance yet equal weight.

Atelier An artist's or designer's studio or workroom.

Attitude A mental position with regard to fact or state; a feeling or emotion toward a fact or a state.

Automatic replenishment system A retailer's auto replenishment system used to keep inventory at optimal stock levels. Retailers use information technology such as bar codes or point of sale scanners to collect the data.

Balance Equal distribution of weight on either side of its vertical axis. In garment design, both sides of the vertical axis mirror each other in appearance.

Bamboo fiber Fiber from the bamboo plant. Bamboo thrives naturally without pesticides or fertilizers and is 100 percent biodegradable: Bamboo fabric is smooth and luxuriously comfortable, and bamboo clothing is also anti-static.

Basic items Clothing items that form the foundation of one's wardrobe; the essentials and the starting point of an outfit.

Batik fabric design Literally, good points or dots in Javanese; a wax-resist dying technique used on textile.

Behnaz Sarafpour Ready-to-wear designer who began using innovative fabrics and intricate designs in her clothing lines in 2008. Sarafpour used organic fabrics and employed natural dyeing techniques in her clothing.

Berlin Capital and largest city in Germany that has also been consistent in making fashion a top priority. Ranked number 11 on the top cities for fashion in 2007.

Bespoke tailor A term that dates from the seventeenth century, when customers would ask for something, or "bespeak," and tailors would then construct garments without the use of a pattern. Synonymous with the term "custom made."

Black Friday The day of store sales after Thanksgiving in the United States, traditionally the beginning of the Christmas shopping season.

Body shapers Shapewear that sculpts your body to help achieve an hourglass figure, examples are girdles, waist cinchers, and long leg shapers.

Boots Fitted covering, often leather or rubber, for the foot and usually reaching above the ankle.

Bra A woman's undergarment to cover and support her breasts.

Budget worksheet A tool; to figure out the amount of money that is available for, required for, or assigned to a particular purpose, as in a clothing budget.

Camel hair Cloth made of camel hair or a mixture of camel hair and wool; usually light tan, and soft and silky in texture.

Camisole A short negligee jacket or a short sleeveless garment for women.

Cashmere Fine wool from the undercoat of the cashmere goat.

Casual cluster Clothing items designed for informal use such as khakis and t-shirts and used to form a group of clothing items for informal activities.

Casual spender About 7 percent of shoppers whose motto is "I don't mind paying more if it means zero effort." The casual spender is not interested in changing how they shop or how much they save.

Catalog shopping To shop from a book containing a complete enumeration of items arranged systematically with descriptive details.

Chambre syndicale de la haute couture The regulating commission that determines which fashion design houses are eligible to be considered haute couture. It promotes, educates, represents, defends, deals with social and working benefits, and advises its members in labor and management relations. It also deals with piracy of styles, foreign relations, and organization and coordination of the fashion collection timetables as well as instituting collective international advertising for the French fashion industry.

Chanel 2/1955 handbag A quilted purse introduced in 1955 by Coco Chanel. For the first time in fashion history a woman's handbag now had a chain shoulder strap that allowed women to sling the handbag over their shoulders and use their hands however they pleased.

Children's category of hangers A wood, plastic, or metal device to hang children's clothing that is smaller in size than adult hangers.

Chroma A quality of color combining hue and saturation; the purity of the color.

Chrome hangers Hangers that are made of chrome or plated with an alloy of chromium.

Chromotherapy Color therapy where color and light balance energy and allow the vibrations of the body to be in a frequency that results in health, welfare, and harmony.

Circumference The external boundary of a figure; a measurement around the body part.

Classic fashion personality A set of distinctive traits and characteristics that are characterized by wearing simple tailored lines in fashion year after year.

Cleavage The depression between a woman's breasts especially when made visible by a low-cut neckline.

Closet organizer An individual or company that organizes your closet by measuring its space, taking an inventory of inventorying your wardrobe, and analyzing your needs.

Clothing cues A clue, identifier, indication, or suggestion perceived by the clothing that you are wearing.

Clothing goals Plans and concepts that direct clothing choices.

Clothing tribe A group of persons wearing common clothing that reveal belongingness to a certain time period or age.

Cluster A collection, grouping, or assortment of clothing; a mass, pile, accumulation or gathering together.

Cluster planning chronicle A record, a worksheet, a journal, and a spreadsheet outlining the clothing items that make up each of your clothing clusters.

Clutch A woman's small, usually strapless handbag.

Coconut fiber Obtained from the fibrous husk (mesocarp) of the coconut fruit (Cocos nucifera) of the coconut palm.

Color The essence of light; color may be described in terms of hue, lightness, and saturation for objects and hue, brightness, and saturation for light sources.

Color Association of the United States In early 1915 the Textile Color Card Association (TCCA) began issuing color forecasts in the form of cards twice a year; goals are to give directions in color trends to the market; to enable different segments of the market to coordinate their products by offering the formulas for the production of each forecasted color; to buy products worldwide knowing they would coordinate at the point of sale; and to serve as an information center for all kinds of color information. In 1955 the name was changed to the Color Association of the United States (CAUS).

Color draping The process whereby color analysis is achieved to identify your correct color choices.

Color seasons There are four seasons of color (winter, spring, summer, and autumn).

Complementary Colors that are opposite each other on the color wheel.

Contrasting In color analysis, no hue in common (e.g., red and blue).

Convertible bra A bra that can be converted from one form or function to another. Great for halter, backless, and strapless garment styles.

Cool hues Colors that appear on the right side of the color wheel and are similar to colors such as the color of sky and water.

Cost-per-wearing formula A method of determining the true value of a garment; the formula is the cost of the garment divided by the number of wearings.

Couture The business of designing, making, and selling fashionable custom-made women's clothing.

GLOSSARY 325

Crocs Crocs™ Shoes. Originally intended as boating/outdoor shoes because of their slip-resistant, non-marking soles. By 2003, Crocs™ Footwear is universally accepted as an all-purpose shoe for comfort and fashion.

Culotte A divided skirt.

Custom Tailors and Designers Association of America (CTDA) Trade association founded in 1880 in Columbus, Ohio as a venue through which ideas and techniques for design, pattern making, fitting, cutting, and tailoring could be shared and exchanged. Membership includes distinguished master tailors, designers, custom clothiers, and direct sellers that create fine custom clothing for discerning clients throughout the United States.

Demi-cup A bra that has partial cups or half cups exposing part of the breast but still allowing for support.

Demographic traits The statistical characteristics of human populations (as age or income) used especially to identify markets.

Denier A unit of fineness for yarn equal to the fineness of a yarn weighing one gram for each 9000 meters. Less than 100-denier yarn is finer than 150-denier yarn.

Department stores A store having separate sections for a wide variety of goods.

Design emphasis A prominence in design; a feature that draws your attention to it.

Detergent A cleansing agent used to remove dirt from clothing; can be in liquid or powder form.

Diamond body shape Body shape characterized by a small frame with narrow shoulders and back, no defined waist, wide midriff, and medium or small bust.

Diamond facial shape Facial shape with a narrow chin and forehead and wide cheekbones.

Dior's New Look Christian Dior's shape of clothing characterized by sloping shoulders, tiny waists, and full hips; launched in the spring of 1947.

Discard To get rid of useless or unwanted clothing; the second step of closet organization.

Discount department stores Sometimes called mass merchant, a retailer that sells large volumes of merchandise at low prices with very little customer service.

Dramatic fashion personality Marked by a set of distinctive traits and characteristics that are characterized by wearing clothing that is striking in appearance or effect.

Dubai A city in the United Arab Emirates that is built around the principles of free trade, foreign investment, and sound business practices. Shopping in Dubai can be a tourist's paradise with Dubai's low import duties and no taxation.

Dyed fabric design A soluble or insoluble coloring matter, the dye, which is used to color fabric.

EBay eBay Inc. An American Internet company that manages eBay.com, an online auction and shopping website where people and businesses buy and sell goods and services worldwide.

Embroidered fabric design Decorative designs with hand or machine needlework on fabric.

Education Evidence of training or practice.

Emphasis Force or intensity of expression that gives impressiveness or importance to something.

Essential Those items of the utmost importance; necessary and indispensible.

Euro hangers Hanger with special contours, construction, and materials where the neck features a "French" collar to protect and maintain the shape of garments with high collars, and a large shoulder preserves the shape of the garment and eliminates hanger marks. The perfect hanger option for hall coat closets.

Fashion Center Business District A nonprofit corporation established in 1993 to promote New York City's apparel industry and to improve the quality of life and economic vitality of Manhattan's garment district.

Fashion follower An individual who imitates or follows the looks and styles of another.

Fashion leader An individual who is first to wear the latest styles.

Fashion mission statement Personal philosophy on your clothing style. A pre-established and often self-imposed objective or purpose.

Fashion personality The totality of an individual's behavior and emotional characteristics as they relate to their fashion choices. The complex fashion characteristics that distinguish an individual.

Fashion week In the United States, American Fashion Designers show their runway collections twice a year, the spring collections are shown in September and the fall selections in February. Fashion designers in other countries hold similar events.

Féederération francais de la couture, du prêt-a-porter des couturiers et des creaters de mode Composed of couture houses and fashion designers of women's ready-to-wear. Created in 1973.

Fit The fact, condition, or manner of fitting or being fitted, as in the way clothing fits the wearer.

Five basic personality types Classic, sporty, natural, romantic, and dramatic fashion personality types.

Flats A shoe or slipper having a flat heel or no heel.

Flip flops A rubber sandal loosely fastened to the foot by a thong.

Footwear Apparel for the feet; shoes and boots.

Forever 21 Los Angeles–based store offering the latest men's and women's clothing at great prices.

Foundation basics The necessary undergarments—bras, panties, body shapers, slips, camisoles, and hosiery—that will shape your body and make or break your image and wardrobe.

Four classic Hermes handbags Haut a Courroies (1892), Bolide bag (1923), the Plume (1930), and the Trim (1958).

Generation A group of individuals born and living contemporaneously.

Generation based clothing Clothing that reveals a certain time period. For example, the mini skirt is reminiscent of Sixties.

Gisele Büundchen Brazilian supermodel known, according to *Forbes*, as the world's richest supermodel. She is the face of more than 20 brands.

Global language monitor Monitors the latest trends in the evolution and demise of languages, word usage, and word choices worldwide.

Goal The end towards which effort is directed.

Golden Mean Ratio A means of separating the body into sections that are easy to dress. The ratio is 3:5:8; the total body is 8 heads tall, the top of the body is 3 heads tall, and the bottom of the body is 5 heads tall.

Green Concerned with or supporting environmentalism.

Grippy hangers A specialty hanger that is suitable for silk, satin, rayon, and other fine garments. Hangers feature a long neck for collared garments and a ball finial on the end for attractiveness. Made of a chrome plated finish with a foam cover similar to motorcycle and bicycle handle bars.

Gucci cane handle handbags Cane handles on the Gucci handbags to compensate for the leather shortage after World War II, (1969–'75).

H&M Hennes & Mauritz AB. A Swedish clothing company, known for its inexpensive and fashionable clothing offerings for women, men, teenagers, and children.

Habit A behavior pattern acquired by frequent repetition or physiologic exposure that shows itself in regularity. A mode of behavior that has become nearly or completely involuntary.

Half-pint body type Petite body type under 5 feet 4 inches tall with a thick lower body and a full, curvy bust.

Half slip Undergarment that begins at the waist and ends at dress length.

Hard and soft goods In retail stores, groceries, toys, and electronics are examples of hard goods, while apparel, accessories, and shoes are examples of soft goods.

Harmony A pleasing or congruent arrangement of parts.

Haute couture The houses or designers that create exclusive and often trend-setting fashions.

Hecto brand paper A brand of tracing paper used to transfer your body image for body type evaluation exercises.

Heel The part (as of a shoe) that covers the human heel and/or a solid attachment of a shoe or boot forming the back of the sole under the heel of the foot.

Hermes Birkin bag A handbag named after the British actress Jane Birkin after Hermès CEO Jean-Louis Dumas discovered she needed a leather weekend bag. Production of the handbag usually takes up to 48 hours. Goat skin lining, metallic hardware—the lock, keys, buckle, and feet studs—all contribute to the handbag's prestige.

Hemp A tall widely cultivated Asian herb that has a tough bast fiber used especially for cordage and that is often separated into a tall loosely branched species and a low-growing densely branched species.

Hermes Kelly bag Designed in Paris, France during the 1930s and named after Princess Grace Kelly of Monaco. In 1956 Princess Grace was shown with the bag on the cover of Life magazine and sales boomed for the handbag after that appearance.

High heels Shoes with a heel height three inches or taller.

HNWIs High net worth individuals with net assets of at least $1 million dollars, excluding primary residences and consumables.

Hosiery Leg coverings that include stockings, pantyhose, tights, and socks.

Hosiery rule Two out of three should match: skirt or trouser bottom; legs; and footwear.

Hourglass body type Defined waist and balanced hips and shoulders; for example 36-26-36 measurements.

Hourglass figures Wide bottom and top and slim, narrow waist.

Hue Color; the attribute of colors that permits them to be classed as red, yellow, green, blue, or an intermediate between any contiguous pair of these colors.

Icon A symbol; an object of uncritical devotion.

Ideal Relating to or embodying an ideal; perfect, conforming to a standard.

Image Mental conception held in common by members of a group and symbolic of a basic attitude and orientation.

Image consultant Specialists in visual appearance, and verbal and nonverbal communications. Working with individual clients, image professionals assist in attaining authenticity, self-confidence, and credibility.

Income A gain or recurrent benefit that results from work or other form of labor usually measured in money; how much you make in a year, i.e. $30,000 per year.

Individuality Total character peculiar to and distinguishing an individual from others.

Ingénue fashion personality A naïve girl or young woman who dresses and looks very youthful in appearance.

Insole An inside sole of a shoe and/or a loose thin strip placed inside a shoe for warmth or comfort.

Institute for Market Transformation to Sustainability (MTS) The institute's mission is to foster and accelerate the global free market transformation to sustainability. The institute's vision is to achieve a sustainable world through transformation of the way we design, make and sell products.

Interest Something that arouses attention.

Internet An electronic communications network that connects computer networks and organizational computer facilities around the world.

Inverted triangle body type Characterized by a large upper half, shoulders, bust, undefined waists, and a slim lower half, small hips, and thin legs.

Inverted triangle facial shape Characterized by a wide forehead and narrow chin lines. Also called heart shape.

John Patrick Designer whose philosophy is "we make sexy, modern, organic clothes for the sexy, modern, organic world." Launched Generation Organic clothing line in 2004.

Karen Carpenter Half of the singing duo The Carpenters, popular during the early Seventies, who garnered three Grammy Awards and an American Music Award. Died of heart failure due to anorexia nervosa in 1983.

Kitten heels Very low heels that are universally accepted by all women and work well for the office and evening attire.

Ku'damm Berlin's most popular shopping street stretching for two miles westwards from the Memorial Church. A wide boulevard flanked by shops, hotels, and restaurants.

Laundry additives Products and substances added to your laundry in relatively small amounts to effect a desired change in properties, such as bleach or fabric softeners.

Learning partner One or two or more persons gathering together to learn material.

Leasing To hold under a lease—a contract by which one conveys merchandise for a specified term and for a specified rent.

Leggings A covering, as in leather or cloth, for the leg; sometimes called "tights."

Lifestyle The typical way of life for an individual, group, or cluster.

Linda Loudermilk Fashion designer. The luxury eco™ category Loudermilk invented with the launch of her line consists of sustainable fabrics she developed and sourced reflecting a respect for nature.

Listener To hear something with thoughtful attention, interpreting the meaning of what is being said.

Loafers A low step-in shoe.

Long Line Bra A bra that reaches the waistline, providing a slimming effect to the midriff area.

Low heels Shoes with a heel height less than two and a half inches.

Manmade fabrics Synthetic fabrics that are produced artificially such as viscose, rayon, acetate, and nylon. Production is by chemical or bio-chemical synthesis.

Marilyn Monroe Alluring American actress who made 30 films during the years of 1947–'62. Monroe is known for her beauty and sensuality.

Mass merchants Also called discount stores; sell large volumes of merchandise at low prices with very little customer service.

Mauveine The first manmade organic dye discovered by William Henry Perkin in 1856.

Metal category of hangers Perfect hangers for long lasting style and quality; can be made in a variety of finishes—brass, chrome, and brushed aluminum.

Milk silk A velvety soft fabric made from milk that rivals the highest silk quality and feels luxurious. Liquid milk is dried and its proteins extracted then dissolved in a chemical solution and placed in a machine that essentially whirls the fibers together. The fibers are then spun into yarn and woven into fabric. Cyran, a Chinese company, produces such fabric.

Minimizer bra A bra that reduces the projection of your breasts by redistributing your breast flesh more under the arms and up towards the chest.

Model stock An assortment of fashion merchandise indicating what should be carried in a particular merchandise category. Inventory is the stock of any clothing item used in a retail store. Inventory systems can be modeled as fixed-order quantity where the same amount of inventory is replenished in each order period.

Mohair A fabric or yarn made wholly or in part of the long silky hair of the Angora goat.

Molded bra A bra with foam added to give it shape and prevent your nipples from showing.

Monique Award-winning plus size comedian and actress who has become a role model for voluptuous women everywhere.

Monochromatic Having or consisting of one color or hue.

Monotone A tedious sameness or reiteration; all one color.

Moscow City capital of Russia that is moving up the ranks of fashion capitals.

Natural fashion personality Characterized by a normal or usual character. Clothing is marked by easy simplicity and freedom from artificiality.

Natural fiber fabrics Created from fibers of animal coats, silkworm cocoons, and plant seeds, leaves, and stems such as wool, cotton, silk, and linen.

Natural wood hangers Durable hangers with a flat construction profile suitable for a wide variety of garments including shirts, blouses, coats, and jackets.

Noe handbag Luis Vuitton bucket-shaped shoulder bag originally designed in 1932 to carry five bottles of champagne.

Non-essential Not essential, not necessary.

Norm Average, a set of standards, representing a middle point.

Notions Small, useful items; sundries. Examples are threads, buttons, and zippers.

Oblong facial shape Facial shape with long and narrow bone structures. Often characterized with a thin, long neck.

Off-price stores Sellers of brand names at 20 to 60 percent less than department and specialty stores.

Oprah Winfrey American television host, media mogul, and one of the most influential and wealthiest women in the world.

Organic Of, relating to, yielding, or involving the use of food produced with the use of feed or fertilizer of plant or animal origin without employment of chemically formulated fertilizers, growth stimulants, antibiotics, or pesticides.

Organic Trade Association (OTA) The Organic Trade Association. The membership-based business association for the organic industry in North America. OTA's mission is to promote and protect organic trade to benefit the environment, farmers, the public, and the economy.

Ott light bulb Full spectrum light bulb that duplicates high quality natural lighting indoors.

Outlet stores A store that sells the goods of a particular manufacturer or wholesaler.

Oval facial shape Facial shape where the jaw is narrower then the cheekbones and is longer than it is wide. Considered to be the ideal facial shape that can wear any hairstyle.

Oval shape Characterized by a thick waist, large bust, and thin legs. Weight gain is usually in the midsection. Also known as apple shape.

Overmeasure The full bust measurement.

Pantone Color Institute Subsidiary of X-Rite Incorporated, a world authority on color and provider of color systems. Founded in 1963 by Lawrence Herbert, the innovator of the Pantone Matching System®, a book of standardized color in fan format.

Panty A woman's undergarment covering the lower trunk and made with closed crotch.

Pantyhose A one-piece undergarment for women that consists of hosiery made with a panty-style top.

Pantyliner Sometimes called an underliner, worn under pants to provide a smooth finish.

Pattern A set of sewing instructions that is printed on tissue paper and is graded to fit a variety of sizes. The tissue paper patterns are sold in packets containing sewing instructions, fabric suggestions and sizing for various body measurements.

Pear shape body type Characterized by a slim upper body and full lower body—large hips, thighs, and bottom; weight gain is below the waist area.

Personal style An individual wearing clothes that are fashionable and popular and exhibiting a part of their personality.

Personality A set of distinctive traits and characteristics such as shyness, assertiveness, or friendliness.

Personality area In wardrobe planning, the face is considered the personality area, the area of concentration.

Personality traits A set of distinctive characteristics such as being friendly, calm, or gregarious.

Personality vendor table A table associating the five fashion personalities—classic, sporty, natural, romantic, and dramatic—with manufacturers that exhibit the look and express the adjectives that describe each personality.

Phillip Lim Clothing designer who debuted his line 3.1 phillip lim to critical acclaim. His organic clothing line Go Green Go is in partnership with retailer Barney's New York.

Pilling To mat into little balls on fabric.

Plastic category of hangers Strong, durable, and economically priced hangers suitable for a wide variety of garments.

Platforms A shoe with a usually thick layer, often cork, between the inner sole and outer sole of a shoe.

Plunge bra A bra with a low center front to accommodate low cut styles.

Primary colors Light is a combination of three primary colors, red, green, and blue.

Printed fabric design Ink or dye is used to impress the design onto the fabric.

Professional Association of Custom Clothiers (PACC) Nonprofit professional associations for individuals engaged in the sewing and design related businesses. PACC is also known as the Association of Sewing and Design Professionals.

Proportion Harmonious relation of parts to each other or to the whole.

Psychographic traits Market research or statistics classifying population groups according to psychological variables such as attitudes, values, or fears.

Pull To remove from a place or situation, such as clothing from your closet. The first step in the three-step closet evaluation.

Push-up bra A bra with additional padding that lifts the breasts and gives the illusion of a full bust line.

Quality A degree of excellence; superiority in kind.

Quality checklist A set of questions to ask yourself as a review to check clothing quality. Questions include those such as "Does the lining lay flat against the garment?"

Racerback bra The straps of the bra form a racer back, curving between the shoulder blades.

Receiver The person receiving your clothing message, acting as a receptacle for the message.

Rectangle body shape No curves to your figure, straight up and down. Weight gain is evenly distributed all over the body.

Rectangle facial shape An oblong facial shape with a square chin. Fullness and width is at the cheekbones.

Recycling To reuse or make (a substance) available for reuse for biological activities through natural processes of biochemical degradation or modification.

Repurposed clothing Clothing that is given a new purpose or new life; redesign and reuse old clothing and make new.

Resources A natural feature or phenomenon that enhances the quality of human life; computable wealth; source of information or expertise.

Retail collective Retail collaboration format that provides retail space and advertising at reduced costs for a group of like business individuals.

Retro Relating to the styles and fashion of the past, especially those from 1975 to 20 years later.

Rhythm Movement, fluctuation, or variation marked by the regular recurrence or natural flow of related elements—line, shape, and form.

Rogan Gregory Designer who successfully merged the concept of cutting-edge fashion with social responsibility via the high-profile clothing line called Edun. His casual clothing collection was produced from organic materials in conjunction with the Dublin-based political activist husband-and-wife duo Paul and Ali Hewson.

Romantic fashion personality A set of distinctive characteristics where the fashion is adhering to a romantic style; one characterized by adventure, mysteryious, idealism and love.

Rome Italian city that recently surpassed Milan as the place to watch for fashion. Rome has haute couture and hosts couture houses Sorelle Fontana, Gattinoni, and Renato Balestra.

Round facial shape Facial shape with full cheekbones and a wide hairline.

Sandals A shoe consisting of a sole strapped to the foot, a low-cut shoe that fastens by an ankle strap, a strap to hold on a slipper, or low shoe or a rubber overshoe cut very low.

Sasawashi Sasawashi products are made from Kumazasa, a plant of the glamineae family found in highlands of mainland Japan and Hokkaido. It is a very durable, washable fiber.

Savile Row A shopping street in Mayfair central London famous for its traditional men's bespoke tailoring.

Seacell A fabric made out of lyocell (a 100-percent wood pulp fiber) and seaweed. The fabric was devised in Germany, and has been certified by the European "echo-label," which promotes green products.

Seamless bra A bra with molded cups and no seams.

Seasonal cluster A group of clothing suitable to be worn only for a certain season; such as skiwear during the winter season or swimwear during the summer season.

Sender That which conveys, transmits, or sends out the fashion message to someone.

Sexy siren alluring personality Characterized by charm and attraction.

Shanghai Known as "the Paris of the Orient," one of the world's busiest ports and regarded as the center of finance and trade in mainland China. The Shanghai government continues to promote fashion in the city.

Shelf bra Constructed for small-breasted women, the cups sit on the breast and allow for support without going braless.

Signature style Something that sets you apart from someone else, it could be just about anything; any accessory or clothing item, a color, hair or eye makeup.

Silent language Clothing is sometimes called this.

Sizing A laundry additive that is used to cover, stiffen, or glaze as if with size.

Slip An undergarment made in dress length and usually having shoulder straps.

Socks A knitted or woven covering for the foot usually worn under shoes and extending above the ankle and sometimes to the knee.

Sole The part of an item of footwear on which the sole rests and upon which the wearer treads.

Sort Placing in separate piles the categories of clothing. Part of the second step in the closet evaluation (choosing to wear, discard, or alter clothing).

Speaker The person conveying the message.

Special occasion cluster A group of clothing items suitable to be worn for special occasions such as birthdays holidays, and weddings.

Specialty category of hangers Hangers that fulfill a specific need, such as children's hangers, padded hangers, inflatable hangers, and blanket and comforter hangers.

Specialty stores A store that carries a deep assortment within a narrow line of goods. Furniture stores, florists, sporting-goods stores, and bookstores are all specialty stores.

Sport cluster A group of clothing suitable to be worn for sports; examples are tennis clothes, golf clothes, or skiwear.

Sports bra A bra that provides support during sports activities and prevents breasts from sagging.

Sporty fashion personality A set of distinctive characteristics where the fashion is related to sports or a physical activity.

Square facial shape Characterized by a wide hairline and jaw. Forehead, jaw line, and cheekbones are almost equal in width.

Status Position or rank in relation to others; high prestige.

Stella McCartney Stella McCartney launched her eponymous label in 2001 as a joint venture with Gucci Group. The brand's luxury ready-to-wear, shoes, bags, fragrances, eyewear, accessories, organic skin care range and performance range with Adidas are available through its acclaimed flagship stores and around 600 luxury stores in key cities worldwide.

Stereotype A standardized mental picture that is held in common by members of a group and that represents an oversimplified opinion, prejudiced attitude, or uncritical judgment.

Stiletto heels A high thin heel on women's shoes that is narrower than a spike heel.

Stockings A type of hosiery that requires a garter at the top.

Strapless bras A bra with no straps that is to be worn with strapless tops and gowns.

Stresser About 16 percent of shoppers whose motto is "I really need to save, but it's such a hassle." The stressers are impulse shoppers, who have hectic schedules and limited time.

Striver About 23 percent of shoppers are strivers whose motto is "I wish I could be a better shopper."

Style A distinctive quality, form or type of something, such as that which is popular, beautiful, graceful, and elegant.

Style mavens One who is experienced or knowledgeable in style and fashion, an expert.

Sustain To give support or relief to, preserving the natural environment.

Sustainable design The art of designing physical objects and the built environment to comply with the principles of economic, social, and ecological sustainability. Also referred to as "green design," "eco-design," or "design for environment."

Symmetrical balance A clothing design when divided in half has similarity in look.

Tap pant Short-shorts with a small flare.

Target market Breaking a market into segments and concentrating your marketing efforts into one or a few key segments.

Taste Individual preference; liking and fondness for a particular something.

Tencel Tencel®, Lenzing Fibers' brand name for lyocell. Tencel® is made from wood pulp cellulose, offers a unique combination of the most desirable properties of man made and natural fibers: soft as silk, strong as polyester, cool as linen, warm as wool and as absorbent as cotton.

Texture The structure formed by the threads of the fabric.

The Bathers French Impressionist painter Pierre-August Renoir's 1887 painting depicting three curvy nude women. The painting is housed in the Philadelphia Museum of Art, Philadelphia.

The Chambre syndicale de la mode masculine Created in 1973 and composed of the Couture houses and Fashion Designers of men's ready-to-wear.

The Three Graces Neo-classical sculpture by Antonio Canova personifying femininity. Becoming one in their embrace, the three slender female figures represent beauty, charm, and joy.

Thepurplebook The original annual directory of the best shops offered by the World Wide Web.

Three color principles Evaluate skin tone, eye color and hair color when analyzing your color season.

Three part closet evaluation First step pull, second step sort, and third step analyze each item of clothing in your closet.

Tights A skintight garment covering the body from the waist down.

Trade journals A magazine, periodical, or publication specific to a particular target market such as *Women's Wear Daily* (*WWD*), a newspaper/magazine specific to the fashion industry.

Traditionalist About 32 percent of shoppers are traditionalists whose motto is "when it comes to shopping, I'm a pro." A disciplined purchase planner, who compiles detailed lists with favorite coupons, who spends an average of 140 minutes in a grocery store each week, and who carefully weighs each purchase decision.

Transumerism The state of being in transition, always on the go, catching a bus, a train, a ship, moving very fast.

Transumers Consumers driven not by the "fixed," but by experiences—entertainment, discovery, the fight from boredom—and who increasingly live a transient lifestyle, freeing themselves from the hassles of permanent ownership and possessions.

Trendy clothing items Clothing items that are very fashionable and up-to-date yet may only last as long as the majority of the population accepts the article of clothing.

Triangle body shape Characterized by a full lower body, wide waist, and small shoulders. Separates are essential for this body type with two different sizes for top and bottom.

Triangle facial shape Characterized by a narrow forehead and wide jaw and chin lines. Also called pear shape.

Tubular hangers Typically the backbone of most closets. Perfect for t-shirts, blouses, and dresses and made of heavy gauge plastic.

Twiggy London-born model who reached supermodel fame in the mid Sixties. A naturally thin girl, Twiggy is known as the pioneer of the waif-like models.

Type-A personality A person possessing a temperament characterized by excessive ambition, aggression, competitiveness, drive, impatience, need for control, focus on quantity over quality, and an unrealistic sense of urgency.

Undermeasure The measurement under the bust.

Underpinning Clothing or an article of clothing worn next to the skin and under other clothing.

Unity A total of related parts; a condition of harmony and accord.

Uniqueness Being the only one distinctively characteristic; without a like or equal.

Upper torso The upper part of the body from the head to the natural waistline (the belly button).

Valentino Italian fashion designer known for opulence, meticulous detailing, and embroidery in his clothing; after 45 years in the industry, Valentino's last collection was shown in Paris, France in January 2008.

Value A principle or quality intrinsically valuable or desirable.

Vamp The part of a shoe upper or boot upper covering especially the forepart of the foot and sometimes also extending forward over the toe or backward to the back seam of the upper.

Variety stores A retail store that sells an assortment of merchandise at inexpensive price points.

Vertically integrated retailer A company's domination of a market by controlling all steps in the production process, from the extraction of raw materials through the manufacture and sale of the final product.

Via Montenapoleone With its narrow side streets branching off, the most elegant street in Milan and one of the most sophisticated in all of Europe.

Vicuna The wool from the vicuña's fine lustrous undercoat; a sheep's wool.

Vintage Garments that come from another era. For clothing to be considered vintage, some historians' require that it must have been created between 1920 and 1975, while others simply maintain that it be at least 25 years old.

Wardrobe selection factors Factors used to select the proper wardrobe—fit, color, fabric, style, quality, and care.

Wardrobe staples Clothing items that have widespread and constant use or appeal; such as black pants or a black dress.

Warm hues Colors that appear on the left side of the color wheel and are similar to colors like those of the sun and fire.

Wear Clothing that is current, in style, and needs no alteration. Clothing items that you carry on a person.

Wedges A shoe having a heel extending from the back to the front of the shank and a tread formed by an extension of the sole.

Wide-set Strap bra Straps that are set wide apart for wide neckline garments.

Wood category of hangers Hangers of wood used to enhance the visual presentation of garments; a perception of quality and elegance, available in a variety of styles and finishes.

Work cluster A group of clothing items, typically 8-10 pieces, to be worn for work, your job, or place of employment.

Zara The flagship chain store for the Spanish Inditex Group owned by Spanish tycoon Amancio Ortega.

Zeitgeist The spirit of a time; the taste and outlook characteristic of a period or generation.

Credits

CHAPTER 1
- 1.0 Courtesy of Fairchild Publications, Inc.
- 1.1 Copyright (c) Johner Bildbyra AB
- 1.2 © Ausloeser/zefa/Corbis
- 1.3a Gustavo Caballero/Getty Images
- 1.3b MICHAEL KAPPELER/AFP/Getty Images
- 1.3c Gustavo Caballero/Getty Images
- 1.3d Steve Mack/FilmMagic
- 1.4a Brian Ach/WireImage
- 1.4b Stephen Lovekin/FilmMagic
- 1.4c Mark Allan/WireImage
- 1.5 © Mary Evans Picture Library/Alamy

CHAPTER 2
- 2.0 © Emmanuel Faure/Getty Images
- 2.1 © Superstudio/Getty Images
- 2.2 REUTERS/Kevin Lamarque

CHAPTER 3
- 3.0 Getty Images/Blend Images
- 3.1 Redraw by Jenny Green
- 3.2a © Chuck Goodenough/Alamy
- 3.2b © Rob Wilkinson/Alamy
- 3.2c Courtesy of The Container Store
- 3.2d Courtesy of The Container Store
- 3.2e Courtesy of The Container Store
- 3.3 Courtesy of The Container Store

CHAPTER 4
- 4.0 Veer
- 4.1 © Pictorial Press Ltd/Alamy
- 4.2 Redraw by Jenny Green
- 4.3a © Allstar Picture Library/Alamy
- 4.3b © Content Mine International/Alamy
- 4.3c © Allstar Picture Library/Alamy
- 4.3d © Allstar Picture Library/Alamy
- 4.4 Redraw by Jenny Green
- 4.5 Redraw by Jenny Green
- 4.6a Courtesy of Fairchild Publications, Inc.
- 4.6b Courtesy of Fairchild Publications, Inc.
- 4.6c Courtesy of Fairchild Publications, Inc.
- 4.7 Lipnitzki/Roger Viollet/Getty Images

CHAPTER 5
- 5.0 © Erica Shires/zefa/Corbis
- 5.1 © Pictorial Press Ltd/Alamy
- 5.2 © Christopher Leggett/Alamy
- 5.3 Redraw by Jenny Green
- 5.4 Marcel Thomas/FilmMagic
- 5.5 Ferdaus Shamim/WireImage
- 5.6 Jeff Vespa/Getty Images
- 5.7 Jeffrey Mayer/WireImage
- 5.8 © Cora Buettenbender/zefa/Corbis
- 5.9 © Luca Tettoni/Corbis
- 5.10a Courtesy of Fairchild Publications, Inc.
- 5.10b Courtesy of Fairchild Publications, Inc.
- 5.11 Courtesy of Fairchild Publications, Inc.
- 5.12a Courtesy of Fairchild Publications, Inc.
- 5.12b Courtesy of Fairchild Publications, Inc.
- 5.13 © Didier Robcis/Corbis
- 5.14a Courtesy of Fairchild Publications, Inc.
- 5.14b Courtesy of Fairchild Publications, Inc.
- 5.14c Courtesy of Fairchild Publications, Inc.
- 5.14d Courtesy of Fairchild Publications, Inc.

CHAPTER 6
- 6.0 Courtesy of Fairchild Publications, Inc.
- 6.1 Photo by Stephen Sullivan for Fairchild Books, Inc.
- 6.2 Photo by Stephen Sullivan for Fairchild Books, Inc.
- 6.3 Photo by Stephen Sullivan for Fairchild Books, Inc.

6.4 Photo by Stephen Sullivan for Fairchild Books, Inc.
6.5 Photo by Stephen Sullivan for Fairchild Books, Inc.
6.6 Photo by Stephen Sullivan for Fairchild Books, Inc.
6.7 Photo by Stephen Sullivan for Fairchild Books, Inc.
6.8 Photo by Stephen Sullivan for Fairchild Books, Inc.
6.9 Photo by Stephen Sullivan for Fairchild Books, Inc.
6.10 Photo by Stephen Sullivan for Fairchild Books, Inc.
6.11 Catwalking.com
6.12 Courtesy of Fairchild Publications, Inc.
6.13 Courtesy of Fairchild Publications, Inc.
6.14 Courtesy of Fairchild Publications, Inc.
6.15 Catwalking.com

CHAPTER 7
7.0 © Jack Hollingsworth/Getty Images
7.1–7.39 Photos courtesy of HerRoom.com

CHAPTER 8
8.0 Julian Ledger Photography
8.1a © Luis Santana
8.1b © Luis Santana
8.2 Kate Spade; classic noel harry
8.3 Courtesy of Sonal Adhikari
8.4 Courtesy of Fairchild Publications, Inc.
8.5 Courtesy of Fairchild Books, Inc.
8.6 Courtesy of Fairchild Publications, Inc.
8.7 Courtesy of Fairchild Publications, Inc.
8.8 Photo by Charles Sykes / Rex USA, courtesy Everett Collection
8.9 © Bettman / Corbis
8.10 Courtesy of Fairchild Publications, Inc.
8.11 Catwalking.com
8.12 Catwalking.com
8.13 Noe; approx: $1,060; 866.VUITTN; www.louisvuitton.com
8.14 Tony Barson/WireImage
8.15 Courtesy of Fairchild Publications, Inc.
8.16 Courtesy of Fairchild Books, Inc.
8.17 Courtesy of Crocs
8.18 Copyright 2007 ML Harris Photography. All rights reserved.

CHAPTER 9
9.0 © Simon Marcus/Corbis
9.1 Courtesy of Fairchild Publications, Inc.

CHAPTER 10
10.0 Veer
10.1 Redraw by Jenny Green
10.2 © Peter Forsberg/Alamy
10.3 © uk retail Alan King/Alamy
10.4 Brian Kersey/Getty Images for Forever 21

CHAPTER 11
11.0 © Matthew Eades for EJF
11.1 AP Photo/Marcio Jose Sanchez
11.2 Courtesy of Norm Thompson Outfitters
11.3 David Silverman/Getty Images
11.4 Courtesy of Norm Thompson Outfitters
11.5 Courtesy of Fairchild Publications, Inc.
11.6 Courtesy of Adidas
11.7 © WWD/Condé Nast/Corbis
11.8 Katy Winn/Getty Images for IMG
11.9 Courtesy of Fairchild Publications, Inc.
11.10 Courtesy of Fairchild Publications, Inc.
11.11 Courtesy of Fairchild Publications, Inc.

CHAPTER 12
12.0 Lara Jade Photography
12.1 Redraws by Jenny Green
12.1a Lester Cohen/WireImage
12.1b © Ted Soqui/Corbis
12.1c Kiyoshi Ota/Getty Images
12.1d Kevin Winter/Getty Images
12.1e Jon Kopaloff/FilmMagic
12.1f George Napolitano/FilmMagic
12.2 Julian Ledger Photography
12.3a Michael Ochs Archives/Getty Images
12.3b Time & Life Pictures/Getty Images
12.3c © Guillaume Horcajuelo/epa/Corbis
12.3d © Alessandra Benedetti/Corbis
12.3e © Mario Anzuoni/Reuters/Corbis
12.4 BCBGMAXAZRIA; Le Journal;Spring 2007

Index

accent pieces, 168
accessories, 5, 36, 209-33
 footwear, 225-29
 handbags, 210-24
 jewelry, 229-33
 packing, 273
 selection factors, 210
accomplishment, 11
accuracy, 11
active lifestyle, 4
 See also sporty fashion personality
Adeli, Katayone, 295
adventure, 11
advertising costs, 242
Africa, fashion weeks in, 253
age group, 44-45
 See also generation
Allard, Lynn, 141
alpaca, 280
AltaRoma Organization, 263
alterations, 61, 73
 See also tailors
alternative designs, 290-91
American English, 262
analogous colors, 65, 118
analyze, 63
Andersonville Galleria (Chicago), 242
angora, 280
anorexia nervosa, 85
antique clothing, 71
anti-shopper, 240
appearance, 93
apple body type, 92, 110
Asia, fashion weeks in, 253-54
assumptions, 9, 26

asymmetrical balance, 132, 135
ateliers, 260
Atlanta, Georgia, 283
attitude, 51
auction web sites, 270
Australia, fashion weeks in, 253
automatic replenishment system, 309
autumn color season, 119, 121

Baby Boomers, 53
backless bras, 183
balance, 132, 135
bamboo, 280-81
Barneys New York, 292, 297
basic items, 168
"The Bathers" (Renoir), 85
batik fabric design, 128-30
beauty, 11
behavior
 habit and, 37
 personal values and, 11-14
beliefs and values, 43, 51-52
Berlin, fashion in, 263
bespoke tailoring, 261
big, beautiful, and loving it (BBLI), 86
biker shorts, 196, 197
bikini panties, 193, 194
Birkin bag, 218, 220
black (color), 117, 126
black jacket, 158, 166
black pencil skirt, 158-66
black pumps (heels), 229
body briefer, 196, 197
body frame measurement, 210-11
body language, 8

339

body scrutiny, 87–88
body shapers, 196–98
body size satisfaction, 86
body tracing, 89–90
body type evaluation, 70, 83–102
    body type recognition, 99–101
    celebrities, 94, 108–9
    fashion industry norm, 84–87
    interesting body shapes, 96–97
    jacket choices for, 141
    major body types, 88
    perfect fit jeans and, 114
    proportion, 95–99
    waists and waist nots, 92–95
Bolide bag, 218, 219
Bombeck, Erma, 237
boots, 227, 229
bra wardrobe, 182–92
    finding correct size, 190–92
    manufacturers, 189–90
Bremer, Jill, 5
British English, 262
budget, 46, 238
budget worksheet, 18, 24
Bündchen, Gisele, 85
business casual, 145
business formal, 145

calm, 11
camel hair, 280
camisole, 45, 196, 197, 198, 199
camouflage, 99
Canada, fashion weeks in, 252
care of clothing, 145–49
Carpenter, Karen, 85
cashmere, 280
casual cluster, 155, 156
casual shopper, 240
celebrities, 4, 315
    color season and, 120–22
    fashion personalities of, 26–28
    figure types of, 94, 108–9
    handbags, 217
    as style mavens, 106–8

Celebrity Copy Cat (web site), 270
Chambre syndicale de la haute couture, 257
Chambre syndicale de la mode masculine, 257
Chanel 2 bag, 221
charity, donation to, 73, 74–75
Chase, Edna W., 41
children's hangers, 67
chroma, 118, 119
chrome hangers, 67
chromotherapy (color therapy), 125
circumference, 91
classic fashion personality, 15, 28, 32, 36
    clustering for, 171
    style and, 307–8
cleaning costs, 238
cleanliness, 12
cleavage, 184, 185
closet evaluation, 59–78
    beginning, 61–63
    discard category, 61, 70–73
    hangers, 66–67
    three parts in, 60–61
    wear process, 60, 64–69
closet organizers, 60
clothing, leasing of, 269
clothing, packing of, 271–72, 273
clothing, recyclable, 282–85
clothing allowance, 238
    See also budget
clothing assumptions, 9, 26
clothing care, 145–49
clothing choices, and proportions, 97–99
    See also wardrobe selection factors
clothing cues, 37
    values and, 10–14
clothing goals, 44, 54–56
clothing message, 25
clothing tribe, 52
    See also generation
cluster concept, 153–77
    cluster groupings, 157–67
    fashion personality and, 171–76
    green (organic), 297–98
    work cluster, 155, 156

cluster planning chronicle, 168, 172
clutch bag, 215
coconut fiber, 281
college students, 4
color, 36, 64, 116-28
    analogous, 65, 118
    complementary, 65, 118
    draping, 122-25
    psychology of, 117, 126
    seasonal theory, 118-22, 123, 126
    universally flattering, 127
color analysis, 122-25
Color Association of the United States (CAUS), 126
color draping, 122-25
colored handbag, 215-16
color wheel, 65, 116, 117-18
communication, 8-9
community, 12
complementary colors, 65, 118
The Container Store, 60, 67
contrasting colors, 118
control brief, 196, 197
convertible bra, 184
cool hues, 117
cost-per-wearing formula, 140
cotton, 129, 279
Cotton, Inc., 114
coupon shoppers, 241
couture, 258, 259-60
CoutureCandy.com, 314
Crawford, Cindy, 304
creativity, 12
crepe, 129
crime investigation, 5
Crocs (plastic shoes), 228
cues, personal values and, 10-14
culotte, 198, 200
culotte slip, 201
customization, 54
Custom Tailors and Designers Association of America, 76
cutting trends, 169

demi-cup bra, 184
demographic traits, 43-47, 86

denier, 204
denim, 282, 311, 314
    See also jeans
Denim King Vintage Wholesaler, 282
Department of Health and Human Services, U.S., 85, 86
department stores, 243
detergents, 148
diamond body type, 92, 110
Dietrich, Marlene, 303
Dior, Christian, 101, 259
Direct Marketing Association, 243
discard category, in closet evaluation, 61, 70-73
discount stores, 243
discovery, 12, 37
discretionary income, 46
dramatic fashion personality, 15, 28, 32, 33, 36
    clustering for, 176
    style and, 308
dramatic style, 4
dress, 312-13
drop waist, 97
Dubai, fashion industry in, 255, 263
dyeing, of fabric, 128-30

earrings, 230
eBay (online marketplace), 270
eclectic fashion personality, 30
eco-friendly clothing. *See* green fashion
education, 45
Edun (t-shirt line), 297
effective communication, 8-9
eggplant (color), 127
1154 Lill (retailer), 54
Ellen Tracy, 141
embroidered fabric, 130
emphasis, 131-32, 143
English, American *vs.* British, 262
environmental movement, 278
    See also green fashion
Erdmark, Tomima, 189-90
Etiquette (Post), 169
Euro hanger, 67
Europe, fashion weeks in, 251

evening bag, 215
excellence, 12
eye color, 122

fabric, 36, 128–38
    design principles, 131–35
    dyeing of, 128–30
    embroidered, 130
    pattern choices, 134, 136–37
    printed and painted, 131
    textures of, 128, 129, 137
fabric design, 128–35
facial shape, hairstyle and, 305–6
faith, 13
family, 13
family life, 52
family status, 46
Fashion Center Business Improvement District (FCBID), 256–57
fashion followers, 46
fashion leaders, 46
fashion magazines, 85, 168
fashion market characteristics, 255–59
fashion mission statement, 18, 23, 25
fashion personality, 3–39, 273
    celebrity table, 26–28
    clustering for, 171–76
    color and, 119
    communication of, 8–9
    defined, 9
    first impressions, 5–7
    five basic, 15
    life lifestyle grid, 16–17
    minor categories, 29–30
    mission statement, 18, 23, 25
    personality cluster, 19–23
    personal style and, 307–8
    total look, 314
    vendor table, 34
    See also classic; dramatic; natural; romantic; sporty fashion personality
fashion weeks, 250, 264
    international listing, 251–54

Fédération française de la couture, du prêt-à-porter des couturiers et des créateurs de mode, 258
femininity, 4–5, 31, 101
    See also romantic fashion personality
Fields, Patricia, 108
figure types. *See* body type evaluation
finishing touch products, 148
first impressions, 5–7, 27
fit, 108–15
    body type and, 109–10
    jeans, 114–15
    sizing and, 112–13
Fitch (consultancy firm), 264
fit style rules, 110–11
flannel, 129
flats (shoes), 225
flip-flops (thongs), 228
footwear, 225–29
Ford, Tom, 181
Forever 21 (retailer), 266, 267
foundation basics, 181–207
    body shapers, 196–98
    bra wardrobe, 182–92
    panty wardrobe, 192–96
    slip wardrobe, 198–201
France, fashion industry in, 257–60
Frey, Alishia, 291
fun, 13

G. I. Generation, 53
Garavani, Valentino. *See* Valentino
generation-based clothing, 43–44, 52–54
Generation C, 53, 54
Generation X, 53
Generation Y, 53
Glancy, Patrick, 37
Global Language Monitor, 250
global view, 13
goals. *See* clothing goals
Go Green Go (organic collection), 295
Golden Mean, 96, 101
Goodwill store, 282, 283
Gore, Al, 278

Graham, Nick, 282, 283
green fashion, 277–99
    defined, 278
    designers, 292–97
    green cluster, 297–98
    natural fibers, 279–81
    Norm Thomsom Outfitters, 287–88
    repurposed designs, 290–91
    sustainability and, 285–86, 289
Gregory, Rogan, 296, 297
Grieve, Julie, 291
grippy hangers, 67
g-string panties, 194, 195
Gucci cane handle bag, 222
Guerra, Concha, 86

habit, 37
hair color, 122, 125
hairstyles, 35, 36
    facial shape and, 305–6
half-pint body type, 92, 94
half slip, 201
handbags, 210–24
    essential, 212–13
    iconic, 218–24
    kinds of, 211–15
    leasing of, 268–69
    trend, 215–17
hangers, 66–67
harmony, 13
    color, 118, 119
Haute a Courroies bag, 218, 219
haute couture, 258, 259–60
health, 52
Hecto brand paper, 89
heel of shoe, 225
height, 93
hemp fibers, 290
Hermes bags, 218–21
Hermes Kelly bag, 221
HerRoom (website), 189–90
high-heel shoes, 225, 226, 229
high net worth individuals (HNWIs), 18

high waistline, 97
H&M (retailer), 265, 267
holiday shopping days, 245–46
hosiery, 202–6
hosiery rule, 206
hourglass body type, 88, 89, 91
    celebrities with, 94, 109
    jacket choices for, 141
    waistline and, 101, 109
hue, 117, 119
    See also color
humorous handbag, 216

iconic handbags, 218–24
ideal body type, 84
image, 303, 304–5, 316
image consultant, 318
image cue, 38
image cue table, 36
image inventory, 308–9
impression. *See* first impressions
income, 45, 46, 238
    See also budget
Indian teal (color), 127
individuality, 52, 56, 282, 304
    See also personal style
ingénue fashion personality, 29
innovation, 14
insole, of shoe, 225
Institute for Market Transformation to Sustainability (MTS), 286
interest, 51
international shopping, 249–74
    fashion market characteristics, 255–59
    listing of fashion weeks, 251–54
    top fashion cities, 255–64
    transumerism, 264–67
    travel packing tips, 271–73
internet shopping, 115, 243–45, 268–70
inverted triangle body type, 88, 91
    celebrities, 94, 109
    jacket choices for, 141
Italian fashions, 261, 263

jackets, 141, 158, 159, 166, 313
Jacobs, Marc, 105, 257
jeans
    customized, 54
    perfect fit, 114–15, 314
    recycled, 282
jersey, 129
jewelry, 229–33
    leasing of, 269
Jouvin, Lisa, 259

Kalisz, Kathryn, 119
kitten heels, 226
Ku-damm shopping center (Berlin), 263

labeling
    care, 145–46
    vintage clothing, 71–72
lace bra, 184
Latin America, fashion weeks in, 252–53
laundry products, 148
learning partner, 87
leasing option, 265
    via internet, 268–69
leggings, 204
lifestyle grid, 16–17, 50
lifestyle, 15, 47
    evaluation of, 48–51
    Italian, 261
    London, 261
    New York, 256–57
    Parisian, 259
lighting, color draping and, 122–23
like.com (web site), 270
Lim, Phillip, 294, 295
linen, 129, 279
liner socks, 205
listener, 9
loafers (shoes), 227, 229
London, 261
long-leg shapewear, 198, 199
long line bra, 184
Loudermilk, Linda, 294, 295
Louis Vuitton, 105, 217, 221

low-heel shoes, 225
Lynde, Paul, 59

Madrid fashion week, 86
Mahagamage, Tony, 282
maintenance issues, 238
Mallis, Fern, 249
manmade fabric, 128
Marks, Leeba, 282
mass merchants, 243
mauveiene, 130
McCartney, Stella, 292
McDonough Baumgart Design Chemistry, 289
McGraw, Phillip, 83
medical socks, 205
Mehrabian, Albert, 8–9
mellow rose (color), 127
Mendelsohn, Hilary, 243
men's ready-to-wear, 258
metal hangers, 67
Middle East, fashion weeks in, 254
Milan, fashion in, 260–61
milk silk (fiber), 295
millennial generation, 53, 73, 291
    recycled clothing and, 282
minimizer bra, 184
Mizrahi, Isaac, 297
model stock, 311
modesty, 52
mohair, 280
molded bra, 184
money, 14, 52
Monique, 86
monochromatic color, 118
monotone, 55, 65
Monroe, Marilyn, 85, 88, 89, 229
monthly budget, 18, 24
monthly specialties, 246
Moscow, fashion weeks in, 264
Myshape.com, 270

National Retail Federation, 242, 243
natural fashion personality, 15, 28, 33, 36
    clustering for, 174
    style and, 308

natural fibers, 128, 279–81
    bamboo, 280–81
    cotton, 114, 129, 279
    hemp, 290
    linen, 129, 279
    silk, 129, 280
    wool, 129, 279–80
natural lighting, 122-23
neutral color bra, 183
New Look, 100, 101
Newton, Isaac, 116
New York City, 249, 255–57
Noe bag, 221
norm, 84
Norm Thomsom Outfitters, 287–88
North America, fashion weeks in, 252
notions, 256

off-price stores, 243
online shopping, 115, 243–45
Organic clothing line, 292–93, 295
organic fashion, 290, 295, 297–98
Organic Trade Association, 290
organize, 64
Orman, Suze, 238
Ott light bulb, 122–23
outlet stores, 243
oval body type, 110
overmeasure, 190, 191

packing, for travel, 271–72, 273
painted fabric, 131
Paltrow, Gwyneth, 106, 108
Pantone Color Institute, 127
pants, 312
    See also jeans
pantyhose, 202–3
pantyliners, 200, 201
panty wardrobe, 192–96
Paris, fashion industry in, 257–60
Parker, Sarah Jessica, 107, 108
Patrick, John, 292–93, 295
pattern choices, 134, 136–37
pattern sizing, 93

Paulin, Helena, 270
Payack, Millie Lorenzo, 250
pear body type, 110
    See also triangle body type
perfect fit jeans, 114–15, 314
Perkin, William Henry, 130
personal image, 304–5
personality, 5, 210
    See also fashion personality
personality area, 99
personality cluster, 19–23
personal style, 303–19
    color choice and, 118
    image and, 303, 304–5
    image inventory and, 308–9
    total look and, 309–16
    vintage clothing and, 71
    See also individuality
personal style evaluation, 41–57
    clothing goals, 45, 54–56
    demographic traits, 43–47
    generation and, 43–44, 52–55
    psychographic traits, 43, 47–51
    values and beliefs, 43, 51–52
personal style journal, 317
petite sizing, 112
pilling, 138
plastic hangers, 67
platform shoes, 225
Plume handbag, 218, 219
plunge bra, 186, 187
plus sizing, 113
Post, Emily, 169
power, 14
Predictive Quantities Index, 250
preferences, 4
Preloved (fashion company), 291
primary colors, 116, 117
printed fabric design, 131
print handbag, 215
Professional Association of Custom Clothiers, 76
professionalism, 316
proportion, 95–99, 132, 134
    footwear and, 226

psychographic traits, 43, 47–51, 86
pull, in closet scrutiny, 63
punk rock clothing, 291
purses. *See* handbags
push-up bra, 186, 187

quality, 138–40
    checklist for, 138–39

racerback bra, 186, 187
Rasband, Judith, 10
receiver, 25
rectangle body type, 88, 91, 99, 109–10
    jacket choices for, 141
recycling, 281–85
reduce, reuse, recycle (three Rs), 281
religion, 52
remain, 64
Renoir, Pierre-August, 85
rentals. *See* leasing option
repurposed designs, 290–91
retail collective, 242–45
retailers, 114
    internet, 268–70
    transumerism and, 264–67
    vertically-integrated, 267
retail formats, 242
retro clothing, 71
rhythm, in fabric design, 131, 132
romantic fashion personality, 4–5, 15, 28, 31–32, 36
    clustering for, 174
    style and, 307
Rome, fashion in, 263
Royal Borough of Kensington and Chelsea, 5
Ruskin, John, 9
Russia, fashion weeks in, 252, 264

sandals, 225, 228
Sarfpour, Behnaz, 296, 297
sasawashi fabric, 295
Savile Row tailoring, 261
savvy savings shopper, 241
Schuller, Catherine, 92
Schwab, Charles M., 3

Sci-Art-global.com, 119, 125
seacell fabric, 295
seamless bra, 187
seams, 139
seasonal cluster, 155, 156
seasonal color theory, 118–22, 123, 126
secondary colors, 116
sender, 25
Sex and the City (tv series), 107, 108
Sex Pistols (punk group), 291
sexy siren alluring personality, 30
Shanghai, fashion in, 264
shelf bra, 187
Shepherd, Cybill, 206
Shikibo Ltd., 281
shoes, 225–29
Shopper Track, 245
shopping
    basics of, 237–47
    holiday shopping days, 245–46
    via internet, 115, 243–45, 268–70
    kinds of shoppers, 240
    planning for, 239, 246
    retail collective and, 242–45
    See also international shopping
Shumsky, Alexander, 264
Siegle, Lucy, 277
signature style, 272, 305, 310
    See also personal style
Silent Generation, 53
silent language, 60
silk, 129, 280
simplicity, 14
sizing, 112–13
    for bras, 190–92
skin tone, 122, 125
slipper socks, 205
slip wardrobe, 198–201
Snow, Carmel, 101
Soap and Detergent Association, 145–46
socks, 204–5
sole of shoe, 225
sort, in closet scrutiny, 63
South America, fashion weeks in, 252–53

spandex, 4
speaker, 9
special occasion cluster, 155, 156
specialty bras, 188
specialty hangers, 67
specialty stores, 243
sport cluster, 155, 156
sports bra, 188
sporty fashion personality, 4, 15, 28, 30–31, 36
    clustering for, 173
    style and, 307
sporty handbag, 216
spring color season, 121
stacked heels, 229
Stanton, Emily, 153
status, 46
Stefani, Gwen, 108
stereotypes, 143
stiletto heels, 226, 229
stockings, 204
    See also hosiery
strap bags, 221
strapless bra, 188
stresser, 240
striver, 240
style, 4
    signature style, 272, 305, 310
    wardrobe selection and, 105, 106–8, 141–45
    See also personal style
style mavens, 106–8
summer color season, 121–22
supermodels, 85–86, 304
sustainable design, 285–86, 289
sweaters, 136, 162–64, 167
symmetrical balance, 132, 135
synthetics (manmade) fabric, 128

tailors and tailoring, 73, 76–77, 115, 238
    Savile Row, 261
tap pant, 201
target market, 137
taste, 4
tencel, 290
texture, of fabric, 128, 129

Thepurplebook, 243, 245
Theron, Charlize, 108
Thomas, Paula Weston, 71
thong-bikini panties, 194, 195
The Three Graces, 85
three Rs (reduce, reuse, recycle), 281–85
tights, 204
total look, 309–16
total package, 318
tote bag, 215
tracing paper, 89
trade journals, 168
trade web sites, 270
traditional shopper, 240
transumerism, 264–67
Trash Clothing, 282
travel, packing tips for, 271–72, 273
trend-spotting chart, 170
Trendwatching.com, 54, 264
trendy clothing items, 168
    See also fashion
    body shapers, 197
    bras, 184
    handbags, 215–17
    panties, 194
    socks, 205
triangle body type, 88, 91, 99, 101
    celebrities with, 94, 109
    jacket choices for, 141
    pear shape and, 110
Trim handbag, 218, 219
Tropical Mixed Used Clothes, 283, 285
true fit sizing, 93–94
true red (color), 127
Trump, Ivanka, 47
tubular hangers, 67
tweed, 129
Twiggy (model), 85
twin set, 165
type-A personalities, 256–57

undermeasure, 190, 191
underpinning, 201
Unified Sustainable Textile Standard, 286

uniforms, 15
union labels, 71-72
uniqueness, 55, 272
    See also signature style
United Arab Emirates, 263
unity, 134, 136
Unsung Designers, 291
upper torso, 96
used clothing. *See* recyclable; vintage clothing

Valentino, 84, 209, 260
value, color, 118, 119
values, clothing cues and, 10-14
values and beliefs, 43, 51-52
vamp, of shoe, 225
variety, 14, 56
variety stores, 242
vertically integrated retailers, 267
Via Montenapoleone (Milan), 260
vicuna, 280
vintage clothing, 70, 71-72, 282
    repurposed designs, 290-91
Vintage Fashion Guild (VFG), 71
visible panty line (VPL), 192, 195
Vogue magazine, 41

waist cincher, 199
waists and waist nots, 92-95, 96-97, 101
Wang, Grace, 291
wardrobe, 35
    costs in, 238

wardrobe selection factors, 105-50
    care, 145-49
    color, 116-28
    fit, 108-15
    style, 105, 106-8, 141-45
wardrobe staples, 154
    See also clustering concept
warm hues, 117
wear process, in closet evaluation, 60, 64-69
web sites, 222-23, 244, 270, 314
    See also internet shopping
wedges (shoes), 225
weight gain, 93
well-balanced wardrobe, 169
Westwood, Vivienne, 291
white blouse, 161, 312
white (color), 117, 126
wide-set strap bra, 188
William Good line, 282
Winfrey, Oprah, 84
winter color season, 121
Witherspoon, Reese, 108
wood hangers, 67
wool, 129, 279-80
work cluster, 155, 156
working professional, 4
World Health Report, 18

Zafu.com, 115, 270
Zara (retailer), 266, 267
Zozlowski, Karen, 169